# FOLLOWING THE TICKER

# *FOLLOWING THE TICKER*

## THE POLITICAL ORIGINS AND CONSEQUENCES
## OF STOCK MARKET PERCEPTIONS

### IAN G. ANSON

SUNY
PRESS

Published by State University of New York Press, Albany

For information, contact State University of New York Press, Albany, NY
www.sunypress.edu

**Library of Congress Cataloging-in-Publication Data**

Name: Anson, Ian G., author.
Title: Following the ticker : the political origins and consequences of stock
    market perceptions / Ian G. Anson.
Description: Albany, NY : State University of New York Press, 2023. |
    Includes bibliographical references and index.
Identifiers: LCCN 2022027842 | ISBN 9781438492292 (hardcover : alk. paper) |
    ISBN 9781438492315 (ebook) | ISBN 9781438492308 (pbk. : alk. paper)
Subjects: LCSH: Stock exchanges—Political aspects—United States. |
    Capitalism—Political aspects—United States.
Classification: LCC HG4910 .A683 2023 | DDC 332.64/273—dc23/eng/20220923
LC record available at https://lccn.loc.gov/2022027842

10 9 8 7 6 5 4 3 2 1

*For Lucy*

Anyone claiming that America's economy is in decline is peddling fiction. What is true—and the reason that a lot of Americans feel anxious—is that the economy has been changing in profound ways, changes that started long before the Great Recession hit, and haven't let up.

—Barack Obama, January 12, 2016


BIGGEST STOCK MARKET RISE IN HISTORY YESTERDAY!

—Donald Trump, March 14, 2020


This sucker could go down.

—George W. Bush, September 25, 2008

# Contents

# Illustrations

## Figures

## List of Tables

# Acknowledgments

Over the span of a decade, one can amass considerable debts. Luckily, mine are mostly debts of gratitude. I owe enormous thanks foremost to my dissertation committee, who shepherded an earlier version of the argument contained in this book through the murky wilderness of my first years in political science. Jerry Wright, my dissertation chair and mentor, was the catalyst for this idea, sparked as it was in his 2012 seminar on inequality in American democracy. Jerry continues to guide my thinking on this subject (and virtually every other subject I think about) to this day. His tireless mentorship is the biggest reason I am a political scientist today, and I will be grateful for the whole of my career.

Margie Hershey was kind enough to let me take a summer independent study course on media and politics early in my graduate studies—a more generous decision than I even realized at the time, and one that led me to quickly discover her unparalleled insights as a mentor. My hope is that readers can see Margie's impact on every page of this volume. Tim Hellwig sparked my interested in economic voting and political behavior in my studies with him, and since then, I have continuously trusted his masterful guidance. Bernard Fraga helped me take what was still a messy idea and transform it into something that might resonate with readers (and methodologists) across the discipline and beyond. And J. Scott Long helped me to understand methods, data, workflow, and how to find passion and enthusiasm for a large-scale project—even when the numbers start to swim.

I owe debts of gratitude to many others at Indiana University (IU) and beyond. My graduate school colleagues endured endless discussions and presentations about economic news coverage and always had the skill (and the endurance) to offer me meaningful feedback. Kirk Harris,

Jason Stone, Ben Toll, Laura Bucci, Rafael Khachaturian, Luke Wood, Katey Stauffer, Nate Birkhead, and many others continue to help me understand the ins and outs of political science (and friendship). I am grateful to others at IU who worked with me, including Ted Carmines, Yanna Krupnikov, Chunfeng Huang, Weihua An, Jack Bielasiak, and my colleagues in the Statistics House and the Indiana Statistical Consulting Center. I am also grateful to my more recent colleagues at the University of Maryland, Baltimore County (UMBC), who offered constant support as I worked on this book throughout my time as an assistant professor. Everyone in the "UMBC political science family" has played a role in supporting me over the past six years, though I am especially grateful to Tom Schaller, Carolyn Forestiere, Tyson King-Meadows, Laura Antkowiak, William Blake, Fernando Tormos-Aponte, Felipe Filomeno, and Christine Mallinson for their guidance, friendship, and support through the book publication process. I am further indebted to Marc Hetherington for his ongoing mentorship and for participants at the Vanderbilt University American Politics speaker series for useful comments and guidance. Thanks also to Jamie Druckman and the Time-Sharing Experiments for the Social Sciences program, the Indiana University Graduate School, and the UMBC College of Arts, Humanities, and Social Sciences for supporting this project.

No one understands the emotional volatility of the book process like family and friends. Whenever my doubts and fears began to outpace my belief in the project, my loved ones always managed to snap me back to a state of determination. I cannot express how grateful I am to my parents, Chris and Gean Anson. They have always believed in me more than I have in myself, and I am still learning from them every day. Thanks also my brother Graham and my friends in Baltimore, Bloomington, the Research Triangle, and beyond, for their unwavering support. I am obligated to mention by name the "GokuUseTheSpiritBomb" group chat. Thanks to my great University of North Carolina alumni friends in that group for their support and for always lifting my spirits with their nonstop banter. And because I promised several people that I would do this: thanks to my cat, Ellie, and my dog, Gus, for all the furry friendship along the way.

Many thanks to my editor, Michael Rinella, who was willing to give this manuscript a shot, and to the anonymous reviewers who provided voluminous, immensely useful feedback on earlier versions of this project. While all remaining errors are my own, I believe that Michael and the reviewers helped make this manuscript a far stronger contribution to the field than it might be otherwise.

Finally, no one is more responsible for this book's completion than my wonderful wife, Lucy. I have been working on this book for as long as we have been married (and throughout the first year of life of our daughter, Rosemary), and it has played a major role in the life we have shared and built together. I am eternally grateful for your patience, your strength, and your optimism, Lucy. I truly cannot fathom the counterfactuals.

# Introduction

In the Spring of 2020, the American economy teetered on the brink of disaster. Amid a global crisis spawned by the COVID-19 virus, millions of Americans suddenly learned their places of work were temporarily closing. Airlines, colleges, restaurants, professional sports teams, and hotels scrambled to adjust to the new social reality. As state governments outlined emergency responses and competed over scarce medical resources, Americans found themselves staring into a deep abyss of economic uncertainty.

All eyes soon turned to Wall Street. After the NBA abruptly suspended its regular season on March 11, Americans began to catch glimpses of the crisis's impacts on the scrolling marquees of the NASDAQ and the Dow Jones Industrial. By March 20, the S&P 500 would lose more than 20 percent of its value, wiping out massive gains witnessed over the prior four years. President Donald Trump was left dumbstruck, uncharacteristically refraining from tweeting about the economy for almost a week after the initial shutdown. While the impacts on the rest of the economy would be felt later, prompting massive stimulus spending to rescue laid-off workers, small businesses, and major industries, viewers were first alerted to these impending struggles by the collapse of core stock market indices.

Americans living through the COVID-19 crisis were accustomed to stock market tickers heralding the arrival of bad news. Black Monday in 1987, the dot-com bubble of 2000, the subprime mortgage crisis of 2007, and September 11, 2001, were all moments during which ordinary Americans' fears were stoked by tumbling share prices. Of course, stock prices also rally in response to good news. When Donald Trump signed the CARES Act into law (a massive stimulus bill that provided over $500 billion in one-time cash payments to taxpayers, among other benefits), stockbrokers responded. As soon as it became clear that the CARES Act

1

would pass, the Dow Jones Industrial Average gained over 2,000 points, the fourth largest daily percentage gain in history.

Diverse mainstream news sources, from cable channels to newspapers, often frame breaking news events in terms of their effects on stock prices. When market fluctuations are especially large, journalists grab viewers' attention with eye-catching graphics, such as colorful red-green candlestick charts or jagged line graphs. Clanging opening bells and the frenzied shouting of Wall Street market makers are intimately familiar sounds to modern news audiences. Simply put, in today's nonstop media environment, stock market coverage is everywhere.

## What This Book Is About

The national recovery from COVID-19, along with its attendant emphasis on stock market performance as a measure of the economy, provides a useful starting point for thinking about the subject of this book. The central premise of this volume is that an intense media focus on the stock market increasingly matters for American politics. As the public seeks out ways to judge incumbent presidents for their performance in office, the stock market is becoming increasingly salient—and increasingly contested—in the minds of loyal partisans.

In 2020, as conservatives and liberals debated the merits of "reopening the economy," the economic toll of the virus became strongly associated in coverage (and in partisan talking points) with the performance of the stock market. In April, President Trump hinted at the chance for a "big bounce" in the stock market after reopening the country, promising that "Our Economy will BOOM, perhaps like never before!!!"[1] Meanwhile, commentators debated the likelihood of a "V-shaped recovery," interpreting the statements of Fed Chairman Jerome Powell in order to gauge whether the pandemic shutdown would have modest or severe long-term economic effects (Stewart 2020). As partisans coalesced around rival talking points, the 2020 Presidential Election loomed—a contest that many political scientists believed would hinge on signals from the faltering economy (e.g., Dassonneville and Tien 2020). All the while, news reports were captivating viewers with up-to-the-minute accounts of the stock market's unprecedented volatility.

Donald Trump's frequent tweets about the stock market in 2020 make sense when we recall that economic judgments shape citizens' behavior at the ballot box. Commentator James Carville once famously summarized decades of political science research on the subject by exclaiming, "It's the economy, stupid!" Presiding over a slumping economy jeopardizes incumbent presidents' chances of ensuring they will stay in office. A booming economy, on the other hand, means that voters will defer their inclination to "kick the rascals out." This straightforward pattern of *economic voting* is one of political science's most enduring discoveries. The economy can make or break an election bid, and politicians know it.[2]

While Carville's exclamation is a great political catchphrase, it overlooks the fact that Americans' economic judgments arise through a complex process of mediated information acquisition (e.g., Brady, Ferejohn, and Parker 2022). Individual voters hold unique perspectives on the issues and events of the day, assembled largely based on their news consumption habits (e.g., Mutz 1992).[3] As a result, voters might disagree about politicians' economic policy proposals. They might also disagree about whether political actions and economic outcomes are causally linked (Hellwig 2014; Evans and Pickup 2010; Healy and Malhotra 2013). Economic voting might be an empirical regularity, but it is much less clear how voters leverage *specific* kinds of economic information to make effective decisions at the ballot box. How citizens form and leverage their economic perceptions constitutes an important area of ongoing scholarly inquiry.

## THE STOCK MARKET AND PUBLIC OPINION: A RESEARCH AGENDA

In today's uncertain political environment, there is another, even more fundamental question, though: Just what exactly *is* "the economy?" Various economic indicators can describe economic reality quite differently, even when reported at the very same time. In this book, I argue that the rise of *stock market indicators* as a resource for economic storytelling is becoming increasingly consequential for public opinion. Stock market data, as opposed to information like wage growth, unemployment, inflation, and GDP growth, tell us very specific, potentially misleading stories about overall economic progress. Since the Great Recession of 2008–09 the United States has heard mostly good news about stock prices, apart from rapid "flash crashes" in 2011, 2015, 2018, and 2020. In each case, the stock market recovered to surpass record highs, aided in part by Fed policies throughout the period that incentivized stock market investment. But when it comes to other indicators of middle-class economic performance, like wage growth and consumer prices, the same period has witnessed more mixed conditions.

The stock market is highly salient in the minds of everyday Americans, in part due to the practices of economic journalists, and in part because middle-class Americans have become more active participants in the financial marketplace. As we will see, these trends mean that stock market indicators are becoming relevant predictors of political judgments.

But despite their surprisingly intimate knowledge of stock market trends, Americans are not always in agreement about the *meaning* of these developments for politics. Republicans and Democrats are beginning to pick partisan fights over these indicators, debating the causes and consequences of stock prices while criticizing or cheering for incumbent politicians. As partisan contestation over the stock market increases, I argue that Americans could increasingly lose sight of other, more relevant economic signals.

Over the course of the present volume, I examine these trends using a two-step approach. First, I study how media and political elites discuss the stock market, with special attention to the agenda-setting behavior of news sources and elites across the partisan-ideological spectrum. Second, I turn to public opinion data and original survey experiments to measure the effects of these media signals. I work to understand how Americans interpret elites' messages to inform their broader political and economic judgments. I also examine the extent to which perceptions of the stock market are biased by individuals' partisan identities. My investigations show that political judgments are becoming increasingly linked to the movement of stock prices in an era of growing economic inequality. "The stock market is not the economy," as recent observers note with alarm (Ryssdal 2018), but today's elite discourse about economic performance—a discourse that media consumers attentively follow—increasingly obscures this fact.

The consequences of these seemingly innocuous trends are manifold for politics and economics alike. Because stock prices portray the economy in ways that are sometimes contradictory to core indicators of middle-class well-being, the stock market ticker can distract from more fundamental economic issues. And because stock prices have often diverged from other core indicators' performance in recent years, stock market perceptions also represent an especially important topic for students of public opinion, inequality, and democratic accountability.

## WHY THE STOCK MARKET MATTERS

The stock market is becoming an increasingly salient topic of discussion in the United States for two primary reasons. First, economic and social trends are causing more middle-class Americans to become interested in (though not intensely affected by) stock market fluctuations. Second, as I discuss later in the introduction and in chapter 1, new professional constraints and demands have caused journalists and media organizations to reorient their economic news values, resulting in increased coverage of stock market data and indicators over the past several decades. As we will see, this agenda-setting effect has manifold implications for public opinion about the economy, including the nature of partisan bias in economic evaluations.

## A FINANCIALIZED ECONOMY

While in the postwar economic boom of the 1950s many middle-class Americans held jobs in thriving manufacturing industries, today's economy is increasingly dominated by the so-called FIRE sector, comprising finance, insurance, and real estate. And as FIRE grows—now over 20 percent of the US economy as a percent of GDP, the public has also become increasingly inundated by stock market news and insights (Bureau of Economic Analysis 2022). The "financialization" of the US economy means that the stock market is a more powerful economic force than it used to be, and attention to the stock market reflects this changing economic landscape.

Americans have also become increasingly interested in the performance of the stock market because of their retirement accounts. Most full-time employees today realize a large fraction of their retirement benefits as stock assets. Whereas in earlier eras defined-benefit pensions would specify the terms of a postretirement income, many employers began terminating their pension programs in the 1980s. In their place are standard 401(k) and 403(b) plans that often provide for employer-matched contributions. In addition, as tax-sheltered IRAs (both traditional and Roth) have gained in popularity over the past four decades, Americans without 401(k) plans similarly became more likely to own and manage stock portfolios as retirement vehicles (e.g., Poterba, Venti, and Wise 2007).

These developments in the retirement savings market put an increased onus on the employee to invest a fraction of their own income to retirement—a process that results in both earnings and benefits flowing to passively managed index funds and other institutional retirement accounts. The stock market, rather than the predefined term sheet of a pension plan, has become a symbol of postretirement prosperity to millions of Americans.

## THE RETAIL REVOLUTION

The rise of so-called "retail investing" has also led to plentiful discussion of the stock market on social media platforms and in the news. In recent years, the growing popularity of low- to no-cost trading platforms has allowed more middle-class Americans the ability to engage in casual investing and day trading as a hobby. Apps like Robinhood promise the ability to instantly buy and sell individual shares of publicly listed companies, yielding worry among some members of Congress about the potential for uninformed hobbyists to lose their savings betting on the wrong stocks (Sorkin et al. 2021).

There is no better recent example of public interest in day trading on the stock market than the frenzy surrounding GameStop, Inc. (GME), which occurred in January of 2021. GameStop, a struggling retail vendor of video games and peripherals, had seen its share prices fall in response to the COVID-19 crisis and the ascendency of digital marketplaces for video games. But when Reddit users on the "WallStreetBets" forum observed that large hedge funds were shorting GME, recommendations to buy shares of GME proliferated on the site.[4] As GME began to surge in earnest on January 26, the topic would soon resonate on more mainstream social media sites like Twitter and later would attract attention on TV and in prominent newspapers. "Stonks" (a tongue-in-cheek misnomer for stocks popular among Reddit users) were the top news item of the day.

The story would continue to attract headlines as GME reached $347.51 per share (over 1,700 percent of its January 11 price) on January 27. The breathless coverage resulted in frenzied buying of the stock, which caused platforms like Robinhood to temporarily halt trading of GameStop shares on their apps. This decision prompted allegations of collusion between Robinhood investors and hedge funds, as those with short positions sought to avoid further losses from the incipient short squeeze. Ultimately, Reddit user and financial analyst Keith Gill, one of the most prominent voices on the WallStreetBets forum, would testify before the House Financial Services Committee along with Robinhood CEO Vladimir Tenev. His testimony continued to raise the media profile of the GME affair throughout the Spring of 2021.

While the direct consequences of the GME saga for partisan politics are currently unclear, the story has far-reaching political implications. Robinhood has since faced increased scrutiny for its business practices, as Reddit users continue to forward increasingly complex theories about market manipulation and the power of hedge funds. Much of the debate in the aftermath of GME's record-setting performance centered on the weakness of retail investors, navigating the markets amongst financial "whales" that can move prices through high-volume transactions and targeted shorts. Financial commentators likened this conflict to a "clash of the classes—proletariat versus bourgeoisie" (Ferre 2021).

Vocal defenders of retail traders have included surprisingly odd political bedfellows, including Representative Alexandria Ocasio-Cortez (D-NY) and Senator Ted Cruz (R-TX). In a series of January tweets, both politicians defended GME investors against hedge funds and the machinations of Robinhood, prompting journalists to note that "for Republicans, the market upheaval was a referendum on elitism," whereas for Democrats, the story was one of "pure corporate greed and the need for greater regulation" (Lerer and Herndon 2021).

As partisan elites on both sides of the aisle made overtures to small-time retail investors, the outcry against large investment firms hearkened back to the Occupy Wall Street movement of 2011 (Gamson and Sifry 2013). In the wake of the global financial crisis, the Occupy movement targeted banks and hedge funds in a similar populist backlash. But in 2021, the protest movement had a somewhat different character. Occupy protesters stood firmly against a system they believed was inaccessible to the middle class and antithetical to democratic principles. In contrast, aggrieved retail investors sought to play a more active role as participants within the Wall Street system. Rather than castigating banks and hedge funds for the erosion of egalitarian democratic principles, members of this online movement have sought to gain fairer treatment as participants in the marketplace.

As more and more Americans transform into seasoned day traders, online stock market hobbyists, and passively invested retirement account holders, one common theme emerges: rapt attention to the stock market as a relevant indicator of economic performance. However, this increased attention to the stock market betrays an unheralded fact about the U.S. economy: almost half of Americans have *no investments in the stock market whatsoever*, and of those who do, most have only a few thousand dollars invested (Parker and Fry 2020; Wolff 2017). When battles between giant hedge funds and small-time investors rage, those Americans without meaningful stock assets are exposed to further barrages of news coverage about wildly fluctuating prices and indices, potentially at the expense of other information that would more accurately describe their own economic prospects.

## WHY THE STOCK MARKET DOES NOT MATTER
## (AS MUCH AS WE THINK IT DOES)

Day trading, individual retirement accounts, and the growth of the financial services sector all point to the seeming importance of the stock market for ordinary Americans' lives. However, these developments obscure an important insight that alters how we should think about the daily rise and fall of stock prices. Despite the growth of the financial sector and the popularity of individual stock market accounts, only around 44 percent of middle-income American households have any stock market assets—including retirement accounts. And of the group that does, the average portfolio is worth just around $12,000 (Parker and Fry 2020).

While Americans have placed an increasing emphasis on stock market data as valuable information for making economic (and ultimately, political) judgments, most Americans have very little "skin in the game." Instead, the very wealthy are those most directly influenced by stock market fluctuations over time (Wolff 2017). Middle-class Americans would perhaps do better to consider other core indicators of economic progress, such as prices and wage growth, to understand how they are truly faring in the present economy. Some commentators have made this observation in starker terms: As the stock market is not a reflection of the "real" economy, "what's bad for America is sometimes good for the market" (Krugman 2020).

The GME story shows how coverage of stock market performance can distract from other economic matters. In January of 2021, media attention to GME was intense. CNBC went so far as to include the price of GameStop alongside the perennially displayed Dow, NASDAQ, and S&P 500 indices on a permanent chyron (Fitzgerald 2021). GME's ascendancy, however, came on the very same day as the release of the Bureau of Labor Statistics' State Employment and Unemployment Report for the second quarter of 2020. This valuable report provides detailed information about jobs and employment in all fifty states. While this report might normally be useful information for journalists seeking to portray economic developments to the public, the eye-catching rise of GME dominated the headlines instead.

## WHY THE STOCK MARKET AFFECTS POLITICS

Because "the stock market is not the economy" (Ryssdal 2018), Americans' increased focus on Wall Street bears consequences for classic theories of democratic accountability. Economic voting theory assumes that voters will go to the polls armed with reasonable judgments about the incumbent's performance on relevant "valence issues" (including the state of the national economy).[5] Nevertheless, political scientists have long questioned the *quality* of so-called economic voting in American democracy (e.g., Bartels 2002; Evans and Andersen 2006). When voters fail to properly weigh the available economic evidence, basic political accountability is put in jeopardy.

In the academic literature, these concerns are generally rooted in two basic observations. The first is that Republican and Democratic identifiers tend to view objective economic developments through politically tinted lenses. These partisan biases are thought to occur because of *partisan motivated reasoning*, a psychological phenomenon that yields bias in individuals' evaluations of a wide array of ideas and facts (e.g., Kahan 2015). If voters filter economic news through party-driven assumptions about the state of the world, the otherwise direct link between economic developments and vote choice becomes far murkier. Republican voters will always assume that Republicans have handled the economy well, whereas Democrats will think the opposite. This bias means that the real economy will have little influence on voters' support for incumbents at the polls.

A second concern is that Americans do not fully comprehend the *unequal* nature of the American economy, even if they can resist the temptation towards partisan bias. Larry Bartels, a prominent political scientist, shows evidence that Americans are more likely to support incumbent presidents during periods when very wealthy citizens experience soaring income growth (Bartels 2009). Surprisingly, however, voters display no similar preference for incumbents who preside over strong income growth for the middle class.

While Carville might have bluntly attested that "it's the economy, stupid," these surprising findings suggest that it's the "economy of the wealthy" that matters most for electoral success—not the economic fortunes of average Americans. Other scholars show that many Americans struggle to understand the income gap between the "one percent" and the "99 percent" (e.g., K.-S. Trump 2018). Americans may correspondingly remain unaware that stock market performance has a much stronger effect on the economic performance of millionaires and billionaires than on the average salaried worker with a 401(k). High-status workers, like CEOs, often elect to take most of their earnings as stock options rather than salary. Another set of very wealthy individuals earn no salaries at all, instead drawing on the proceeds of their massive investment portfolios to pay the bills. If middle-class Americans prioritize the stock market as a source of vital economic information, the electorate may inadvertently reward incumbents when these wealthy groups prosper—even during periods of stagnant middle-class economic performance.

Given these developments, it is increasingly important to examine what Americans know and think about the stock market, how their beliefs are formed, and how their perceptions affect their political judgments. What do American media say about the economy, and to what extent do ideological and "mainstream" media rely upon stock market information over other indicators? What do partisan elites say about stock market performance (if anything at all)? What do Americans ultimately believe about the stock market—and how do these perceptions drive their evaluations of political actors?

## SUMMARY OF FINDINGS: STYLIZED FACTS ABOUT STOCK MARKET PERCEPTIONS

My answers to these questions are informed by descriptive analyses of media and public opinion, followed by causally identified survey experiments. They uncover a pattern that supports a theory characterized by partisan motivated reasoning, political credit-taking and blame-giving, and hidden agenda-setting effects. They reveal the increasingly salient and politicized nature of stock market perceptions in a polarized and unequal society.

By describing the "economic media agenda" across a wide variety of contemporary sources, I first show that media sources have devoted a huge amount of attention to stock market information since the 1980s. More so than any other economic indicator, including jobs reports and inflation data, average Americans can expect to learn something about stock prices when they seek out economic news on any given day. This pattern of *stock market media saturation* endures regardless of a source's medium, market, or ideological slant. Americans are paying attention, too. Despite their inherent partisan biases, Americans know a lot about the stock market, and they increasingly use this reserve of stock market knowledge to evaluate incumbent presidential performance.

Media saturation also helps to explain why partisan political elites have generally avoided public discussion of the stock market until very recently. The abundance of stock market coverage in media has historically kept mentions of stock market performance away from the persuasive arsenal of partisan elites as the constant flow of new information constrains the framing efforts of partisan message senders.

However, Donald Trump's efforts to take credit for the stock market during his presidency represented a sudden exogenous shock to the economic information environment. Americans' stock market perceptions during the Trump era present a critical test of media effects, pitting presidential framing efforts against the effects of longstanding media agenda setting. Are stock market perceptions polarizing in response to this new-found form of elite credit-claiming?

The present analyses reveal that these recent cueing efforts helped foster new forms of partisan bias in Americans' economic beliefs. When stock prices rose during the Trump administration, Republicans became more likely to believe that the stock market *mattered* for the health of the overall US economy. Democrats, on the other hand, became increasingly doubtful of the stock market's importance for economic progress. This finding represents a new development for theories of political and economic accountability. It points to the notion that "factual polarization" is currently reaching into the realm of economic indicators, compounding more familiar biases in overall economic perceptions. Now, different economic signals are themselves coming to bear different *meanings* for Republicans and Democrats, resulting in further challenges to democratic accountability.

Overall, then, the book's findings reveal that contemporary hyperattention to the stock market bears two major political consequences. First, the rise and fall of stock market indicators appear to increasingly matter for elections and political judgments. Because Americans hear so much about the stock market in news, they apply this knowledge to evaluations of economic and political reality through mostly *automatic* cognitive processes. Second, in service of partisan congenial interpretations of reality, Republicans and Democrats are beginning to adjust their beliefs about the way the stock market shapes economic outcomes. Despite the surprising accuracy of Americans' beliefs about the performance of the stock market, bias lurks below the surface—an important lesson about the strength and flexibility of partisan perceptual screens.

In the next sections, I briefly review current scholarly perspectives in the study of economic perceptions before previewing the primary theoretical contributions of this volume. I conclude by providing an outline of the remaining chapters that describes my aims, analyses, and findings in greater detail.

## Economic Perceptions: Contemporary Approaches

Most Americans are highly attuned to the state of the nation's economy (Druckman, Peterson, and Slothuus 2013). As we will see in later chapters, the public's economic perceptions are also not substantially influenced by gender, racial, generational, or even class distinctions. When asked about the state of the economy, low- and high-income Americans often make surprisingly similar judgments. Citizens' perceptions reflect real economic developments that have been discussed in the news, growing more pessimistic during downturns and more optimistic during expansions (e.g., DeVries, Hobolt, and Tilley 2018; Goidel and Langley 1995; MacKuen, Erikson, and Stimson 1992; Nadeau et al. 1999; Sanders 2000). Americans even use mediated information to build reasonable expectations about the future economy (Soroka, Stecula, and Wlezien 2015).

But when we disaggregate economic perceptions across Republican and Democratic party lines, this seeming consensus comes apart at the seams (e.g., Bartels 1992; Brady et al. 2022; Evans and Pickup 2010). Partisan disagreement in economic evaluations has increased considerably since the 1970s and 80s, in tandem with more general forms of political polarization. When Republicans say the economy is booming, Democrats are often more skeptical, like during the last year of the Trump administration. When Democrats are enthusiastic about economic progress, like they were at the tail end of the Obama administration, Republicans are generally much more pessimistic.

In recent years, these polarized economic perceptions have shifted seismically in response to presidential election results. During the Obama administration, Americans experienced a slow but steady economic recovery from the challenges of the Great Recession. Over these years, Obama-backing Democrats became ebulliently optimistic about economic performance. Republicans, on the other hand, maintained perceptions that were no less pessimistic than they had been in 2009, during the peak of the crisis—right up until the inauguration of Donald Trump (Bartels and Bermeo 2013).

In 2017, Republicans' pessimism suddenly vanished, as the Trump administration rode into office on the tailwinds of nearly a decade of recovery efforts (Lowrey 2018). Meanwhile, Democrats' optimism has flagged since Trump's inauguration, despite strong performance across indicators such as unemployment, the stock market, and business activity (Boskin 2018). Partisan identities, combined with the partisanship of the incumbent, now help to determine more than any other factor whether members of the public fall on the optimistic or the pessimistic side of the economic perceptual spectrum.

This pattern has evolved over time. Surveys in the modern period have consistently shown that the sitting president is the primary recipient of blame and credit for overall economic performance (Rudolph 2003). While presidents might find this attribution of responsibility to be a bit unfair given the complexity of the global economy, Americans often point the finger for these developments at the most visible political figurehead.[6]

We have some indication that state economies and their political features also play a role in driving economic judgments. Nevertheless, most of the evidence suggests that national political circumstances are far more important for citizens' overall judgments (Ansolabehere, Meredith, and Snowberg 2014; Clark and Makse 2019; Dickerson and Ondercin 2017). Scholars have recently pointed out that American politics is also becoming increasingly nationalized, and this presidential link to economic outcomes is no exception (Hopkins 2018). The party of the incumbent president is now more important than ever in explaining whether Republicans will be more enthusiastic than Democrats about the economy, or vice versa.

Existing work on economic evaluations therefore paints a gloomy picture for democratic accountability because of partisan bias. We know that regardless of the true state of the economy, "bias will find a way" to satisfy partisans' need to feel good about their party (Bisgaard 2018). Even in the face of overwhelming evidence to the contrary, partisans will adjust their views about who is responsible for current economic conditions to maintain a biased perspective. Americans' economic perceptions reflect a society that is falling victim to increasing "belief polarization" (Gerber and Green 1999). While their reported perceptions may partly reflect efforts to "cheerlead" for their preferred party, Americans appear to be more likely than ever to judge the economy through partisan-tinted lenses (Berinsky 2018).

## PERCEPTIONS OF STOCK MARKET INDICATORS

While much is known about the contours of Americans' overall economic perceptions, far less attention has been traditionally paid to what Americans believe about more specific economic trends. Many prior studies have examined unemployment, inflation, and GDP growth as sources of economic information, evaluating the degree to which these objective indicators influence economic beliefs and political evaluations (e.g., Bartels 2002; Bisgaard et al. 2016; Conover et al. 1986; Evans and Andersen 2006; Mutz 1998; Nadeau et al. 2000). While aggregate-level analyses show that unemployment and GDP growth both matter in driving political judgments, it is not always clear that Americans are specifically attentive to the nuances of these economic trends. Most Americans are poor guessers when asked to identify the current unemployment rate or the rate of inflation (e.g., Lawrence and Sides 2014).

Mutz (1998) argues that mediated reports of economic trends are essential for Americans to grasp current economic performance, simply because of the US economy is so large and complex. As a result, economic news reporting is a critical factor in determining whether a given economic indicator influences Americans' broader views of current and future conditions. Inflation, unemployment, wage growth, sales, commodity prices, and many other sources of economic data are only well-understood by Americans when they are reported on by mainstream media sources (Larcinese et al. 2011).

Existing research also points out that the economy's vast complexity bears consequences for the links between the objective movement of indicators and Americans' economic judgments (e.g., Jerit and Barabas 2012). Notably, Parker-Stephen (2013) posits that partisan biases will be inhibited when economic indicators all move together in a positive or negative direction. When the "burden of evidence," however, is fragmented, with some economic indicators showing gloomy results, and other indicators showing reason for optimism, this ambiguity leads to more room for partisan bias. When economic indicators disagree, Americans' economic judgments become far more partisan in nature due to the inherent ambiguity of economic progress (see also Bisgaard 2015).

Over the past decade, we have witnessed a changing economy that has increasingly privileged attention to the stock market. Nevertheless, the stock market has remained a chronically understudied subject in the relevant literatures over the same time period (but see Fauvelle-Aymar and Stegmaier 2013). Americans are increasingly attuned to the stock market, with major consequences for theories of partisan bias and political opinion formation, as the information environment adapts to the expectations of an increasingly financialized society. Despite these trends, relatively little is currently known about the causes and consequences of Americans' beliefs about the stock market.

In the next section, I briefly outline a theory that explains why and how the stock market has become central to Americans' perceptions of economic reality—and what these expectations mean for voting and political behavior.

## How the Stock Market Shapes Public Opinion

In developing a theory of the stock market's effects on public opinion, I argue that *data*—specifically the *hyper-availability of stock market data*—represent an overlooked determinant of Americans' factual economic perceptions. More specifically, while a huge volume of existing research has shown that media agenda setting influences citizens' beliefs, I trace economic agenda setting to the government institutions and private groups that produce the raw numbers used in journalistic reports.[7] I expect this "data-driven agenda-setting" to shape the salience of the stock market for Americans' overall judgments of economic reality. Echoing Parker-Stephen's (2013) "tides of disagreement," this form of agenda setting should influence the degree to which Americans are willing to internalize (or rationalize away) the reality of specific economic developments. When we consider the process through which economic data are currently produced, and the imbalances in coverage that might result, new lines of theorizing emerge about the newfound salience of the stock market in shaping Americans' opinions and attitudes.

In conventional accounts of economic agenda setting, journalists and politicians affect the objective knowledge of Americans through their communication strategies (e g., Druckman 2001). However, I assert that the norms and practices of "data generators" are equally important. This is because the availability of raw economic data can reshape the strategic considerations of both partisan elites and the press.

Relevant data generators include the Bureau of Labor Statistics, the Federal Reserve, the Census Bureau, stock markets, and a host of private firms and economists. These actors contribute to an unintentional process that causes journalists—and subsequently, citizens—to focus their attention on stock market indicators, merely because a much larger and much more frequent volume of statistics about stock market trends exists than for other economic topics. The technologies that generate and report economic statistics yield imbalances in the *availability* of data on a day-to-day basis. These imbalances affect journalists, who seek to efficiently provide the public with economic information at a rapid pace. Providing audiences with up-to-the-minute stock market news is a quick and relatively effortless method to create economic reporting that can be disseminated on a predictable basis. Stock prices have become quotidian fodder for the vast content demands of the twenty-four-hour news cycle (Bucy, Gantz, and Wang 2007).

While data generation is likely an important driver of a wide array of public attitudes, in the present volume, I study stock market perceptions as a critical case. Media saturation helps to explain the surprising accuracy of Americans' stock market perceptions—and, as we will see in chapter 4, the influence of those perceptions on presidential approval. Modern agenda setting helps to explain the ascendant salience of the stock market in an era of nonstop news.

INFORMATION SATURATION AND ELITE INFLUENCE

Partisan elites must also navigate this imbalanced information environment. Elites will often comment on news stories when they are useful vehicles for the assignment of blame or credit. Much current research is interested in the conditions under which elites succeed or fail in these persuasion efforts (e.g., Druckman, Peterson, and Slothuus 2013). When it comes to the economy, members of the president's party will often attempt to highlight stories that show evidence of economic progress, while the opposition will seek to undermine the president's reputation as an economic manager by repeating talking points about economic stagnation.

Elites often perform this credit and blame assignment using strategic *media framing* (Scheufele 1999; Scheufele and Tewksbury 2006). Partisan elites craft persuasive messages, which selectively present and interpret information, framing news stories in ways that support partisan-congenial narratives. However, these messages are not always successful in their persuasive power. Much current scholarship has sought to detail the limits of elite framing attempts (Anson 2016; Druckman 2001; Lecheler and De Vreese 2012; Nicholson 2011).

Journalistic agenda setting represents one important limit on the success of elite framing efforts. In particular, I argue that media hyper-attention to the stock market will dissuade politicians from mentioning stock prices as a tool for assigning credit and blame. The vast availability of this information makes framing difficult as Americans will likely already possess a clear understanding of the relatively unambiguous rise or fall of stock prices prior to the moment when framing efforts are deployed.

Attempts to "swim upstream," against the tide of journalistic agenda setting, are therefore expected to be rare. However, if they happen, partisan cues could signal to audiences that the stock market is a relevant indicator not only for attention, but for partisan contestation. In this way, an entrepreneurial politician might reflect recent trends towards public interest in the stock market by claiming credit for rising stock prices. As we will see later, Donald Trump's bombastic rhetoric about the stock market represented exactly such a shift in framing behavior. As attention to the stock market's performance became a hallmark of his presidency, so too did this framing behavior generate new attitudes towards the stock market among Republicans and Democrats in the electorate.

## Partisan Identities and Economic Progress

When economic reports are disseminated to citizens through media reports and politicians' statements, cognitive processes spring into action. Partisan motivated reasoning holds that partisans will interpret newly acquired information through the lens of their deeply held psychological group attachments (Bolsen, Druckman, and Cook 2014; Kunda 1990; Slothuus and De Vreese 2010; Taber and Lodge 2006). Partisans not only engage in *self-selection* in deciding which kinds of news to consume; they also make conscious and subconscious decisions to *accept* or *reject* new information. As a result, the most pressing question in the study of motivated reasoning is not *whether* it has an impact on partisans' judgments, but rather *when* and *where* its impacts can be constrained.

It currently remains unclear whether Republicans and Democrats can agree on economic specifics—and if they can, *which* specifics are characterized by the most and least agreement (c.f. Jerit and Barabas 2012; Parker-Stephen 2013; Bisgaard 2019). Seemingly benign variation in Americans' exposure to data about different economic topics, such as commodity prices and consumer confidence, can shape the way that partisan-motivated reasoning exerts itself upon the overall political judgments of partisans.

These trends towards disagreement are indicative of a broader phenomenon of "factual polarization." In the present era, partisan identities fundamentally shape the way many citizens interpret the world around them. Partisanship, much akin to a religious affiliation, is a *social identity*. Party identifiers interpret social meaning through the lens of their group attachments, linking their self-esteem and sense of self-worth to the successes and failures of the party (Green, Palmquist and Schickler 2004; Layman, Carsey, and Horowitz 2006). While contemporary partisans are not as ideologically extreme as the party elites they look to for guidance in the world of politics, patterns of in-group partisan favoritism are currently intensifying (McCarty, Poole, and Rosenthal 2016).

One consequence of this "team" mentality is that Republicans and Democrats are much more likely to view members of the opposing party in a negative light when compared to members of their own party. Partisans in the electorate may not be as ideologically extreme as their elite counterparts, but many experience intense emotional, or *affective*, reactions to matters with relevance to their partisan identities. We have become a nation of partisans who "disrespectfully agree," according to Lillianna Mason (2018). Many partisans experience intense affective reactions to members of the other party, despite holding relatively moderate issue positions.

In addition to these intensely negative views about the "other team," partisan social identities also reshape Americans' perceptions of objective reality. Republicans and Democrats interpret real-world developments through the lens of a "preferred world state," which is informed by their group membership. The preferred world represents the way things *ought* to be, given the presupposition that members of the in-group are superior to those of the out-group. Social psychologists have dubbed this phenomenon motivated reasoning because it reflects the notion that partisan identifiers are "directionally" motivated to see the world in a manner that trends towards congenial interpretations (and away from "disconfirming" evidence).

Motivated reasoning leads partisans to learn about, interpret, and justify current events in ways that support their party's claims to superior morality and performance in office. Partisans also pay greater attention to information when it is provided to them by trusted party elites. They will correspondingly find reasons to ignore or discredit information that contradicts the preferred world interpretation of reality, and they will resoundingly reject information that comes from outgroup sources. Cue-taking, the process through which partisans make snap judgments about the validity of information, helps to explain why so many partisans quickly dismiss their opponents' claims (Bullock 2011; Flynn, Nyhan, and Reifler 2017; Kam 2005).

Party identities are evolving in the present period. They are increasingly aligning with the other deeply held identities and group loyalties of the electorate. Citizens' racial, religious, gender, and cultural identities are becoming more strongly associated with the partisan divide (Abramowitz

2018; Harsgor 2018; Mason 2016). There is even some indication that partisans are changing some of their other identities to better fit the descriptors that characterize the in-party group. Republican Protestants, for example, have increased their religiosity to better match their Republican identities, while Democratic Protestants have diminished the strength of their religious attachments in recent years (Campbell et al. 2018; Margolis 2018). Conceiving of the world in a partisan-directional fashion can not only reshape what we think: it can also reshape who we claim to be.

Partisan identities are also coming to reshape not only our knowledge of "the facts," but also our interpretations of real-world developments (Bisgaard 2015). Modern framing and agenda setting of the stock market may not lead to increasing disagreement over whether the stock market is going up or down. Instead, because of its hypersaturation in media, partisans may come to contest the *meaning* of stock market data. Rather than disputes over the objective record of stock market performance, "economic narratives" represent a new dimension of partisan bias. If strategic elites use stock markets in their framing efforts, contemporary partisans may react by developing increasingly sophisticated forms of expressive bias.

## Plan of the Book

The above theory traces new patterns in Americans' beliefs about the stock market. These patterns originate in media agenda setting, obtain nuance through partisan elite communications, and influence downstream aspects of citizens' attitudes and political behavior. Below, I briefly outline how the book approaches each part of this theory through a multifaceted research agenda. From studies of economic news coverage to elite messaging, I first examine contemporary economic discourse among journalists and political elites. Then, I turn to studies of public perceptions, integrating insights from the earlier media analyses to test the effects of agenda setting and framing behavior. I conclude with tests of citizens' political judgments and a broader discussion of the stock market's impact on future political outcomes.

### CHAPTER 1: DATA-DRIVEN AGENDA SETTING: HOW STOCK MARKET INDICATORS SHAPE CITIZEN PERCEPTIONS

The first chapter expands upon the theory briefly introduced above. Chapter 1 reviews existing research on agenda setting and framing before applying these lessons to a theory of Americans' stock market perceptions. I explain why Americans' beliefs about economic specifics deserve increased scrutiny in public opinion research. I also show why stock market perceptions have important consequences for theories of retrospective accountability.

Next, I describe how motivated reasoning can be conditioned by the contours of the stock market–saturated information environment. I do this by describing the process in which information about the economy is disseminated from reporting agencies to journalists. These stylized facts show us that not all economic information is created (or at least reported) equally: stock market data are produced continuously, while other information trickles out from reporting agencies on monthly or quarterly bases.

These imbalances in the information environment are expected to have consequences for citizens' perceptions of the economy and presidential incumbents. In the remainder of the chapter, I explain how and why the stock market is coming to play a more central role in American public opinion. These expectations, relying on theories of automaticity, explain that Americans are likely to evaluate presidential incumbents, as well as the overall nature of the economy, through stock market knowledge that is relatively free of partisan bias.

CHAPTER 2: "FOLLOWING THE TICKER:" MEDIA AGENDA SETTING AND STOCK MARKET DATA

In chapter 2, I trace the expectations developed in chapter 1 using observational analysis of news media. I describe the ways in which economic indicators are discussed in economic news through an analysis of news stories in print and on cable news. I analyze a dataset of *New York Times* economy stories from 1980 through 2020, followed by a set of thirteen daily newspapers and two cable news sources from 2015 through 2020. These descriptive investigations help us better understand when and why news sources (including partisan media) discuss the stock market. Through an automated content analytical strategy, I show that the contemporary economic news agenda is saturated with media mentions of the stock market relative to indicators like unemployment, wage growth, and prices.

The results show that this stock market saturation occurs regardless of the ideological proclivities of the source in question. While the *New York Times* dataset shows clear evidence of stock market indicator saturation, the data collection performed from 2015–2020 allows us to see whether this agenda-setting behavior holds true in other contexts. The results show that news sources in media markets as diverse as Oklahoma City,

Minneapolis, and San Francisco all privilege the stock market over other indicators. Cable news sources also talk about stock market performance more than other topics, irrespective of the networks' partisan slant.

CHAPTER 3: GRAPPLING WITH BULLS AND BEARS: HOW CONGRESS DISCUSSES THE ECONOMY

I next engage in a descriptive examination of economic messages conveyed to the public by partisan elites. This analysis relies upon a large-scale effort to monitor the official Twitter accounts of all members of the Senate and the House of Representatives from 2015 through 2020. I analyze a repository of more than 1.2 million tweets using the same text-as-data approach developed in chapter 2. This strategy allows us to learn what economic topics were mentioned by Republican and Democratic members of Congress over time.

The results of this analysis show that congressional Twitter discussions of the economy generally follow a pattern of credit-claiming and blame-giving, consistent with traditional accounts of strategic framing. Partisan elites are less likely to discuss economic data when it saturates the information environment. Instead, elites choose more opportune economic data for framing. These results help us understand why, traditionally, stock market performance is almost never discussed by members of Congress in their communications. These partisan elites prefer instead to discuss unemployment and trade when they persuade audiences about the state of the economy.

However, these elite economic messages are evolving. I show evidence in chapter 3 that Republican members of Congress are becoming increasingly interested in claiming credit for stock market performance. This phenomenon intensified from 2017 through 2020, when Donald Trump took to Twitter in his official capacity as president of the United States. Each additional Trump stock market tweet led to a rise in Republicans' mentions of the stock market. Democrats, too, are increasingly willing to mention the stock market in service of ideological framing. Due to the creativity of entrepreneurial partisan elites, the past several years have witnessed a rise in partisan contestation over stock market performance.

CHAPTER 4: THE POLITICIZATION OF STOCK MARKET PERCEPTIONS

Based on the findings from chapters 2 and 3, chapter 4 develops expectations about bias in partisans' economic perceptions. The chapter's findings support the hypothesis that beliefs about stock market performance are relatively immune to partisan bias. They also support the assertion that the stock market is an increasingly powerful predictor of presidential approval, due to the accuracy and salience of these perceptions. Combining the data presented in earlier chapters with a large repository of surveys, the chapter's analysis allows for a study of the effects of the media environment on economic perceptions and political support over time.

In this chapter, I present results from a dataset consisting of nearly two hundred survey items from a wide variety of sources spanning 1980 to the present. The data collection totals more than five hundred thousand unique records of nationally representative American survey participants, many of which specifically measure Americans' beliefs about the movement of the stock market.

Using hierarchical regression models, I first measure the sources of influence on bias in partisans' stock market perceptions over time. Outpacing the effects of the state of the economy and the demographic characteristics of partisans, the theoretically relevant features of the information environment, including media saturation and the presence of elite framing, help us determine when and where partisans' stock market perceptions become irreconcilably biased.

In a follow-up analysis, I also study partisans' rationalizations about the *meaning* of stock market data. This empirical analysis is inspired by recent literature which studies "bias below the surface" of partisans' evaluations of reality. The study examines eleven survey items that ask partisans whether "the stock market matters" for what happens in the broader economy. The results reveal that in recent years a partisan gap is developing in these "economic narratives." Republicans came to believe that the stock market mattered more for the economy during the Trump administration, while Democrats' support for this notion remained unchanged. This lurking form of bias represents a new direction for research on motivated reasoning and economic perceptions.

CHAPTER 5: FRAMING THE STOCK MARKET: EXPERIMENTAL EVIDENCE

In chapter 5, I examine stock market perceptions from an experimental perspective. I trace whether frames provided by partisan elites affect the economic attitudes of citizens under varying conditions. In these tests, I show how motivated reasoning conditions receptivity to messages with and without partisan source cues. Contrary to the expectations of existing work on cueing, these studies show that exposure to congenial information only allows partisans to adjust their beliefs in a pro-inparty direction when it comes to *some* economic topics.

When exposed to congenial news stories about the stock market, partisans do not engage in biased updating—even when the news is associated with an in-group source. This result is consistent with the idea that partisans have been *pre-exposed* to large amounts of stock market information. This pre-exposure is strong enough to mitigate the effects of a persuasive message. The saturation of stock market information in the information environment helps to explain why partisans do not update their stock market perceptions in line with the messages of trusted party elites. Nevertheless, partisans also appear to be pre-exposed to messages about the *meaning* of stock market data, suggesting again that bias lurks below the surface of stock market perceptions.

CONCLUSIONS

I conclude by describing how the book's main findings fit within the extant literatures on framing and priming effects, economic perceptions, motivated reasoning, inequality, and political accountability. These discussions reveal the ingenuity of the persuasive communications efforts of modern elites, as well as the asymmetric nature of motivated reasoning in the realm of economic perceptions. They also illuminate several warning signs for scholars of economic inequality and performance voting.

Nevertheless, I also point to several ways in which the present volume's findings are promising for democracy. The results of the present volume show that partisan motivated reasoning is rivaled in many circumstances by a genuine desire to accurately understand economic reality. These instances show how information saturation can help to determine when and why partisans will see the world in fundamentally different ways and how journalists might help them reach fleeting points of agreement.

Chapter 1

# Data-Driven Agenda Setting

## How Stock Market Indicators Shape Citizen Perceptions

Citizens largely form their economic perceptions by reading, watching, and listening to the news (e.g., Mutz 1992). In this chapter, I explain how citizens' economic perceptions are influenced by the contours of the modern "economic information environment" and how, in turn, those perceptions influence political attitudes and beliefs. Motivating these insights is a basic initial observation. News reporting on the economy is tinted by an overlooked form of agenda setting that privileges *stock market* information over many other possible forms of economic reporting. While economic facts like wage growth, inflation, and unemployment are disseminated at regular intervals by official and expert data sources, the stock market is a far more frequent distributor of raw economic information than any of these other sources. Continuously measured indicators of stock market performance inform journalists and consumers each business day, while other indicators are measured and disseminated at monthly or quarterly intervals. This seemingly innocuous imbalance in the *availability* of economic data changes the behavior of journalists, pundits, and even incumbent politicians, setting off a chain reaction that shapes citizens' economic beliefs and establishes patterns of partisan consensus and conflict over economic performance.

As we will see, one result of stock market-oriented coverage is that Americans' broader economic and political judgments are increasingly influenced by stock market fluctuations. This pattern of influence occurs through a largely automatic cognitive process: The positive or negative tone of stock market coverage tints audiences' attitudes when they perform broader information searches about the state of the world. Due to its overwhelming prevalence in news, even Americans without stock market portfolios are becoming more attuned to the movement of core stock market indices, with consequences for their economic and political perceptions.

A second consequence relates to the opinions of Republicans and Democrats. Perceptual biases inform the way that partisans perceive the world around them—a natural outgrowth of a phenomenon called "partisan motivated reasoning." When a topic like the stock market saturates the news environment, however, partisan motivated reasoning can be constrained (Jerit and Barabas 2012). This means that while Republicans and Democrats might disagree on a wide variety of factual topics, such as the size of America's trade imbalance or the amount of foreign aid doled out by an incumbent president, Americans' beliefs about the performance of the stock market are expected to be far less polarized along partisan lines.

Nevertheless, increased attention to the stock market can allow alternative forms of partisan bias to emerge. I assert that a recent increased in framing efforts by partisan elites has led to new disputes about the *meaning* of the stock market for the broader economy. Republicans, following the persuasive efforts of Donald Trump and congressional Republicans from 2017 through 2020, have come to assign greater importance to the stock market as a relevant performance cue; Democrats have correspondingly reduced the importance they assign to stock prices as a relevant economic signal.

This recent development has generated an important theoretical test, of interest to political communication scholars. It pits the power of media agenda setting against the persuasiveness of partisan elite framing. Ultimately, I argue that the emergence of "partisan narratives" about stock market performance shows us that elite frames are surprisingly powerful, even in the presence of intense media agenda setting (c.f., Parker-Stephen 2013). When Americans make cognitively effortful attempts to interpret the meaning of stock market reports, exposure to elite messages can foster disputes over causal interpretations, attributions of responsibility, and the basis for credit and blame for national economic performance. These mutable "economic narratives" are normatively concerning, given the existence of a disconnect between recent stock market performance and the objective economic prosperity of the American middle class.

## Plan of the Chapter

The present chapter proceeds in four parts. In the first section, I develop a theory of agenda setting in economic news. This theory explains how modern "news values"—the practices of journalists—are shaped by the prevalence of stock market data in the daily flow of economic information. The result is an increased willingness among journalists to cover stock market developments in their economic reports. Second, I theorize the consequences of this agenda-setting behavior for partisan elites' efforts to frame the economy. I argue that elites' framing of credit and blame for economic developments is sensitive to media agenda setting, resulting in an unwillingness among most politicians to use the stock market as a performance cue. Third, I theorize the downstream consequences of these agenda-setting and framing processes for the salience of stock market performance among members of the American public. A wealth of knowledge about the stock market among the American public means that such indicators are exerting a growing influence on Americans' broader economic and political attitudes. Finally, I explore the possibility that the *meaning* of the stock market is a topic of increasing political contestation. By reviewing the contemporary literature on partisan bias and motivated reasoning, I make the case that recent elite framing of the stock market could lead Republicans and Democrats to dispute interpretations of the stock market rather than give biased accounts of its recent performance. Altogether, these expectations point to the possibility that the stock market is becoming increasingly consequential for Americans' political judgments.

## Data-Driven Agenda Setting: A Theory of Modern News Values

Members of the media play a crucial agenda-setting role in modern democracy (e.g., Boydstun 2013; Mutz 1992). Their practices and values are important determinants of what topics are discussed—and not discussed—by the public (Gans 1979). Existing research has carefully and extensively documented the pivotal role of media agenda setters in determining how economic news is conveyed to the public (e.g., Soroka, Stecula, and Wlezien 2015).

But as journalists work to fulfill their public responsibility by reporting accurate information, they confront many constraints.[1] In this section, I posit that the *availability* of economic data is a major driver of economic journalists' reporting practices. As we will see, this means that on an everyday basis, journalists are expected to focus a great deal of their attention on *stock market data* as a source for producing quick, easily digestible economic news stories. The result is a news environment in which stock market reports are far more plentiful than any other form of economic reporting.

*News values* are essential considerations that help journalists determine what is newsworthy (e.g., Harcup and O'Neill 2001). Historically, news values like timeliness (producing stories quickly), unexpectedness (focusing on unexpected developments), personalization (telling stories with personal interest angles), and overall story impact have allowed professional journalists to regularly produce quality journalism even under the pressing constraints of deadlines and budgets. When it comes to modern American news values, however, perhaps the most prominent constraint facing journalists is the nonstop demand for timely content.[2] In the twenty-four-hour news cycle, extremely short production times lead journalists to prioritize stories that they can quickly and efficiently produce. As a result, busy, stressed journalists often develop pragmatic shortcuts to aid in rapid story selection and production (Boydstun 2013). Timeliness considerations affect journalists across a wide range of publications and news outlets: regardless of medium, size, geographical scope, or even ideological slant, the pressure to produce content quickly yields the same kinds of time-saving shortcuts.

When these individual heuristic practices are aggregated across the field of journalism, time-saving habits come to shape the overall agenda of the news in powerful ways. Journalists might still prioritize news values like completeness (getting the whole story), impact (finding the story that is most meaningful to consumers' lived experience), or slant (presenting partisan-leaning news to political audiences), but in modern news, the sheer demand for content is an extreme pressure that overwhelms most other considerations (Bucy et al. 2014).

## News Values and Economic News

While news values influence journalists across the field, the economics beat poses a unique set of challenges (Hayes 2014; Shaw 2015). This is because government, academic, and private economists are continuously producing a deluge of sophisticated statistics that report the detailed inner workings of the US economy. The effective presentation of data is a critical news value in modern journalism: it gives credibility to reporters hoping to impress readers with the accuracy of their technical reports (Harcup and O'Neill 2017). But while journalists in most fields are hard-pressed to dig up relevant, high-quality data to support their stories, there is simply far too much economic data available to reporters. As agencies and firms release technical economic reports to their specialized audiences, it is the responsibility of professional journalists to filter, select, aggregate, decipher, and present the meaning of these findings to their audiences.

Journalists attempt to present dry, technical economic information in a compelling way. In twenty-first-century journalism, profit-motivated private media firms face staunch competition while operating in a highly fragmented media environment (Ostini and Ostini 2002). Even technical, data-driven topics like the economy can draw in audience interest and therefore bolster razor-thin profit margins if stories can be sufficiently eye-catching (e.g., Hamilton 2004). As the Bureau of Labor Statistics, the US Census Bureau, the Bureau of Economic Analysis, and a host of private economic firms continuously pump out the tickers, tables, reports, and graphics that inform skilled observers, news values cause journalists to react in predictable ways. Despite attempts to provide high-impact coverage, reporters are constrained by time and the technical nature of many reports. Using their expertise, economic journalists navigate their information-rich environment to produce simple, salient economic reports. As we will soon see, this often takes the form of a major reliance upon stock market indicators relative to other forms of economic reporting.

## FEATURES OF ECONOMIC JOURNALISM

Before going further, it is instructive to review what else we currently know about the practices of economic journalists. The study of economic news is a surprisingly robust scholarly field, in part because of the well-known importance of economic news reports for public attitudes like presidential approval (e.g., Boydstun et al. 2018; Nadeau et al. 1999; Wlezien et al. 2017). We know of several ways that modern news values can cause economic journalists to fail to reflect "economic reality" in their coverage (e.g., Larcinese, Puglisi, and Snyder 2011).

*Negativity bias,* for example, occurs when journalists respond to the psychological proclivities of individual news consumers (Vliegenthart et al. 2021). Journalists have a distinct tendency to assign greater importance (and therefore greater coverage) to news that tells us of negative, alarming, or threatening developments. The reason for this bias is akin to the reason why local television stations often exhibit "ambulance chasing" and "if it bleeds, it leads" styles of reporting (Fallows 1996). Viewers are transfixed by shocking and gruesome stories, in part because the brain is highly attuned to the occurrence of, or the potential for, threats to our safety and that of our communities (Martin 2008). Shocking, negative stories may provide valuable information about how to avoid falling victim to a similar outcome as the ones described therein. This means that journalists' (and viewers') attention naturally gravitates towards the alarming and the grim.

These evolutionary psychological developments work to influence the overall *tone* of economic news (e.g., Soroka et al. 2018; Vliegenthart et al. 2021). The economy is often presented in a way that magnifies negative developments and cautions against wholesale positivity when a new development signals a strengthening economy. Journalists likely engage in this behavior either because they are aware of the attention-grabbing nature of negative news or because they are also susceptible to negativity bias. Of course, some ideological media will try whenever possible to report economic news with a "congenial" (or party-serving) tone (Larcinese et al. 2011). But regardless of a source's partisan agenda, negativity bias often still plays a role in shifting the economic discourse towards pessimism.

This phenomenon is also conditioned by a second trend, in which news sources pay greater attention to abrupt shifts than to smooth over-time trends (a news value known as *frequency*; O'Neill and Harcup 2017; Soroka 2006). In response to the profit motive of contemporary journalism, economic journalists seek to present economic news in a way that is as attention grabbing as possible. Journalists overlook "flat" trends in favor of sharp movement in other economic series due to the eye-catching nature of economic shocks. While it seems quite justifiable to focus on such surprises in coverage, especially because unexpected events portend broad consequences for financial markets, attention to volatility can conceal important long-term patterns. Consider, for example, sluggish long-term wage growth or inflation rates that chart slowly rising costs in basic goods and services. While journalists do occasionally remind audiences of these economic patterns, daily coverage of unvarying trends can become repetitive.

These patterns in news coverage speak to the idea that "the economy" is not a single, continuously observed phenomenon. Instead, journalists can influence our beliefs about the economy when they shift the focus of their coverage from one data source to another. By discussing unemployment in one story, reporters might ignore a second indicator, such as manufacturing productivity. The question then becomes: What data are most frequently reported by economic journalists, and why?

## THE "INDICATOR STORY"

Economic news is a specific genre of writing with a highly structured format. This is partly because journalists rely on specific, familiar data series to support their short-term descriptions of economic developments. This is a primary reason why a complete understanding of agenda setting in economic news must take economic indicators into account. The economic story format normally involves the discussion of one specific trend or data release. Consider, for example, an economic news story found in the pages of *USA Today* (Shell 2017). The article, from January 4, 2017, reads as follows:

> **Stock Markets Start January with a Bang; For First Time Since '13, S&P 500 Posts Gains on First Trading Day.**
>
> What a difference a year makes. The U.S. stock market kicked off the first day of trading of 2017 with solid gains, a year after plunging in the opening session of 2016 on its way to its worst week to start a year ever.

As we can see from this opening paragraph, the article clearly describes the focus of the day's economic developments as movement in the S&P 500, a measure of stock market performance. It provides a general description of the valence of the development, indicating that stock market conditions are greatly improving (by using terminology like "solid gains"). Economic journalists must work hard to convey the meaning of important developments of the day to their nontechnical audiences. They will therefore rely on a standard set of descriptors to explain many developments. The article next provides context about this improvement in stock prices: "Last year, the large-company stock index cratered 1.53% on January's first trading session—its sixth-worst Day 1 percentage loss and worst annual kickoff since 2001—on its way to a worst-ever first week of the year decline of 5.96%, according to S&P Dow Jones Indices. The S&P 500, however, rebounded and finished 2016 up 9.5%."

This historical context demonstrates that the day's stock result is dissimilar to last year's performance, further bolstering the notion that the day's news is reason for optimism. It also provides a brief definition of the S&P 500. The article concludes with a series of quotes from economic experts, offering interpretations of the development with varying sentiments: "'When the final week of 2016 ended on a flat note, many people were wondering whether the Trump rally was fading,' says Nick Sargen, senior investment adviser at Fort Washington Investment Advisors. 'The strong opening (today) suggests that it may have more legs to it.'"

Finally, economic journalists also seek to provide explanations for the developments in question. In this case, the author describes changes to the Chinese economy, a lack of panic triggers, a less threatening Fed, and reduced pension fund selling as potential causes later in the article. But overall, the article clearly reports a shift in one specific economic indicator, as exemplified by its structure and the vocabulary included throughout. The message is clear: many other things are happening in the economy today, but the important thing to know is that the stock market is exhibiting surprising bullishness.

In subsequent discussions, I refer to this kind of writing as an indicator story. It focuses on one major economic development using boilerplate language to convey positive or negative valence to readers. The indicator story genre is commonplace in economic news coverage. Scholars like Amber Boydstun (2013) have shown that journalists are highly receptive to any practice or strategy that might help them save time, given ongoing cuts to newsrooms and the difficulty of moves to rapid-fire digital marketplaces (Grieco, Sumida, and Fedeli 2018). Boydstun's (2013) analysis of the national issue agenda shows that journalists attempt to save time by returning to issues they have recently covered. This behavior causes certain stories to receive outsized agenda attention for longer periods of time than might be warranted. Journalists, having already invested the effort necessary to learn background information about an issue or topic, will seek to fall back on that work in subsequent weeks to meet deadlines.

Because of the highly structured, conventional style of economic story writing, many journalists rely on time-tested strategies for collecting and writing about economic indicators (Damstra et al. 2021). While it might initially seem like the expanded space constraints afforded by the contemporary twenty-four-hour news cycle would increase the number of economic developments discussed by economic journalists, the indicator story genre results in a daily economic news agenda that often remains limited to a narrow set of economic indicators. Journalists turn to the same kinds of familiar data day by day, month by month, to provide quality reports on the state of the economy. Such behavior hints at the potential for large imbalances in the topics of economic coverage over time.

## The Life Cycle of Economic Data

Journalists produce indicator stories that attempt to highlight the most important recent economic developments (Damstra et al. 2021). As every day brings a new onslaught of brand-new economic data with varying consequences for the broader economy, we might expect these topics to span a wide variety of subjects over time. However, economic journalists face a second constraint when seeking to provide an audience with economic news updates: much of the data provided by government agencies and private firms are released on a monthly or even a quarterly basis. Journalists might jump at the opportunity to provide their audience with information about things like national GDP growth, but such a story can only include "fresh" data a few times per year. In contrast, new data pertaining to a specific form of economic activity—the movement of stock markets—can be accessed by journalists on a continuous, up-to-the-minute basis.

In tables 1.1 through 1.8, I provide a nonexhaustive account of important sources of economic data that journalists and economic experts rely upon for information. These tables are derived in large part from the indispensable work of Baumohl (2012). These indicators form the backbone of journalists' sourcing of raw economic information. In each table, I provide a description of the frequency with which the source in question releases the economic report. The tables arrange these reports loosely by topic.

The differences between the ubiquity of the varying types of economic information presented in the tables are immediately apparent. Almost all core economic indicators, such as price indices, consumer confidence, and unemployment reports, are aggregated on a monthly or quarterly basis. Journalists wait with anticipation for the Bureau of Labor Statistics (BLS) jobs report each month; upon receipt of these statistics, they are often inclined to feature them in the next day's economic news. The same goes for a variety of other types of economic data. Americans wait each quarter, for example, for the GDP report furnished by the Bureau of Economic Analysis to describe the overall productivity of the US economy.

While it may seem strange for so much of the nation's economic data to be so infrequently released in a world of up-to-the-second news production, these delays are quite reasonable given the painstaking measurement strategies employed by data producers. Much of the information

Table 1.1. General Economic Growth Indicators

| Economic Report | Frequency | Source |
| --- | --- | --- |
| Gross Domestic Product | Quarterly | BEA |
| Index of Leading Economic Indicators | Monthly | The Conference Board |

Table 1.2. Labor Statistics

| Economic Report | Frequency | Source |
| --- | --- | --- |
| Employment Situation | Monthly | BLS |
| Weekly Unemployment Insurance Claims | Weekly | DOL |
| Help-Wanted Ad Index | Monthly | The Conference Board |
| Corporate Layoffs | Monthly | Challenger, Gray, and Christmas |
| Mass Layoffs (MLS) | Monthly | BLS |
| Labor Productivity and Costs | Quarterly | BLS |
| Employer Costs for Employee Comp. | Quarterly | BLS |

Table 1.3. Indicators of Sales, Spending, and Goods

| Economic Report | Frequency | Source |
| --- | --- | --- |
| Personal Income and Spending | Monthly | BEA |
| Retail Sales | Monthly | US Census Bureau |
| E-Commerce Retail Sales | Quarterly | US Census Bureau |
| Weekly Chain Store Sales | Weekly | ICSC/UBS |
| Durable Goods Orders | Monthly | US Census Bureau |
| Factory Orders | Monthly | US Census Bureau |
| Business Inventories | Monthly | US Census Bureau |
| Industrial Production | Monthly | Federal Reserve Board |
| ISM Manufacturing Survey | Monthly | Institute for Supply Mgmt. |

Table 1.4. Indicators of Credit and Housing

| Economic Report | Frequency | Source |
|---|---|---|
| Consumer Credit Outstanding | Monthly | Federal Reserve Board |
| Cambridge Consumer Credit | Monthly | Cambridge Credit Counseling |
| Housing Starts and Building Permits | Monthly | U.S. Census Bureau |
| Existing Home Sales | Monthly | Nat'l Association of Realtors |
| New Home Sales | Monthly | U.S. Census Bureau |
| NAHB Housing Market Index | Monthly | National Association of Home Builders |
| Mortgage Applications Survey | Weekly | Mortgage Bankers Association |
| Construction Spending | Monthly | US Census Bureau |

Table 1.5. Indicators of Consumer Confidence

| Economic Report | Frequency | Source |
|---|---|---|
| Consumer Confidence Index | Monthly | The Conference Board |
| Survey of Consumer Sentiment | Biweekly | University of Michigan SRC |
| ABC/Money Consumer Comfort Index | Weekly | ABC News/*Money Magazine* |
| UBS Index of Investor Optimism | Monthly | UBS/Gallup |

Table 1.6. Indicators of Trade

| Economic Report | Frequency | Source |
|---|---|---|
| International Trade in Goods and Services | Monthly | BEA |
| Current Account Balance | Quarterly | BEA |
| Import and Export Prices | Monthly | BLS |

Table 1.7. Indicators of Prices and Wages

| Economic Report | Frequency | Source |
|---|---|---|
| Consumer Price Index (CPI) | Monthly | BLS |
| Producer Price Index (PPI) | Monthly | BLS |
| Employment Cost Index | Quarterly | BLS |
| Real Earnings | Monthly | BLS |

Table 1.8. Stock, Bond, and Other Market Indicators

| Economic Report | Frequency | Source |
| --- | --- | --- |
| Yield Curve on Treasury Securities | Continuous | U.S. Treasury |
| Commercial Paper Rates | Daily | Federal Reserve Board |
| Dow Jones Industrial Average | Continuous | S&P Dow Jones Indices |
| Standard & Poor's 500 | Continuous | Standard & Poor's |
| Nasdaq Composite Index | Continuous | Nasdaq, Inc. |
| Russell 2000 | Continuous | FTSE Russell |
| Brent Crude Oil Futures | Continuous | Intercontinental Exchange |

presented in the tables above was generated from surveys, which require intensive planning, exhaustive data collection efforts, and careful data analysis.

Of the economic reports presented in the tables, one subset of data sources stands out as wholly unlike those presented elsewhere. Table 1.8 provides a very brief and incomplete list of *market-based* indicators of economic developments, such as the S&P 500, the Dow Jones Industrial Average, and measures of commodities trading. These up-to-the minute statistics measure the heartbeat of America's financial sector.

Unlike the other indicators discussed above, journalists do not need to wait weeks, months, or quarters to learn about their movement. Instead, they continuously monitor this information, either firsthand or by reading market summaries. As a result, when journalists seek out the data that will allow them to write indicator stories about the economy's performance, they may find themselves reaching most often for continuously compiled indicators of stock, bond, and commodity markets to inform the subjects of their writing.

The demand for up-to-the-minute media reports is only increasing in contemporary society, as smartphone use, fast internet connectivity, and cable television saturation allow for virtually nonstop news consumption. As the twenty-four-hour news cycle continues to accelerate, and as social media continues to outpace traditional news sources as key drivers of the agenda, journalists may find themselves turning even more frequently to continuously updated indicators to satisfy audiences' demand for nonstop news. Consider, for example, how the jump from network TV news to twenty-four-hour cable news gave audiences the ability to watch a larger volume of news at any time of day. This development necessitated the invention of new ways to feed breaking news to audiences, such as the "scrolling marquee" and picture-in-picture (PIP) insets.

While economic news might have garnered a brief mention on a half-hour news program in the 1970s, the cable audiences of the '90s soon found themselves exposed to fast-moving stock market tickers and up-to-the-second commodity price updates on cable news channels. The scrolling ticker, native to cable news, is just one example of a technological development that favors even more constant discussions of *up-to-the-minute* economic indicators. Today, we see these scrolling marquees on twenty-four-hour news networks like CNN, FOX News, and MSNBC just as often as we do on dedicated business news networks like CNBC and Bloomberg TV.

Monthly or quarterly data, in contrast, are generally only worthy of extended discussion on the day they are released. While previous generations might have been frequently exposed to market reports featuring graphs and stock listings in the business sections of newspapers, today's cable TV consumer is continuously bombarded with even more frequent and eye-catching technologies to convey data—oftentimes, stock market data—to viewers.

Altogether, then, the preceding section has laid the foundation for a basic claim with several downstream implications: *Economic journalists are expected to report stock market conditions more often than other data due to the stock market's up-to-the-minute data generation process.* In the next section, I consider the first of such implications by introducing a new set of actors, partisan elites, to the information environment. How might we expect elite economic discourse to respond to the modern proliferation of stock market coverage in economic news? Understanding these patterns might help us better anticipate the effects of stock market news on citizens' perceptions and attitudes, a subject that I take up in the final sections of the chapter.

## Elite Framing and Economic News

Thus far we have sought to explain why news values might cause journalists to report on the stock market more often than other indicators like unemployment, wage growth, and inflation. In the present section, I explain how these news values, and the information environment that results, can influence the behavior of partisan elites. Specifically, I consider how partisan actors (such as incumbent politicians and ideologically slanted media elites) use *framing* to convince audiences to see the economy in a way that makes the in-party look good, and the out-party look bad.

While framing is incredibly common in today's information environment (as well as the subject of thousands of published books and articles), framing the economy is a specialized endeavor.[3] When partisans find a way to construct a compelling frame, the signals they send to rank-and-file party members will quickly exacerbate partisan disagreement and lead to polarized attitudes among the public. But framing is not always successful, due in part to contextual moderators that can ramp up the difficulty of persuading audiences (Anson 2016; Lecheler and DeVreese 2019). One such moderating environmental factor is an abundance of high-quality information about a topic or development. Because media agenda setting inundates audiences with high-quality information about stock performance, framing stock market developments as "partisan-congenial" becomes harder. Elite signals about stock market performance are therefore expected to be rarer than communications about other economic data. Nevertheless, when they do occur, elite frames about the stock market could have subtle effects. They are unlikely to have direct effects on Americans' views of the basic facts of stock market performance. But they could persuade audiences to reshape their views about what the stock market means for broader economic and political outcomes.

### Blame and Credit: Why Elites Frame

Despite the inherent difficulty of framing the economy, partisan elites have good reasons to actively try to influence their constituencies' economic beliefs. This is because officeholders seek election above all else. Once in office, their foremost goal is to remain in office (Mayhew 1974). Thankfully for these instrumentally motivated politicians, incumbency can afford distinct advantages in the ability to frame. Members of Congress, for instance, employ dedicated staffers who work almost perpetually to communicate the work being done in Washington for voters back home (Herrnson 2015). Through Twitter, Facebook, email lists, public appearances, floor debate, mail, and many other channels, contemporary politicians and their staff constantly signal to constituencies that conditions are improving—all thanks, of course, to their hard work in Washington.

We see this behavior occur most notably in the realm of *pork*: specific lines in appropriations legislation that bring distinct economic benefits back home to a state or district (Grimmer 2013; Grimmer, Westwood, and Messing 2014). Recent scholarship has shown that a large volume of elites' communications to constituencies make mention of pork. In this way, members of Congress (MCs) signal to wavering prospective voters that local interests are still at the heart of their agendas in Washington. Appropriations are also useful items to point out to constituencies because they could help offset prevailing negative economic conditions. In economic hard times, MCs can highlight their work in helping the constituency to win grants, projects, and contracts. Considering this kind of signaling, it is no wonder that so many MCs win re-election over and over, despite Congress's notoriously abysmal levels of overall public approval—and the public's willingness to fire incumbents when the economy is struggling (e.g., Erikson and Titiunik 2015).

There might be circumstances, however, where MCs will buttress their statements by framing the basic economic facts. But how and when are incumbent politicians willing to make mention of these "valence" considerations?[4] Are Republican and Democratic elites willing to tell a story to their constituencies, and to the broader public, that conflicts with prevailing information about recent economic developments? Or will politicians feel constrained, unwilling to present economic information in a way that might otherwise resonate with the preferred-world state of co-partisans?

Together with journalists' news values, I expect economic data generation to yield a patchwork pattern of economic discourse from political elites. MCs will attempt to frame the national economy by reaching for whatever economic topic is most *congenial* to partisans at that moment. For example, when unemployment rises, the out-party members might increase their discussion of jobs, hammering the incumbent's tarnished reputation as an overseer of job growth. The in-party members might search for another indicator, like key commodity prices, to assuage the public (and to distract from the jobs issue). In other cases, though, the economic data will be left out of the conversation altogether. Specifically, I expect stock market coverage to normally fall outside the realm of consideration of elite framing efforts, due to its intense saturation in contemporary media discourse. When it comes to the stock market and its ubiquitous daily news coverage, most elites will decide the topic is simply "too tough to frame" (e.g., Amsalem and Zoizner 2022; Glazier and Boydstun 2012).

## FRAMING THEORIES

To further explore this notion, I find it useful to review contemporary framing theories. Most current discussions of elite framing distinguish the concept from other media effects by emphasizing framing's ability to affect *interpretations* of issues or developments in news (Entman 1993). So-called "emphasis frames" help to connect the "what" with the "why" and "how" in the minds of the public by offering explanations for the origins, status, and possible solutions to the issues of the day. Frames even go so far as to explain whether an issue deserves to be thought of as a problem in the first place (Chong and Druckman 2007).

The contemporary information environment is replete with frames. Each time a new issue appears on the public agenda, political elites, pundits, interest groups, and other communicators race to provide audiences with explanations that contextualize (and often assign responsibility for) political developments. A salient example is the Patient Protection and Affordable Care Act of 2010, which sought to overhaul the American healthcare and insurance market. Immediately upon the introduction of this plan by Democrats in Congress, opponents of the legislation branded it "Obamacare," a frame designed to attribute responsibility for the outcomes of the act to President Barack Obama (Fowler et al. 2017). In the months and years that followed, the term "Obamacare" was even adopted by proponents of the legislation, so much so that it is now the law's most recognizable moniker. To the extent that the frame was designed to link responsibility for the outcomes of the law to Obama's presidential performance and legacy, it can be considered a resounding success.

Conservative attempts to frame the slow, uphill economic recovery of the years immediately following the Great Recession as "Obamanomics" were slower to catch on. However, President Obama himself once lamented his lack of attention to the politics of framing the economic facts. "The mistake of my first term—couple of years—was thinking that this job was just about getting the policy right," Obama said in 2012. "The nature of this office is also to tell a story to the American people that gives them a sense of unity and purpose and optimism, especially during tough times" (Leonhardt 2012). Framing is one of the foremost objectives of contemporary politicians, from presidents to MCs to local representatives.

## Constraints on Framing

Politicians use frames to explain the meaning of an economic development to a sympathetic audience. But these efforts are likely to be substantially constrained by the nature of information itself. Even the craftiest political communicator will encounter difficulty framing news if there already exist clear, undisputable causes and consequences for a development (Glazier and Boydstun 2012; Jerit 2008). One example of these constraints can be seen in 2008, when the Emergency Economic Stabilization Act or "bailout bill" was introduced near the end of the George W. Bush administration. At that time, the bill was seen by Secretary of the Treasury Henry Paulson as a near imperative. The public, however, could not be convinced of the bill's moral or practical utility. Americans were also unconvinced that the economy would be getting better anytime soon. More than 70 percent of surveyed respondents would voice their disapproval of Bush in tracking polls in October of that year, nearing all-time records for negativity. Most Americans couldn't be swayed by even the most powerful efforts to sell Bush's economic competence.

In a circumstance like this, we would expect Republican MCs—who shared the president's party identification, and therefore at least part of the blame for poor conditions according to the public—to simply stay far away from any mention of the economy in their political communication (Brown 2010). Any attempt to convince an audience that the economy would be getting better soon would probably be viewed with incredulity or scorn. Instead, MCs might talk up developments in their states or districts, emphasizing local strategies to help reeling constituents find their economic footing.

An economic and political outlier, 2008 was a rare moment in which the public agreed the economy was in dire straits. In other times, the public reports mixed, uneven, and even contradictory economic beliefs. Over the past few decades, these mixed views have been justifiable, largely due to the actions of the Federal Reserve in bolstering financial markets. Stock market indicators have shown impressive strength, rising to all-time highs despite occasional flash crashes. Other indicators like wage growth and net national savings continue to justify more pessimistic outlooks, while still others have shown mixed results. At any given moment, different economic indicators have painted different pictures of a complex American economy.

Given these mixed, uneven economic signals, we might expect partisan elites to feel few constraints when framing the economy. Elites might be willing to bring up any economic fact that appears congenial to the partisan preferred-world state of their co-partisans in the public. When a copartisan president resides in office, it might make sense for partisan elites to talk up a booming stock market. When in opposition, it might make more sense to point out rising commodity prices or weak wage growth in service of critiques of the incumbent president. Nevertheless, regardless of the performance of a given economic indicator, elites must still contend with an information environment in which some indicators (such as the stock market) are presented to audiences constantly, while others are rarely reported.

The reporting frequency of economic indicators is expected to constrain economic framing. Elites' efforts to claim credit (or lay blame) using stock prices might be quickly contradicted by ubiquitous updates about those same prices' rise or fall. Thus, highly saturated stock market indicators are difficult to frame due to their inherent capacity for rapid change. This situation resonates with a study conducted by Redlawsk, Civettini, and Emmerson (2010), in which sudden exposure to large amounts of disconfirming information about a candidate became "too much" for partisans to ignore. The saturation of economic data can prove to be an insurmountable hurdle for elites when new developments contradict their framing efforts.

When it comes to other indicators, however, elites might find the news environment to be relatively devoid of coverage for long periods. If new data reports about a core economic indicator only come out once per month, elites will enjoy a period in which they might contest the meaning (or even the valence) of a specific economic indicator. An unemployment rate of 4.3 percent might be interpreted as a positive development by economic journalists, having seen those rates fall more than expected since the last Bureau of Labor Statistics release. But in the month-long gap between BLS reports, political elites have room to claim credit, deflect blame, and even reinterpret the meaning of a 4.3 percent unemployment rate altogether. This means that in the case of less continuously reported economic data, political actors will relish the opportunity to "fill in the blanks" for partisans eager to engage in motivated reasoning.

Framing can be powerful. A recent study from Denmark showed that Danish citizens reacted strongly to a shift in one party's stated position on the nation's debt (Bisgaard and Slothuus 2018). After assuming office, partisans who had in earlier times argued that the national debt was a dire problem began to sing a different tune. Quotes from prominent partisan actors were broadcast heavily in media thanks to the attention-grabbing nature of the debt issue. The contours of public debate about the nation's fiscal situation shifted in line with the strategies of party elites. Partisans in the electorate responded by diminishing their level of concern about the national debt.

This empirical example was one of the first to show that party leaders' depictions of economic reality can powerfully reshape the beliefs of rank-and-file party members. When elite communications are particularly newsworthy, the agenda-setting and framing efforts of journalists can be reshaped by a desire to convey these statements to the public. While the practices of mainstream "watchdog" or "guard dog" journalists can constrain partisan actors, those actors can also see their frames amplified by explicitly partisan media. When partisan elites consistently speak out about certain kinds of economic data, partisan media will shift their focus accordingly.

## FRAMING THE STOCK MARKET: EXCEEDING CONSTRAINTS?

Thus far, we have seen evidence that economic framing is a crucial tool for elites, despite scope considerations that sometimes render it powerless. Nevertheless, we know that occasionally elites can reshape political and economic discourse unilaterally, causing co-partisans to develop new interpretations of reality. For instance, initial public support for the War on Drugs was thought to stem almost entirely from Nixon's public communication efforts—a surprisingly powerful framing effect (Whitford and Yates 2009). When presidents orient their communication strategies around subjects that are difficult to frame, sometimes the public will respond by changing their interpretations of the *why* and the *how* of a new development.

Presidential efforts to frame the US economy using stock market performance represent a critical test of framing theory. If presidents do discuss the stock market, their frames have the potential to reorient Americans' understanding of the economy itself, as Americans may come to value the information as a more salient contributing factor to personal and sociotropic economic performance. However, Americans' understanding of the stock market's *performance* is unlikely to be swayed by these communication efforts. Therefore, we might expect presidents to succeed in claiming credit for stock market developments when the stock market is booming—but potentially see that strategy backfire when the market craters. As we will see, this risky strategy was employed with varying levels of success by President Donald Trump, whose term in office exhibited a strikingly unorthodox communication style.

Altogether, I anticipate a situation in which elite framing of the stock market is rare overall, yielding relatively accurate and unbiased stock market perceptions among American partisans. However, there remains the possibility that elite framing of the stock market, when it does occur, will have implications for partisans' *interpretations* of the US economy. In the next sections, I turn my attention away from the information environment and towards the psychology of citizens. Having reviewed theories of agenda setting and framing as they pertain to stock market perceptions, I next seek to explain how Americans will contend with these mediated signals. As we will see, Americans *process* stock market information according to their partisanship and their attentiveness to the news media. To understand the nature of this information processing, I next build upon a rich theoretical literature in the realm of political psychology.

## How Citizens Process Stock Market Information

Classical theories of democracy assume that citizens are well informed on current events and political issues. But in reality, many economic and political facts are beyond the knowledge of most citizens (e.g., Flynn, Nyhan, and Reifler 2017).[5] Many "rationally ignorant" Americans are quick to *confidently* report opinions and perceptions that indicate a basic lack of political awareness. But while there is generally only one way to be right, there are many ways to be wrong. In this section I discuss Americans' processing of stock market information, developing expectations about the way in which citizens update their economic perceptions in response to this uniquely salient economic indicator. I assert that due to the *automaticity* of most Americans' economic information acquisition process, contemporary Americans know a surprising amount about the day-to-day performance stock market, even if they have little interest in the topic. Superseding the rational ignorance of the public due to its ubiquitous coverage in news, stock market performance is therefore expected to increasingly drive economic and political beliefs in the contemporary period.

In reviewing the literature on partisan motivated reasoning, I also discuss ways in which partisans might develop inaccurate beliefs about the performance of the stock market. Following the logic of the above section on framing, I make the case that Republicans and Democrats will exhibit *less* biased overall perceptions of the stock market when compared to other common economic indicators. The salience and ubiquity of the stock market in American media is expected to yield mostly accurate, politically consequential stock market opinions among middle-class Americans. But as discussed above, partisan-motivated reasoning theory asserts that *interpretations* of the stock market are a viable response to persuasive elite frames.

## LEARNING ABOUT THE STOCK MARKET

Citizens' perceptions of reality, from economic progress to the state of domestic and international affairs, are thought to derive from a complex psychological process. Most of the time, Americans consume information in news, accept it as relevant and accurate, and then store it in their long-term memory for later retrieval or "sampling" (Zaller 1992; see also Taber and Lodge 2006; Lodge and Taber 2013). This "receive-accept-sample" or R-A-S framework is a cornerstone of modern political psychology. While variously critiqued by more recent work (e.g., Feldman, Huddy, and Marcus 2012), the framework is a good starting point for understanding why the stock market looms large in Americans' understanding of the economy. According to the model, citizens must be attentive to learn things from news. Just as important, they will decide whether to reject a news item as irrelevant based on *cues* about its origin and content. Do Americans receive stock market news, and if so, do they deem it worthy of their consideration?

While the receive-accept-sample framework might make it seem like such economic details would rarely wind up stored in Americans' memory, even relatively inattentive people can learn things about the economy when they are haphazardly exposed to news (Entman 1989; Mondak 1993). Some Americans are highly attuned to news, as well as to cues that help them sort out the credibility of a source. But most news consumers are incidentally and uncritically exposed to a given day's headlines. In fact, most Americans receive much of their news information automatically, before they have had a chance to consciously assess the information's meaning, provenance, or partisan consequences (e.g., Bargh and Ferguson 2000; Petty and Cacioppo 1986). While stereotypes of highly partisan "news junkies" glued to twenty-four-hour cable television are common in American discourse, the fact remains that relatively few modern consumers consciously and intentionally sit down to consume news with any regularity (Park and Kaye 2020).

## AUTOMATICITY

An automatic response to news yields greater susceptibility to framing and agenda-setting effects (e.g., Lecheler and DeVreese 2012). While most

Americans lack the sophistication necessary to identify and resist these media effects, some possess the experience and knowledge necessary to spot persuasion and to ignore hostile communicators. But inexperienced, casual, or occasional news consumers are less able to or willing to seek out news that best fits their proclivities. Instead, many Americans are coming to adopt a "news-finds-me" attitude to information acquisition, in which regular intentional news consumption is thought to be unnecessary due to social media exposure (Gil de Zúñiga, Weeks, and Ardèvol-Abreu 2017). The result has been a decline in current events knowledge, and with it, a diminution of the political sophistication needed to counteract framing and agenda-setting effects.

The present chapter has detailed the potential for a strong media agenda setting effect that privileges stock market information over other economic data. The casual news consumer is expected to be highly vulnerable to this agenda setting effect for two reasons. First, most audience members consume news in a scattershot fashion, obtaining a somewhat random sample of the available stories and headlines. Because of the high prevalence of stock market stories in day-to-day coverage of the economy, this random sample is more likely to contain stock market stories than other economic information. Chronic news consumers will eventually learn about BLS unemployment reports, inflation updates, or GDP reports, when these stories release at their regular monthly or quarterly intervals. But obtaining a smaller random sample of the news reduces the likelihood of obtaining this information (Price and Czilli 1996).

Second, audiences without much experience as news consumers will find it harder to parse the day's economic news (Nelson, Oxley, and Clawson 1997). A sophisticated audience will be able to determine the significance of current trends and events, using cues to understand what the day's updates mean for the broader economy. Others might have a harder time understanding the relative significance of various news reports. An unsophisticated audience, having fewer pieces of information about a topic in memory, will be more likely than sophisticated consumers to dramatically revise their perceptions of an issue when they stumble upon a news item (e.g., Zaller 1992). Stock market performance may not be as inherently meaningful to a sophisticated consumer, who knows that a multitude of economic indicators are required to explain the present status of the American economy. But to a casual consumer, it is not immediately clear that an economic "indicator story" does not represent a complete account of the economy.

Ultimately, though, sophisticates and nonsophisticates alike are susceptible to media agenda setting vis-à-vis the stock market because of our predisposition to automatically react to *message tone* (e.g., Soroka and McAdams 2015, Knobloch-Westerwick, Mothes, and Polavin 2020). Dramatic developments receive increased attention because they cause us to experience a state of emotional arousal. This arousal further increases the degree of automaticity of our information processing, leading us to remember details about stories even if we might otherwise give them little credence. Because of the daily rise and fall of stock prices, frequent stock market "indicator stories" provide audiences with clear and attention-grabbing positive or negative tone. Audiences often remember the positive-negative *valence* of communications, even when they fail to remember the details (e.g., Gomes, Brainerd, and Stein 2013). Critically, this means that even if a consumer has little interest in the topic of stock markets, media agenda setting will mean that they will *recall the valence of stock market reports* when they perform an "information search" to update their overall economic perceptions (Lau and Redlawsk 2006).

Together, these observations from the literature on information acquisition lead to the following expectation: *Relative to other kinds of economic information, Americans will possess increasingly accurate, informed perceptions of the stock market, and will use these accurate perceptions to update their economic and political judgments.*

## Partisans, the Stock Market, and Perceptual Biases

While Americans are expected to possess a surprisingly strong understanding of the stock market, opportunities for biased perceptions of the stock market could still arise due to the psychology of *information processing.* Biased perceptions are the subject of much ongoing debate in political science. While many longstanding critiques of American democracy focus on a lack of basic political knowledge among members of the public (Delli Carpini and Keeter 1997), motivated reasoning theory asserts that partisans are misinformed due to the "perceptual screens" of their social identities. It is one major reason why classical democratic theory (in which enlightened voters make informed decisions at the polls) falls flat according to some contemporary observers (e.g., Achen and Bartels 2017).

Under motivated reasoning, conscious or subconscious processing of relevant information leads partisans to draw biased conclusions about factual elements of an event, circumstance, or issue. For example, when a partisan makes a wildly incorrect estimate of the number of attendees at an inaugural ceremony, they have likely consumed information about the event through a biased cognitive lens (Schaffner and Luks 2018). As a result, committed Republicans and Democrats can come to surprisingly different conclusions.[6] Factually incorrect, plausible premises will be readily internalized if they soothe partisans' self-esteem.

Motivated reasoning has been variously described by existing scholarship in psychology and political science. One way to think about the phenomenon is from the perspective of Bayesian statistical theory (Kahan 2015; Ditto and Lopez 1992). So-called "Bayesian updating" is a surprisingly simple idea at its core. People hold a set of prior beliefs and attitudes in their minds, and weigh these "priors" against any new evidence they might encounter. Suppose, for instance, that we asked a group of Americans to guess the likelihood of the unemployment rate rising in the next month. Our interviewees could take a rational approach, reflecting carefully on everything they had learned about the unemployment rate in the recent past. If they were then presented with a new, pessimistic news story about unemployment, they would weigh the impact of this news in their minds, guided by the information they already possessed.

The news story would therefore influence our interviewees' perceptions, but the degree of this influence would depend upon their pre-existing knowledge of the issue. The information gleaned from the story might substantially reshape perceptions, if the story seemed credible enough and if interviewees knew little about the current jobs situation in the United States. If interviewees had a great deal of recent, high-quality information that suggested the unemployment rate was in good shape, however, only marginal perceptual adjustments would occur.

In this way, some respondents would come away having dramatically increased their fear of rising unemployment. Others' perceptions would be relatively unchanged. But if any of these individuals were prone to partisan motivated reasoning, a critical step in their Bayesian updating process would have been twisted by the emotional and cognitive impacts of political group attachments, leading to unexpected patterns in the group's unemployment expectations.

## The Partisan Preferred-World State

Party identification, the so-called "unmoved mover" in the study of public opinion, causes Americans to feel a deep sense of attachment to partisan political actors.[7] Current research shows that this social identity causes us to become intensely antagonistic towards members of the opposite party, even if we share a good deal of common ground when it comes to policy positions (Mason 2018). Social identity theory tells us that we do this because we are quick to link our self-esteem to our group attachments (e.g., Huddy 2001). As a result, when partisans reflect on facts that signal the successes or failures of our in group, the desire to see the "home team" win can distort the Bayesian updating process.

Under motivated reasoning, information is weighed according to its implications for the reputation of the political in group. New information is compared to a set of biased priors referred to by some scholars as the "partisan preferred-world state" (e.g., Parker-Stephen 2013). This preferred world is founded on the default assumption that members of the in group are superior to members of the out group. For example, a Democrat would argue that Joe Biden is a better economic manager than Donald Trump because members of the in group possess positive characteristics like intelligence and decisiveness—useful traits for an economic manager. According to a Republican's preferred-world state, however, the Democrats are only intelligent and decisive when it comes to deceiving voters; economic management is best left to the (Republican) experts.

Biased perceptions of the facts arise even when partisans confront exactly the same news stories. If the information contained in a news story is *congenial* to a Democratic preferred-world state, many Democrats will happily assign the story importance when they update their prior beliefs. But if a news item is congenial to Democrats, it is likely *disconfirming* to Republicans. Loyal Republicans might look upon the information from a default position of skepticism. They will assign little importance to the story, and most Republicans' (partisan-congenial) prior beliefs will emerge unscathed. As a result, Republicans and Democrats will soon possess differing appraisals and interpretations of a factual development—*even if they have consumed the exact same information.*[8] Partisans are subconsciously unwilling to account for facts that might damage their group-oriented sense of self-esteem.

A NEED FOR ACCURACY

Motivated reasoning is a powerful obstacle to retrospective accountability, potentially disrupting one of the simplest and most convincing mechanisms for ensuring that we reward and punish elected leaders for their performance in office (Achen and Bartels 2017; Fiorina 1981). However, there exists at least one conflicting motivation that can challenge partisans to update their beliefs about the world in potentially disconfirming ways. Partisans balance a need to preserve their preferred-world state against a need to hold *accurate* beliefs about the world (Bisgaard 2015; Arceneaux and Vander Wielen 2017; Kunda 1990; Parker-Stephen 2013). Americans could be motivated by accuracy because they are aware of certain responsibilities inherent to democratic citizenship.

When voting, citizens will often perform an "information search" of relevant data about the rival candidates; this process allows them to make a confident, minimally informed decision. Even if that decision is often biased by motivated reasoning, there is still an innate desire among many citizens to make "good," or at least justifiable, political choices (Lau and Redlawsk 2001). The same logic applies to knowledge about the economy: responsible citizens might feel an innate desire to retain an accurate understanding of vital economic signals, in order to properly appraise the health of their communities, and to take appropriate action at the ballot box or in other areas of their civic lives in response.

Knowing things about the state of the economy is also a basic survival instinct. It is rationally advantageous to have up-to-date knowledge about America's economy, in the event of a catastrophic reversal of economic fortune (Soroka 2006). After having seen the disastrous consequences of the financial crisis of 2008–09 and the effects of the COVID-19 shutdown, it stands to reason that contemporary Americans prioritize accurate, up-to-the-minute information about the economy. No one should want to be the last to know about a stock market crash or an announcement of mass layoffs.[9]

However, recent studies argue that that these accuracy motivations are only rarely at the forefront of partisans' minds. In politically charged circumstances, motivations tend to increase, rather than diminish, in strength (Levendusky 2018). When partisans discuss issues that are especially central to the current contours of partisan debate, the willingness to engage in motivated reasoning intensifies (Slothuus and De Vreese 2010). We also know that only the most politically sophisticated members of the public possess strong enough accuracy motivations to reliably challenge directional motivations, even though motivated reasoning is cognitively costly (Leeper and Slothuus 2014). The empirical research on the subject has arrived at a pressing question: When can partisans agree on the facts?

## Partisan Bias in Context

While partisan-motivated reasoning is an enduring psychological phenomenon, partisans' attitudinal biases can grow and shrink due to several contextual factors. These factors can be related to developments in the real world, or they can be determined by the information environment—including the framing and agenda-setting behavior of news sources and party elites (Amsalem and Zoizner 2020). Below, I review these contextual limits on partisan biases, to help explain why the stock market is unique among economic indicators in its effects on motivated reasoning behavior.

Partisan attitudinal polarization decreases when real-world circumstances become indisputably good or bad. One of the most striking examples of this phenomenon—reflecting partisan agreement on a normally contested issue—occurred during the Great Recession of 2008–09 (Bisgaard 2015; Stanig 2013). As the George W. Bush administration struggled desperately to assuage public fear about the dire economic circumstances, both Republican and Democratic identifiers had no choice but to agree that the economy was in very bad shape. Not even the most head-in-the-clouds optimists were willing to suggest the economy was good (or even middling) during that time. As the subprime mortgage crisis crushed the stock market, triggered mass foreclosures, and obliterated decades worth of Americans' savings, both Republicans and Democrats commiserated.

After President Obama took office in 2009, partisans of all stripes continued to agree on the dismal state of the economy. In the months that followed, recently appointed Secretary of the Treasury Timothy Geithner tried to persuade the public that doubling down on the Bush-era Troubled Asset Relief Program (TARP) was a good idea (Geithner 2014). As the Obama administration struggled with the optics of the recovery program, Republicans and Democrats alike remained deeply worried about the future of the economy. In a time of crisis, motivated reasoning was pushed aside by justifiably pessimistic beliefs (Redlawsk, Civettini, and Emmerson 2010).[10]

This episode accords with a theory of "ambivalence" forwarded by Lavine, Johnston, and Steenbergen (2012), who argue that conflicting considerations can eventually suppress partisans' confidence in their directionally motivated perceptions. Enough bad news can eventually break down partisans' motivated reasoning as it becomes too cognitively costly to engage in effortful mental gymnastics (Pennycook and Rand

2019). Given enough countervailing information, accuracy motivations eventually win out over partisan biases.

In times with more ambiguous economic performance, partisan elites loom as prominent culprits in driving widespread disagreement on the facts (Bisgaard and Slothuus 2018; Leeper and Slothuus 2014; Mullinix 2016; Slothuus 2016). The public looks to elite members of America's two major parties to learn about new political issues that have arisen on the agenda, and elites respond with framing efforts (as discussed above; see also Bullock 2011). In most cases, partisan elites are eager to discuss performance issues with their constituencies. These discussions frame current events in ways that help facilitate motivated reasoning. For instance, Mullinix (2016) shows that among Republicans, exposure to persuasive messages arguing for specific tax reforms produced a positive shift in support for such changes to tax policy. Studies have shown that when partisan elites signal that an issue is of great importance to a party's overarching goals, party adherents become increasingly willing to use motivated reasoning to guide their opinions.

In the present moment, partisan elites are highly polarized.[11] Unlike earlier eras of American politics, Republican MCs are almost unanimously conservative, while Democrats are consistently liberal. It is therefore quite commonplace for party elites to attempt to persuade their constituencies using intensely ideological, polarizing cues. One needs only to peruse the Twitter feeds of prominent contemporary politicians to discover many cues designed to reinterpret (or flatly contradict) seemingly incontrovertible facts. In the era of seemingly nonstop campaigning, these cues are yet another reason why we might anticipate widespread "factual polarization" in the American public.

The evidence reviewed above suggests that the most *ubiquitous* facts will challenge motivated reasoning because elites will struggle to effectively frame these issues. In an important early study, Jerit and Barabas (2012) examine partisan perceptual biases across a wide variety of facts. They scour surveys for political questions with "right" or "wrong" answers, including beliefs about the effectiveness of vaccines, the cost of prescription drugs, and the parties engaged in international conflicts. Surprisingly, the authors find that issues receiving a *greater* amount of coverage in news prompted more partisan-congenial responses than those receiving little news coverage. Instead of helping partisans to learn the "right" answers, news exposure only served to increase biased responding.

When it comes to the economic facts, we might expect to see a somewhat different pattern. As I discuss below, this is because economic agenda setting and elite framing of the economy are quite different from media effects in other realms. Audiences become accustomed to learning about certain kinds of economic data over months and years of daily economic updates. Other topics, like a ruling on a vaccine lawsuit or allegations against a pharmaceutical executive, will "explode" on to the news agenda and then disappear (Boydstun 2013). These stories are soon replaced by new topics with new reporting conventions and data sources. Meanwhile, economic data enjoys steady, ongoing daily coverage, even during periods of relatively "slow news."

As Jerit and Barabas (2012) theorize, vocal, committed partisans possess decidedly nonmedian news consumption habits, yielding susceptibility to framing even on highly visible issues such as stock market performance. Selective exposure is a phenomenon in which partisans come to exclusively trust certain media sources because those sources present viewers with unmistakable ideological slant (Barberá et al. 2015; Stroud 2008; 2010). Viewers learn that the opinions and information presented in these media are likely to support the partisan preferred-world state, and consequently favor those sources above others. This brand loyalty makes partisans more likely to commit information to memory if it comes from these sources. When partisan-tinted facts are presented on these networks, viewers will automatically update their priors without much cognitive investment.

While intense partisans often desire to learn "selective facts" that support the preferred-world state, most Americans possess a far more balanced news diet than the stereotypical hardcore Fox News or MSNBC consumer (e.g., Barberá et al. 2015). Regardless, the phenomenon of selective exposure complicates the seemingly straightforward assumptions of earlier sections. Perhaps partisan biases will influence stock market perceptions if partisan elites (and their TV host allies) are willing to provide intense enough framing efforts. To better understand this empirical question, a thoroughgoing study of the economic content of both mainstream and ideological news, as well as the messages of partisan elites, is required—an analysis I perform in later chapters.

## Will Bias Find a Way?

The preceding section provides some encouraging reminders that motivated reasoning can be constrained in special circumstances. But recent research on partisan-motivated reasoning suggests that in such cases, "second-order" biases can still emerge in response to elite framing efforts. Below, I describe my expectations for second-order partisan biases in the case of the stock market. I argue that such biases are more consequential for Americans' economic beliefs than previously thought.

In a study of economic attitudes during the Great Recession, political scientist Martin Bisgaard (2015) shows that bias can still "find a way" to tint partisans' attitudes. Studying economic perceptions in Britain before and after the occurrence of the worldwide financial downturn sparked by the Great Recession, Bisgaard (2015) shows that even as partisan survey respondents began to agree about the direness of the circumstances, a second bias began to emerge. Partisans began to polarize in terms of their *justifications* for the economic collapse, as those who identified with the party in government began to assign responsibility for economic conditions to nongovernmental actors. Conversely, members of the out parties became much more willing to blame the government for current economic conditions.

Perhaps, then, even unambiguous economic trends cannot fully stop partisans' willingness to defend their preferred-world states—though it can bring basic economic perceptions closer together. Bisgaard's (2015) study shows us that bias can often be more nuanced than it might initially seem. Because the partisan preferred-world state is complex, partisans can develop new justifications to reduce the cognitive dissonance of believing uncomfortable facts (Anson 2017). However, these justifications are surprisingly *effortful*. Maintaining the preferred-world state requires the expenditure of scarce, jealously guarded cognitive resources (Kahan 2015). Some partisans will be unwilling or unable to invent a meaningful and internally consistent partisan-congenial explanation for a given economic development because it is mentally draining.

To develop biased justifications for bad news more efficiently, some partisans will therefore look to trusted sources for hints. In particular, motivated reasoners will adopt "economic narratives" offered to them by *partisan elites*, such as the president and members of Congress. Elites work hard to continuously frame new developments using congenial partisan explanations. But even if partisan audiences are continuously fed these biased messages, I argue that they will rarely hold incorrect beliefs about whether stock prices are going up or down. Instead, they will more likely respond to these framing efforts by changing the way they *think about the economy*.

Given the complexity of the US economy, partisan framing of the stock market might offer Americans the ability to conform to the partisan preferred-world state by adjusting their beliefs about whether the stock market *matters* for the broader economy. While many Americans might normally agree that the stock market has little bearing on their day-to-day economic potential, the opportunity to cheerlead for their favorite politicians might be enough to reshape these fundamental "economic narratives" about how the economy works. Revising one's economic narrative is in many cases *easier* than updating one's attribution of responsibility for economic performance, as was observed in Bisgaard's (2015) study. Instead of crafting tortured narratives about how a president's recent actions directly boosted or depressed stock prices (which fluctuate for countless reasons), partisans can simply argue about whether stock prices are good signals of overall economic prosperity.

## Summary of Expectations

The present chapter's arguments can be summarized in a series of stylized expectations:

- *The stock market is the most frequent source of economic data in economic news stories—even when those sources have ideological leanings.*

- *The stock market is among the least likely economic indicators to be discussed by political elites in their economic framing efforts.*

- *Republicans and Democrats are most likely to express unbiased judgments of the stock market relative to other economic indicators.*

- *Stock market performance influences Americans' presidential approval ratings, even after compensating for other features of the economy.*

- *Americans' interpretations of the stock market's effects on the broader economy are increasingly influenced by partisanship.*

## Conclusion:
## Stock Market Performance and Economic Voting

Economic indicators are interrelated. Some constitute leading, and others, lagging, signals of overall economic progress. Economic theories like Okun's law posit relationships between classes of indicators that help professional economists make complex projections about the future (Okun 1970). Some indicators help us understand the basic "inputs" of economic activity in America, while others help us understand how those activities have influenced the perceptions and behavior of everyday participants in that economy. That having been said, there is one other way in which these economic indicators differ in their meaning. Some are useful tools in helping us understand the economic performance of average Americans, while others describe a more selective group of earners. This latter group of Americans has recently been identified in political discourse as "the 1 percent"—those families who straddle the highest echelons of America's wealth and income distributions (Piketty and Saez 2006).

In the post–Great Recession American economy, inequality is a fact of life. Since the early 1980s, we have witnessed a trend in which a growing disparity between the incomes of the nation's most ascendant earners and everyone else. Most memorably captured by the rhetoric of Bernie Sanders in the Democratic primary of the 2016 Presidential Election, the concept of "the 1 percent" is now commonplace in public discourse (Jacobson 2017). Focal events like Occupy Wall Street in 2011 captured the frustration of many Americans who witnessed the uneven effects of the recovery from the Great Recession (Gamson and Sifry 2013).

Since 2009, economists have tracked the 1 percent's steady climb into the economic stratosphere, as well as the relative stagnation of the living standard of middle-class America (e.g., Piketty and Saez 2006; Piketty and Saez 2014). While wages have risen marginally since 2009, these changes are being offset by dramatic increases in the cost of a variety of important goods and services, most notably college education and housing—once thought to be gateways to prosperity for the middle class. The rapid multiplying of the income levels of the wealthiest Americans stands in contrast to this muddled economic situation. The 1 percent enjoyed rapid recovery from the Great Recession and the COVID-19 economic shutdown. In the wake of these focal events, the richest Americans compounded their intergenerational wealth, while most others experienced decreased social and economic mobility.

Very wealthy Americans not only differ from members of the middle class in their degree of prosperity. These individuals also obtain income much differently than middle-class people. As Hacker and Pierson (2010) show in their political account of today's "gilded age" of economic inequality, very wealthy Americans are much more likely to hold specific professional titles, like CEO, than average. These job descriptions come with special perks beyond salary, which include stock options as a form of compensation. Some wealthy Americans have no formal job title as they rely upon dividends generated by their stock portfolios to supply their entire incomes. Thus, while most Americans derive their regular incomes from wages, the economic performance of very wealthy Americans is much more directly influenced by the movement of the stock market.

Of course, many working Americans also have a stake in the stock market. Many Americans with steady white-collar employment have 401(k), 403(b), or other employer-sponsored retirement accounts. Every month, salaried workers save a fraction of their incomes (an amount that is sometimes matched by their employer) in index funds. But while we might expect the economic performance of average Americans to track with the stock market for this reason, the *volume* of stocks held by average Americans is surprisingly low. Because middle-class Americans' stock market investments are so paltry on average, the relationship between the stock market and the economic fortunes of the majority is weak.

Even many employees with sponsored retirement accounts decline to use these options until late in life. According to the Economic Policy Institute, nearly half (47 percent) of American families aged thirty-two to sixty-one had saved nothing for retirement as of 2013, a decline of 7 percent from 2001 (Morrissey 2016). As Americans accumulate debt and struggle to afford a variety of goods and services, saving has fallen off the back burner as an economic priority.

This means that many lower- and middle-income Americans are relatively uninvested in the stock market. Caner and Wolff (2004) demonstrate that Americans across the economic spectrum have anemic stock portfolios. In fact, around half of Americans have no exposure to the stock market whatsoever. Instead, Americans' well-being is much more sensitive to other economic indicators. Their ability to afford a basic market basket of goods is dependent upon whether their wages keep up with new bouts of inflation (Storm 2017). The lower middle class is sensitive to U-6 unemployment, as it reports the fraction of the population that faces unemployment or underemployment at any given time. Americans are also highly sensitive to real estate values and the cost of rent, in a time when fewer and fewer people can gather the resources necessary to invest in a home.

Overall, the most impactful economic indicators for the well-being of the middle class are only indirectly associated with the movement of markets. However, as we have seen above, this class of indicator is expected to be among the most frequently aggregated and frequently reported indicators in news. It is, consequently, also less likely to be subject to partisan framing than other indicators. We might further expect that the American public will have a mostly unbiased, well-informed appraisal of market conditions at any given time.

These patterns mean that the success and failure of incumbents will rise and fall in tandem with the economic well-being of the wealthy more so than the prosperity of the middle class. In Achen and Bartels' (2017) pessimistic account of US elections, even myopic, uninformed voters are expected to respond to valence information to make choices between candidates. The problem is that this information is sometimes irrelevant to the observed performance of candidates (much like the occurrence of shark attacks in coastal towns). If the movement of the stock market has few direct effects on middle-class Americans' prosperity, "following the ticker" is a suboptimal—and possibly misinformed—way to reward and punish incumbents.

Compounding the problem is the fact that voters' perceptions of other core economic indicators are highly biased (e.g., Bartels 2002; Evans and Pickup 2010). Partisan motivated reasoning means that many voters' unemployment, inflation, and GDP growth perceptions do little to aid them in rational decision making. Many co-partisans of the incumbent will insist these indicators show signs of great economic progress, even if they do not; co-partisans of the opposition will insist the opposite. As a result, when voters perform "information searches" that allow them to make political judgments using the reward-punish logic of economic voting, they will recall stock market performance more accurately than other economic signals. The "economy of the wealthy," as described by this indicator, will form an unbiased, rational basis for economic voting decisions. If the evidence in later chapters supports the present expectations, the stock market would therefore occupy a heretofore unheralded role in driving the American economic vote (Fauvelle-Aymar and Stegmaier 2013).

## Summary

In this chapter, I have traced a theory of political communication that explores the norms, practices, and strategies of economic data producers, journalists, and political actors. These news values help to explain the centrality of the stock market as a driver of Americans' economic and political perceptions. Such patterns have far-reaching consequences for elite communications, partisan biases, and elections in an era of continued polarization and economic inequality.

The present theory is not altogether controversial: After all, we have seen many instances in this chapter of academic studies and historical examples which corroborate the influential role of framing and agenda setting in reshaping Americans' perceptions. However, this story also makes it clear that to understand the contours and impacts of economic news on public opinion, we must examine the specifics of economic journalism. Expectations about partisan bias in climate change beliefs, war casualties, foreign affairs, and crowd sizes can only be understood after a thorough examination of how such topics are discussed in the information environment. The same can be said of perceptions of the stock market—an understudied subject in the existing literature in public opinion and political psychology.

The next chapter works to evaluate the present expectations by studying the content of economic news. In a large-scale content analysis of more than thirty years of economic news stories across a variety of media sources, I show that daily-aggregated economic indicators far outpace monthly and quarterly indicators in terms of overall presentation volume. This agenda-setting behavior is insensitive to medium, local market, or publication type. By intensely scrutinizing the contours of daily coverage of the economy, the upcoming chapter reveals that stock market coverage dominates a wide variety of news sources across the ideological spectrum.

Chapter 2

# "Following the Ticker"

## Media Agenda Setting and Stock Market Data

The "information environment" is an encompassing concept. It includes all the news conveyed to Americans daily through media and other sources—from friends, neighbors, "mainstream" news outlets and wire services, pundits, Internet acquaintances, and even personal experience. In the sections that follow, I engage in a descriptive analysis of the *economic* information environment, as it was observed by Americans, over the past several decades. In chapter 1, I argued that one cannot understand Americans' economic perceptions without first understanding how journalists present news about the economy, given that much of the economic information we learn comes to us through mediated sources (Mutz 1992). Because mainstream journalists face deadline pressures and other constraints on their ability to describe the economy in detail, I expect modern news values to produce a high volume of stock market reports relative to other types of economic data.[1]

The present chapter tests these claims. I do this by examining the economic news agenda in the pages of the *New York Times* from 1980 through 2020, and in a more diverse but more recent dataset, spanning only the period from 2015 to 2020 due to limited data availability for some sources. The goal of these analyses is to study journalists' economic agenda-setting practices, and to see if they hold across diverse economic, ideological, regional, and intermodal contexts.

There are good reasons to believe that ideological slant, regional focus, medium, and the state of the economy might all influence the agenda-setting behavior of the press. However, the results of this study show that relative to other data series that are mostly collected on a monthly or quarterly basis, daily stock market reports prevail as the most widely discussed topic—largely irrespective of these contextual features. The results show that stock market reports saturate economic news across a wide variety of sources, even when the stock market's performance is not congenial to the partisan or ideological proclivities of a given news source. Modern news values mean that most of the time, when Americans read or watch economic coverage, they will be exposed to at least some information about the stock market.

## Expectations

Economic journalists find themselves constrained by the fact that some information, such as the official calculation of GDP, U-3 unemployment, consumer confidence, and measures of sales and manufacturing, are reported at infrequent intervals. This is in part because such information is difficult to compile, requiring skilled experts and specialized tools. Other economic information, like stock prices and commodity prices, are available during the business day on an up-to-the-second basis. Thanks to the efforts of stock exchanges like the New York Stock Exchange, stock prices are conveyed to journalists virtually instantaneously. This imbalance in the availability of economic data is expected to spill over to influence the economic news agenda on any given day.

This agenda-setting behavior is expected to endure over the long term, even though the most "newsworthy" economic indicator varies from day to day. Take, for example, the BLS's monthly jobs report—a vital source of economic data that receives intense coverage on the day it is released. Unemployment (measured by the BLS using a variety of statistics at the national and state levels) fluctuates across time in response to economic conditions. While unemployment is highly salient for most news consumers, journalists cannot always reach for this indicator to fill the economic "news hole." But one day per month, the release of an unemployment report will occur, causing journalists to delve into the data to interpret the report's meaning. If the unemployment trend is better or worse than anticipated, the coverage may be even more intense. The surprising figures might reformulate audiences' expectations about the broader economic environment.

While these spikes in coverage are an important feature of good agenda setting, I argue that *long-term* imbalances in coverage are just as consequential. Journalists must make choices about economic topics even on a "slow economic news day." What they choose to report on, as discussed in chapter 1, partially comes down to the availability of data on a quarterly, monthly, or daily basis. Daily aggregated indicators fluctuate more quickly than unemployment, wage growth, and GDP growth, meaning short-term shifts will attract more attention on any given day due to journalists' focus on movement over stasis in economic data (Soroka 2006). Because many Americans learn from news haphazardly and infrequently, this aggregate, long-term behavior is consequential for citizens' beliefs and perceptions.

Based on the preceding discussion, I propose the following initial hypothesis:

H1. Stock market indicators will receive more coverage in major news sources over the long term than other common economic indicators.

This pattern is also expected to hold despite fluctuations in the status of the real economy. While it is certainly true that dramatic, eye-catching shifts in economic data will reorient the economic news agenda in favor of whatever data have spiked or plummeted, these surprising developments can only be reported after the data have been aggregated and reported by the firms and agencies that produce them. Even when compensating for the movement of the real economy, I expect the stock market to prevail as a more salient feature of economic coverage than other core indicators on average:

H2. When compensating for fluctuations in the observed economy, major new sources' economic agendas will favor stock market data over other common indicators.

Of course, stock markets are not the only sources of daily-aggregated economic data. Many price indicators, including commodities like crude oil, refined gasoline, and crops, are also available to consumers on an instantaneous basis. As discussed in the introduction, however, the stock market is further expected to occupy a primary role in economic news coverage because of audience demand. As more Americans turn their attention to the stock market due to their experimentation with day trading or their desire to monitor passively managed retirement accounts, reporters will respond with even more stock market coverage. Thus, even when compared to other daily-aggregated indicators like gas prices, major stock indices are expected to appear most frequently in news coverage.

## AGENDA SETTING ACROSS NEWS SOURCES

Much has been written about how journalists decide on the most important stories and story details of the day. The aptly named volume written by Herbert Gans, *Deciding What's News* (1979), gave readers a close-up insight into the practices of journalists. This study, along with a wealth of communication research that has followed its trajectory, shows that agenda setting often conforms to a "follow-the-leader" approach. Journalists are keen to observe what other sources are covering, even across different media. This effect is compounded due to the nationalization of news, as well as the looming presence of major newswires such as the Associated Press. A small number of on-the-ground reporters make story choices that are echoed by other journalists in far-flung newsrooms (Boyle 2001; Meraz 2009).

The news agendas of specific metropolitan news organizations are therefore not always determined solely by journalists working in those newsrooms. Sources like the *Baltimore Sun* or WRAL-TV (a local NBC affiliate in Raleigh, North Carolina) often look to the top stories and headlines produced by large, national-level sources like the *New York Times* to determine their content (Golan 2006). Follow-the-leader journalism helps journalists produce cost-effective and timely coverage of national affairs.

In addition to these "intermedia agenda-setters," smaller news organizations also search for cues related to the news agenda among national wire services. International wire service agencies are often large public companies, such as Reuters (based in the United Kingdom) and the Agence France-Presse. In the United States, the Associated Press prevails as the most important wire service, operating as a nonprofit cooperative that employs journalists in more than 250 locations around the world (Associated Press 2018). Wire services directly summarize and report much of the economic data described in chapter 1, so even journalists who are not economic experts can quickly and easily digest the day's economic news.[2]

Finally, patterns of ownership also work to influence the agendas of specific news outlets. The aforementioned *Baltimore Sun*, for example, gleans many of its national stories from the collective information gathering capacity of its parent corporation, Tribune Publishing. Concentration of ownership in media accelerates the trend towards top-down agenda setting (Baker 2006; Noam 2016). A 2017 report by the Pew Research Center identified just five companies—Sinclair Broadcasting, Gray, Nexstar, Tegna, and Tribune—as owning almost 40 percent of all local TV stations in the United States (Matsa 2017). Similar trends have occurred in the realm of newspapers, as declining profits have forced many local papers to cede ownership to national conglomerates. Just as independent local news organizations turn to large news organizations for help in setting their news agendas, so too have large conglomerates begun buying up independent news producers with an eye towards asserting their own visions of what is newsworthy.[3]

Together, the availability of wire services, the conglomeration of ownership, and the practices of busy journalists lend support for the expectation that national economic news will be remarkably similar in coverage style across a wide variety of sources. While the advent of social media as an alternative to traditional news means that important parts of the economic information environment might come from other "bottom-up" sources of influence, we cannot forget that much of the content shared and cited on social media still derives from the work of professional reporters (Meraz 2009; but see Singer 2018). Even though audiences now play a much larger role in determining the news agenda, the discussion of new developments in economic affairs is still quite likely to be passed from economic data producers to wire services and national sources, to local sources and social media, and finally, to consumers.

The availability of economic content in the daily news diet of Americans is therefore highly contingent upon the conventions and practices of journalists at prominent media organizations. As we saw in chapter 1, to practice expedient and effective reporting, this means that the daily news agenda will depend upon what kinds of economic data are most readily available for journalists to write about on any given day. We can summarize this expectation in H3:

H3. Among national and regional daily newspapers, stock market data will occupy a greater share of the economic agenda than other common indicators.

Daily newspapers can also tell us whether the phenomenon of imbalanced indicator coverage is attenuated by local forces. This is because newspapers serve a diverse array of markets, seeking in each case to cater to their audience.[4] Some newspapers, like the *San Francisco Chronicle*, serve communities with high concentrations of white-collar jobs, high average rents, and relatively high median incomes. Others, like the *Daily Oklahoman*, serve cities with relatively large volumes of industrial jobs and low median incomes. Media markets also differ across a variety of other factors, including size, region, and ideology.

That having been said, there is little *a priori* evidence to suggest that journalists reporting for these daily newspapers will practice unique economic agenda-setting behavior. Compared to sources like *USA Today*, reporting about the national economy among local-market newspapers should not be radically different. The pressure to produce content, the need to fill the "news hole" with relevant data to constitute stories—none of this situation is better or worse for journalists at the *Journal News* of Westchester, New York, than it is for the staff of the *Reporter-News* of Abilene, Texas.

In fact, theories of "pack journalism" suggest that smaller newspapers with fewer reporters on staff will look to the agenda-setting behavior of large national papers as a cue for their own subject matter (McDevitt 2003; Sabato 1991). Facing looming budget cuts and layoffs, journalists will pay attention to the stories reported by major players in the market to help guide their decision. making. They may do this regardless of whether their papers serve boom towns like Nashville, Tennessee, or rust-belt cities like Dayton, Ohio. And, of course, cash-strapped newsrooms will also be more likely to slot Associated Press stories into their pages when covering national topics. Economic news is a prime candidate for newswire coverage, especially when a paper's skeleton-crew staff lacks the expertise to effectively interpret raw economic data.

Furthermore, the concentration of ownership of newspapers across the country might mean that local journalists will be pressured to draw from a parent company's national source material to supplement their own reporting. When it comes to national economic news, we might be especially likely to see reports drawn from sources outside the locale. In fact, all of the newspapers mentioned in the paragraph above, from the *Nashville Tennessean* to the *Abilene Reporter-News* to *USA Today*, are owned by a single parent company, Gannett, which supplies national news stories to each source via a network of reporters.

## THE CABLE NEWS AGENDA

Finally, we must also consider whether cable news coverage of the economy differs from that of newspapers. This variation may stem from differences in the magnitude of the "news hole" on cable TV relative to other media (e.g., Prior 2007). The news hole is a vital concept in the study of agenda setting and media effects. It can be most intuitively thought about from the perspective of daily print newspapers. In this case, the "hole" is a physical space on the page where a column can be fit. Any given column will be space-limited by advertisements and other copy that demands room on the page. The agenda-setting behavior of print journalists is strongly influenced by these space constraints, causing some stories and story details to be dropped in favor of others.

In contrast, filling the vast twenty-four-hour televised "news hole" with content requires a great deal of creativity and strategic behavior. It might require the same information to be repeated several times across many hours of coverage or a large amount of interpretive dialogue about the day's top stories. Since cable news can also convey information to viewers in multiple ways simultaneously, scrolling marquees and graphics can surround the primary on-screen content, yielding even more space for recurring updates.

Together, these features of cable news suggest that *repetition* is a useful strategy for journalists hoping to cover the twenty-four-hour news hole. As a result, we might expect mentions of daily-aggregated economic information to be repeated even more frequently on cable news than print sources. On days when salient monthly or quarterly economic reports are released by official sources, we may also see stories about unemployment or GDP growth repeated ad nauseum. But as we have seen above, on most days, scrolling marquees can be more easily filled with continuously updated stock market information.

There is one other reason why cable TV might differ in its economic news agenda relative to print media. The format of many cable news segments is designed to fill the news hole with opinion and debate—much of it partisan in nature. While many cable shows like CNN's *The Lead with Jake Tapper* might briefly present headlines of the day pertaining to economic matters before moving on to other content, shows replete with interview and discussion segments might result in vastly different patterns of economic mentions. Fox News Channel's *Your World with Neil Cavuto*, MSNBC's *Morning Joe*, and CNN's *Anderson Cooper 360°* all present headlines interspersed with live interviews, roundtables, and other formats designed to keep audiences engaged. These interviews and discussions have important consequences for the economic content mentioned on cable, specifically because of the hosts' and guests' penchant for interpretive (and often partisan) discourse.

Partisan elites often appear on cable news to debate policy positions, discuss headlines, or offer careful partisan interpretations of recent trends and events. Free-flowing discussion formats cede much of the economic agenda to those elites, meaning that economic mentions are likely to be influenced by two primary factors. In addition to the long-term frequency of data reporting, the preferences of partisan elites also shape the economic news agenda on cable channels. This means that in addition to the forces that increase the attractiveness of the stock market for agenda setting, *partisan congeniality* may also play a role in determining the cable news agenda. Newsrooms that intend to support the positions of one political party over the other may select economic news stories that make the incumbent administration look especially good or bad. Supporters of an incumbent will choose to feature positive economic developments, while the incumbent's detractors might choose to feature negative ones instead.

Together, these expectations can be expressed as H4a and H4b below:

H4a. Cable news broadcasts will prioritize stock market indicators over other economic information, regardless of the partisan congeniality of recent stock market performance.

H4b. Cable news broadcasts will prioritize partisan-congenial economic information over other economic information.

As we will see in chapter 3, partisan elites are highly attentive to certain types of information, such as the unemployment rate, to craft persuasive, partisan-congenial frames. As a result, the cable news agenda should reflect a balance between journalists' news values—influenced by the pressure to fill the news hole with available content—and the priorities of guests (and even anchors) with clear partisan preferences.

## Studying the Economic News: A Lexical Methodology

To assess these hypotheses, I employ a methodology known as automated content analysis (ACA). While contemporary social scientists and linguists often use highly sophisticated algorithms to analyze the nuances of text as a form of data, the present study calls for a straightforward method. To examine the economic news agenda, I employ a *dictionary-based* form of lexical analysis, which tallies the occurrence of words and phrases (known as N-grams) related to topics of interest.[5] Dictionary-based approaches are commonplace in the study of political texts and news content (Grimmer 2013).

However, no existing lexical dictionary is exactly suited for the present analysis. Dictionary-based methods have been used to great effect in existing studies of economic news, allowing us to learn a great deal about topics like tone and negativity bias (e.g., Young and Soroka 2012; Wlezien, Soroka and Stecula 2017). But this study requires a robust *indicator-specific* economic lexicon that identifies the frequency and density of mention of a wide variety of economic data. Amassed in a dictionary format, this lexicon would ideally allow for the easy identification of mentions of economic indicators in plain text. It might also allow us to discriminate between descriptions of the US economy and other irrelevant uses of economic terminology (consider, for example, the myriad uses of terms like "job" and "inflation" in news). A dictionary that classifies economic news tone, despite its excellent performance in its intended application, would not yield an effective test of the above hypotheses.

To classify economic news reports (and, as we will see in chapter 3, the communications of political elites), I created a specialized dictionary with the assistance of two advanced undergraduate research assistants. The dictionary was assembled by examining samples of economic news stories that were randomly selected from a much larger dataset of *New York Times* articles spanning 1980–2020. These articles were drawn from the Nexis Uni (formerly LexisNexis) platform, selected based on search criteria that limited the sample to news stories with an economic focus (see the appendices for a description of the search string content). Overall, the search yielded 50,071 articles to be used for analysis. Of those articles, I selected 250 through a random draw to serve as a training set. I also selected 200 random articles to serve as a test set, which allowed us to validate the effectiveness of the lexicon.

Each of us carefully read all the economic news stories in the training set, identifying and recording any words or phrases in the text that made explicit reference to an economic indicator. An "explicit reference" conforms to one of two cases. The first is if a word or phrase accompanies a numeric economic statistic (e.g., coders reading the phrase "The first quarter of last year witnessed GDP growth of 1.5%" would select "GDP growth" as a relevant economic mention). The second category is less cut-and-dry, as coders were instructed to capture any phrase which was used in conjunction with a message indicating the *directionality* of economic performance (e.g., "The government's leading index showed major gains this quarter" would merit inclusion of the phrase "leading index"). Next, phrases fitting either of these two criteria were labeled for inclusion in one of nine categories, each corresponding to one of the broad indicator categories described by Baumohl (2012) and introduced in chapter 1.[6] Our initial set of terms constituted 289 unique words and phrases.

One way to identify whether the coders were successful at creating a reliable dictionary of economic terms is to check if different coders spotted the same words in the same sample of news stories. The initial common code proportion, a measure of intercoder reliability that is suited to this kind of exploratory coding, was 75.1 percent. After discarding terms that failed to be agreed upon by coders, 241 words and phrases that clearly and unambiguously denoted mention of an economic indicator in the news remained. This set of terms is a useful, if basic, tool for measuring when each of our nine economic topics were brought up in economic news. In subsequent tests of the lexicon, we found that the dictionary yielded a testing accuracy rate of 97 percent. A comparison of hand-coded and machine-coded classifications from the 200 test-set documents determined that our lexicon inadvertently coded noneconomic content as references to economic indicators only 3 percent of the time. Further details regarding the dictionary, its validation, and its contents can be seen in the appendices.

## Study 2.1: The Economic News Agenda, 1980–2020

To assess H1 and H2, I first examine the economic news as it was presented in the *New York Times* from January 1980 to January 2020. The *New York Times* does not reflect the *entire* economic agenda across the period in question—nor should we expect it to. As we will see in study 2.2, there is some degree of heterogeneity in economic coverage across various news sources, meaning we should remain cautious about applying study 2.1's insights to other sources for which we lack long-term archival data. Nevertheless, the *New York Times* is often used as a stand-in for the information environment in scholarship on economic news (e.g., Fogarty 2005; Goidel et al. 2010; Hester and Gibson 2003). As a prominent national source, it is a leader in agenda setting that many other news outlets look to for newsworthiness cues (Page and Shapiro 1984; Sabato 1991). Its status as a preeminent American newspaper also makes for a more challenging test of the present hypotheses. Having a well-staffed newsroom makes for a longer newspaper, potentially leading to more plentiful economic news content (and discussion of diverse economic indicators) relative to other sources.

Data collection was performed through a comprehensive (and labor-intensive) search for economic news articles spanning the available *New York Times* transcripts on Nexis Uni. While Nexis Uni stores a reliable archive of many newspapers dating back to as early as 2015, the *New York Times*'s data series includes full-text articles dating back to 1980. Earlier transcripts are available, but many are limited to abstracts and therefore are not appropriate for the present analysis.

It is important to study H1 and H2 across this extended time span. Over four decades, the American economy experienced everything from recessions to economic booms. Stock markets surpassed record levels, crashed abruptly, and rose to still greater heights. Inflation climbed precipitously and then receded; the national debt swelled to a prodigious size, and trade imbalances became more lopsided. Manufacturing shriveled as trade deficits became more pronounced, while Silicon Valley established itself as the preeminent global force in the information technology sector.

Through it all, however, economic journalists presented the news according to standard conventions. These behaviors yielded surprisingly consistent patterns over time. As we will soon see, journalists set the agenda from 1980 to 2020 in predictable ways. Most important, they privileged daily aggregated stock market data over other common indicators, especially those reported to the public at monthly and quarterly intervals, like unemployment, wage growth, and trade statistics.

ECONOMIC DISCOURSE IN THE *NEW YORK TIMES*

A first glimpse at the economic discourse seen in the pages of the *New York Times* across the past four decades is captured in figure 2.1. This figure shows the average number of mentions per article of nine economic indicator categories across the entire period under study. Each of the nine categories includes a robust lexicon of economic terms related to the topic: for example, the "employment" category includes terms like "unemployment," "job growth," and "jobs." For further details on the economic lexicon, see the appendices. Across more than forty-five thousand individual news articles that make mention of the economy, the evidence is relatively clear: *New York Times* coverage describes the performance of the financial sector far more than any other indicator category.

Figure 2.1 demonstrates that keywords related to financial markets (including "stock," "bond," and "commodity markets") constitute the most frequently mentioned indicators in the series. In fact, across the forty years of coverage, we see that financial market keywords are mentioned more than three times per *New York Times* economy-focused articles. This volume of reporting can be contrasted with scarcely mentioned indicators, such as "trade," "wages," and "consumer confidence," which are all mentioned less than one time per article. Interestingly, this first glimpse at the results shows that commodity prices are the second most

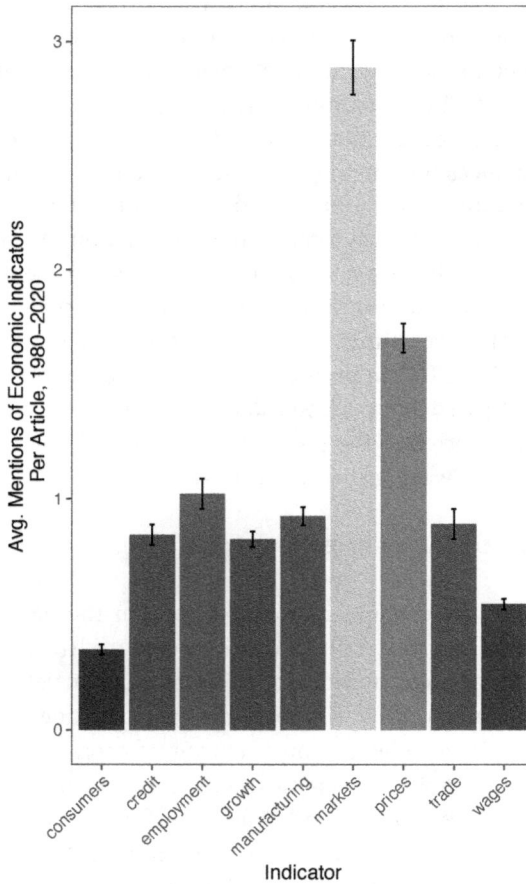

Figure 2.1. Average mentions of nine indicators per article, *New York Times*, 1980–2020. *Source*: Author's own material.

frequently mentioned genre of economic indicators, perhaps also because these prices are aggregated daily and are therefore convenient data for journalists seeking to efficiently fill the "news hole." However, even though prices update more frequently than government reports on GDP growth and wages, discussions of prices are still not as prevalent as mentions of financial market indices.

Of course, this first look at the data could be very misleading. It might be that certain articles about stock and bond markets simply include long descriptions that make many repeated references to different financial market indices, whereas unemployment, manufacturing, credit, and other economic issue areas are mentioned only briefly in the same number of shorter articles. To assess these considerations, I next disaggregate the economic news agenda across time and by article.

## Economic Indicators across Time

While an aggregate view of economic indicator mentions is still useful for our purposes, it does not help us to fully assess H1 and H2. These hypotheses make assertions about over-time agenda differences; that is, prices and stock market data are expected to saturate economic news despite the occasional emergence of other major economic stories. To assess the volume of economic news across the period in question, figure 2.2 depicts over-time movement in the rate of mentions of different indicators, quarterly, from 1980 through 2020.

Figure 2.2 depicts a comparison between the over-time mention volume of financial markets and a highly salient monthly aggregated indicator: unemployment. We can glean several important details about *New York Times* economy coverage from this figure. First, the economic news agenda is quite volatile across time. This volatility also corresponds with basic expectations given what happened to the US economy over the period covered by the data. Stock market booms and crashes, for instance, are accompanied by spikes in mentions. Unemployment mentions spike later, as unemployment is a lagging indicator.

We see several instances in which mentions of financial markets began to reach fever-pitch levels of coverage—especially during major financial events like the 2007–2009 bear market caused by the Great Recession, the crash of 1987 colloquially known as "Black Monday," and the massive coverage of COVID-19 in the spring of 2020. During the subprime mortgage crisis and the COVID-19 crisis, we see many mentions of unemployment,

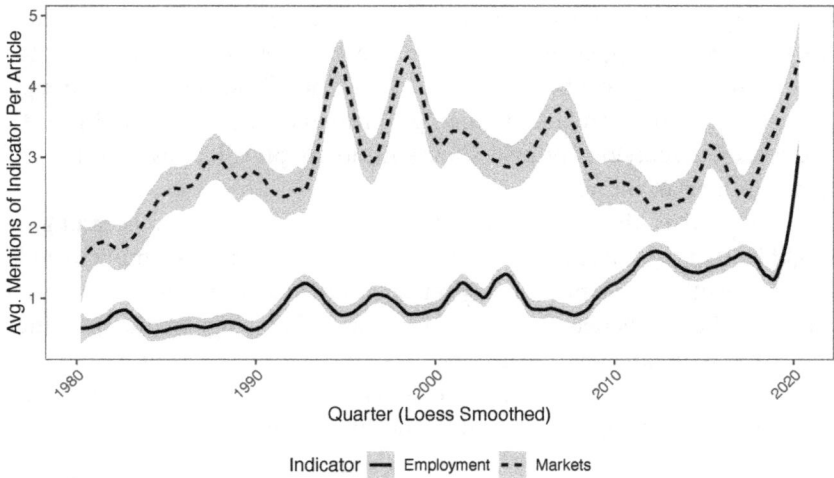

Figure 2.2. Loess smoothed quarterly mentions of employment and stock market indicators per article, *New York Times*, 1980–2020. *Source*: Author's own material.

as the labor market spiraled into disastrous territory in both cases. Certain hot-button BLS reports also clearly achieved a high level of attention in news, including the aforementioned October 2012 job market report that conservatives suspected would help Obama win re-election.

Despite these trends, the two series depicted in figure 2.2 also show important differences between unemployment and financial markets as topics of discussion. At no point does unemployment surpass financial markets in coverage volume. In 2004, coverage spiked largely because unemployment numbers showed surprising improvement. But in 1992, and 2020, the unemployment numbers became too worrying to ignore in daily commentary, as the figure had ballooned to 7.5 percent in that year. In each case, these short-term spikes in mentions tell us that economic news is accurately tracking the real economy. The more important story for our purpose, however, is that during 2020, 2004, and 1992 financial market indicators were still mentioned more frequently on average than the pressing matter of unemployment across the full length of each quarter.

While this first cut at the data shows a clear distinction between the number of mentions of different indicators, the scale can be some-what misleading, given that it is merely capturing the *average* number of mentions of an indicator per article. A relatively long article about the stock market might contain ten mentions of that indicator, while five other articles might make no mention whatsoever. As a result, we can also consider what percent of articles in the dataset make at least one mention of any of the nine indicator categories captured by the dictionary. Figure 2.3 shows this distribution across the entire period in question.

Compared to figure 2.2, figure 2.3 shows that the rank order of economic indicators, from most to least frequently mentioned, is effectively unchanged. However, figure 2.3 shows that the number of articles mentioning specific indicators is more evenly distributed than the average

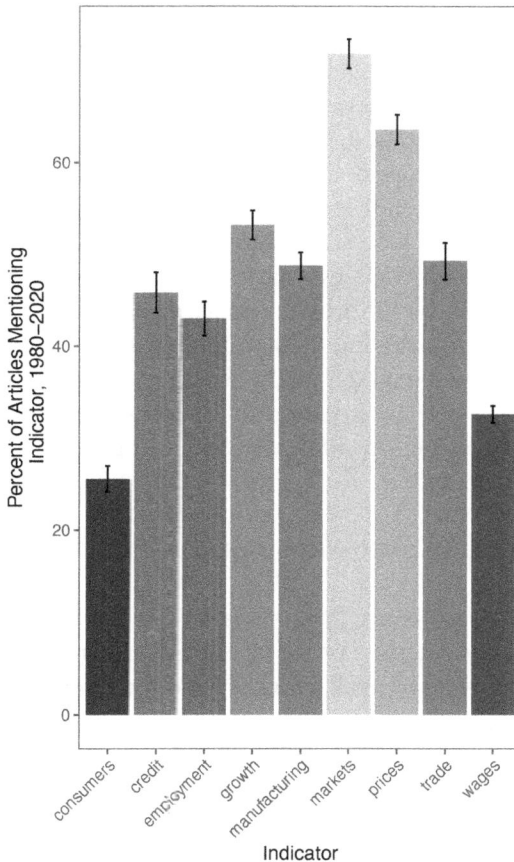

Figure 2.3. Percent of articles referencing nine economic indicators, *New York Times*, 1980–2020. *Source*: Author's own material.

number of indicator mentions per article. In addition to the fact that some news stories make repetitive mention of indicators like the stock market and prices, many stories about *other* topics also appear to contain mentions of financial indicators.

Stories with headlines featuring mentions of unemployment, for example, might mention the stock market towards the bottom of the page or vice versa. Stories about inflation might discuss prices as part of the interpretation of the causes or consequences of movement in that indicator. As a result, the percentage of "indicator stories" making at least one reference to any given economic indicator is high. It may be that many stories discuss the stock market and prices because these are leading, rather than lagging, indicators. Or, as can be seen through a qualitative reading of many "indicator stories," daily aggregated economic information is simply "tacked on" to the end of many news articles about the economy without any meaningful interpretation or narrative link.

One example of this former style of reporting comes from Paul Davidson's (2009) coverage of a relatively obscure economic indicator. RV sales are a good leading indicator of economic expansion because they are expensive splurges that lock buyers into a whole host of related expenses (like gasoline and camping fees) that people anticipate paying for in the future. In Davidson's (2009) article, various explanations for a rise in RV sales are mentioned, including the notion that the stock market had witnessed gains. A late paragraph in the article makes several mentions of stock performance. Even when economic journalists describe developments as obscure as the ownership of motor homes, the stock market is often mentioned in conjunction.

## Modeling the Economic News Agenda

To more formally assess the hypotheses set out at the beginning of this chapter, I next present the results of analyses designed to examine the relationships between the "real" economy and the economic news agenda. I perform two tests in this vein. First, I create a cross-sectional time series regression model that is designed to understand why some indicators are so frequently mentioned in economic news. To do this I account for three primary sources of influence on topic mentions. First is the volatility of an economic indicator, which should be positively associated with indicator mentions. For example, when gas prices become volatile, we would expect this volatility to catch the attention of journalists hoping to inform readers or viewers about an unexpected economic shock. Next, I capture the absolute value of an economic indicator's performance. Were gas prices to creep slowly upwards (without any major volatility), the news might similarly focus its attention on that indicator when it eventually approaches record highs. Last, I account for the frequency with which economic indicator data are released by official sources (daily, monthly, or quarterly), to assess the theoretical expectations described above.

In a second test, I scrutinize the features of two specific economic time series, the stock market and unemployment, using specialized time series methods. These latter models allow me to determine whether real stock market performance and the real unemployment rate, respectively, significantly influence the volume of news about those topics. If so, the evidence would indicate that journalists are mostly responsive to an indicator's performance and volatility in deciding whether to mention it in news. If not (as we might suspect in the case of the stock market), the evidence would suggest that journalists cover some topics reflexively, regardless of variation in recent economic performance.

The nine indicator categories we have examined thus far are somewhat abstract, as they represent broad collections of the specific data releases described in Baumchl (2012) and reproduced in chapter 1. This makes it difficult to effectively measure their "real" movement over time. A single quantitative measure of the stock market's performance, for example, will fail to capture the fact that different indices and stock exchanges all performed differently across the time span. However, by constructing a dataset of economic indicators as they were measured across the period in question, I perform rough tests of the effects of the "real" movement of economic indicators on the topics in economic news.[7]

All independent variables in the analyses to follow were measured on a quarterly basis. Data were gathered from the St. Louis Federal Reserve's FRED economic dataverse. For unemployment, growth, and prices, I rely upon the standard FRED measures of the official national (U-3) unemployment rate, Gross Domestic Product (GDP), and the Consumer Price Index, respectively. For a measure of wages, I rely upon median usual weekly earnings among employed full-time wage and salary workers. For the topic of credit and debt, I use a measure of total outstanding consumer credit owned and securitized. To measure stock markets, I rely upon the Wilshire 5000, a broad index of publicly traded stocks. For trade data I use the GDP Terms of Trade index, a measure of the relative competitiveness of US exports, and for manufacturing and sales I use the NAICS score, a standard measure of industrial productivity. Altogether, these data series do not come close to describing the entire economy. But for our purposes, they might get us closer to understanding why economic news mentions increase or decrease over time.

Several measures can be used to evaluate the effects of the real economy on economic news. In the first model presented below, model 2.1, each economic indicator variable $x_{it}$ corresponds to the $i$th economic topic at time $t$. One way to think about economic influence on the news agenda is to think about the degree of *volatility* in $x_i$ across time. If an economic indicator rapidly changes in its value, it may surprise observers and merit increased reporting. This volatility is represented in the analyses below by a standardized measure of quarter-over-quarter change in each indicator's total value: $\Delta x_{it}$. Because of the negativity bias inherent in economic news, however (e.g., Soroka and McAdams 2015), I further disaggregate volatility in the regression context by including a second term, $|\Delta x|_{it}$, or the absolute value of an indicator's quarter-over-quarter volatility. Because a regression model measures the independent effects of each included variable, when both $\Delta x_{it}$ and $|\Delta x|_{it}$ are included in a model together, the two variables separately measure the positive/negative *direction* of volatility. $\Delta x_{it}$ comes to represent what happens when an indicator experiences a negative shift. In contrast, $|\Delta x|_{it}$ expresses what happens when an indicator shows improvement.

Of course, volatility is not the only reason to cover an economic topic in news. I also measure the current level of an indicator's performance by assessing whether an indicator is at historically high or low values at time $t$. I capture this variable by calculating the standard z-score for each variable and time point, $z_{it} = \left(\frac{x_{it} - \mu_i}{\sigma_i}\right)$. This score compares an indicator's current value to its standardized historical average since 1980. Z-scores also have the added benefit of easy interpretability.[8]

Finally, I measure each indicator's frequency of data collection. This is captured by a measure *Periodicity*$_i$ that includes "daily," "monthly," or "quarterly" values in a trichotomous scale. This last score is determined by calculating the modal reporting frequency among the indicator categories described in chapter 1's tables 1.1–1.8. For example, the general category of unemployment is determined to have a modal frequency of "monthly," because four out of the seven common unemployment indicators listed in table 1.2 are reported on a monthly basis. Table 1.8 also shows that stock markets and prices merit "daily" periodicity scores.

*Model 2.1: The Economic News Agenda in Context*

Model 2.1, presented below in table 2.1, is a linear panel model (LPM) that estimates the effects of economic volatility, economic performance, and reporting frequency on the rate of mentions of nine economic topics (Ansolabehere, Lessem, and Snyder 2006; Larcinese, Puglisi, and Snyder 2011).[9] The model accounts for over-time and topic-specific variance while estimating the effects of the real economy. I estimate model 2.1 including $\Delta x_{it}$ and $|\Delta x|_{it}$ to separately estimate the effects of positive and negative economic shocks on indicator mentions, respectively. I present the results of a random-effects model with two-way estimators, though these modeling decisions were robust to alternate specifications (see the appendices).

Table 2.1. Panel Linear Regression Model Predicting Mention of Indicator Topics, *New York Times* Coverage of the Economy, 1980–2020

| | |
|---|---|
| $z_{it}$ (Performance Level) | −0.058 |
| | (0.063) |
| $\Delta$ (Negative Volatility) | 0.087*** |
| | (0.009) |
| $|\Delta|_{it}$ (Positive Volatility) | −0.046*** |
| | (0.017) |
| Monthly Periodicity | −1.872*** |
| | (0.378) |
| Quarterly Periodicity | −1.296** |
| | (0.567) |
| Constant | 2.618*** |
| | (0.327) |
| Observations | 1,215 |
| $R^2$ | 0.091 |
| Adjusted $R^2$ | 0.087 |
| F Statistic | 121.056*** |

Note: *p < 0.10; **p < 0.05; ***p < 0.01.

We can see from table 2.1, above, that the real economy strongly influences the economic news agenda, though primarily through volatility, rather than an indicator's current performance. This latter variable has no significant effect on topic mentions in the model ($\beta$ = –0.058, p < 0.1). But when an economic indicator reports sudden changes in performance, the news agenda responds by increasing or decreasing mentions of that indicator. Interestingly, in model 2.1, a standard deviation increase in *negative* volatility serves to *increase* the rate of mention of an indicator by around 0.087 mentions, or about one mention in every 12 articles (p < 0.01). Positive shifts, on the other hand, seem to depress the rate of mention of an economic indicator, though this effect is smaller ($\beta$ = –0.046, p < 0.001).

These findings make some intuitive sense from the perspective of economic journalism. Especially strong or weak quarterly performance can influence long-term agenda setting, as these values work as prisms through which other short-term economic matters can be interpreted. Major dips in the stock market, such as the Dow's nosedive in March of 2020, often provoke a flurry of attention from journalists given the eye-catching (and alarming) nature of the numbers. However, when these fluctuations give way to long-term trends, the news might overlook the subject until another burst of short-term volatility.

Of course, these patterns should not be interpreted without several caveats. A quarterly unit of analysis may be too long to capture the true impact of some economic indicators on news coverage. Day traders scrutinize up-to-the-minute volatility in stock prices as opportunities to buy and sell. A surprising jump in the New Home Sales measure reported by the U.S. Census Bureau on a single day might similarly cause investors to buy stock in companies like Ryan Homes, a major East Coast housing developer. Over the length of an entire quarter, these shocks are less visible, limiting the explanatory power of the volatility variables included in the model.

The third and final source of variation explored in figure 2.4 is the frequency of an indicator's reporting availability, as captured by daily, monthly, and quarterly data reports. Compared to figures 2.2 and 2.3, the coefficients presented in table 2.1 help us to evaluate H2 in a more robust statistical setting. The table's coefficients report the influence of indicator reporting periodicity after compensating for shifts in the real economy. This is an important detail because it allows us to understand whether media are saturated by daily aggregated indicators like the stock market and prices merely because those indicators are more volatile.

Instead, the coefficients reported in model 2.1 show that an indicator's reporting frequency exerts a strong independent effect. Relative to daily reported indicators, monthly reported indicators are referenced in economic news about 1.9 times less per article from 1980 through 2020 ($p < 0.001$). Quarterly reported indicators fare better relative to monthly aggregated data, though they are still reported about 1.3 times less per article across the same period ($p < 0.001$). These differences are large and statistically significant. They show us that journalists' practices help to explain what gets discussed in economic news, even as those indicators bear witness to a variety of real conditions.

## Model 2.2: Predicting Stock Market Mentions

Following recent scholarship, I next employ an ARIMA time series modeling framework to assess the effects of the real economy on stock market mentions (Damstra and Boukes 2021; Vasileiadou and Vliegenthart 2014). This modeling strategy allows us to robustly examine the effects of the real economy on the news agenda, although it does not allow for a simultaneous examination of all nine indicator topics, as was the case in the PLM models above. But by focusing on stock market mentions as a single time series, we can evaluate whether stock prices cause shifts in agenda-setting behavior. From earlier analysis and figures 2.1 and 2.2, we know that stock market coverage is usually more prevalent than other economic topics in news. But is this agenda-setting behavior reflexive—due mostly to the effects of journalists' news values—or does the stock market's inherent volatility cause journalists to report on it more frequently than other indicators?

We can test this question by examining an ARIMA(0,1,1) model of stock market mentions that takes $z_t$ (a z-score derived from the Wilshire 5000 index), $\partial_t$ (negative volatility in the same index), and $|\partial_t|$ (positive volatility) as the independent variables. For comparison, I also include a model of unemployment that uses the same predictor variable transformations. Data for the unemployment model are based on the FRED standard national unemployment rate measure. For modeling details, including a discussion of the model selection and time series diagnostics, see the appendices.

Table 2.2 shows that while stock market mentions are sensitive to stock market volatility more so than the current value of the Wilshire 5000, unemployment mentions are more sensitive to the current unemployment rate and less sensitive to changes in that rate. A one standard deviation fall in the price of the Wilshire 5000 (roughly 3.8 percent of its value) is expected to yield around 1.3 more mentions of the stock market per *New York Times* article, all else equal (p < 0.05). A one standard deviation positive shift, however, is expected to *decrease* coverage by around 1.6 mentions per article (p < 0.01). Once again, we see a pattern consistent with the idea that stock market coverage increases in response to major crashes and dips in stock market indices. Of course, it is important to remember that even in times of relative calm, stock market mentions normally remain high, perhaps why we see no consistent effect for the performance variable.

The unemployment rate, however, evinces a somewhat different pattern. Volatility seems to have little consistent effect on media mentions of the indicator, though the current unemployment rate does exert an influence on the volume of mentions in news. A one standard deviation increase in the unemployment rate is associated with a small but significant increase in coverage of the indicator ($\beta = 0.09$; p < 0.001). This pattern is likely more characteristic of other quarterly aggregated economic topics. Because unemployment only officially changes each month with the BLS's updates, it is more likely that reporters will remind readers of its value when it becomes

Table 2.2. ARIMA Models Predicting Stock Market and Unemployment Mentions

| | Stock Market Mentions (Model 2.2) | Unemployment Mentions (Model 2.3) |
|---|---|---|
| Constant (Drift) | 0.004 (0.02) | 0.008 (0.01) |
| MA(1) | −0.48 (0.08)*** | −0.38 (0.10)*** |
| $z_t$ (Performance) | 0.02 (0.04) | 0.09 (0.03)*** |
| $\partial_t$ (Negative Volatility) | 1.28 (0.62)* | −0.08 (0.40) |
| $|\partial_t|$ (Positive Volatility) | −1.61 (0.47)** | 0.66 (0.48) |
| AIC | 123.21 | −99.4 |
| Ljung-Box Q | 18.4 | 7.13 |

Note: ***p < 0.001; **p < 0.01; *p < 0.05. Standard errors in parentheses.

steadily higher. Large shifts in unemployment, like the one witnessed during the COVID-19 crisis, are rarer, and therefore harder for journalists to incorporate into coverage given their volatility-focused news values.

Altogether, the analysis in study 2.1 helps us to assess H1–H2 from an over-time perspective. We see evidence that the stock market, a daily-aggregated economic indicator, receives outsize coverage in news, but especially during dips and crashes. Economic news coverage tends to emphasize the stock market over the long term, due to a combination of prevailing news values and the attention-grabbing nature of stock market volatility.

While the four-decade time span of study 2.1 is useful for uncovering these patterns, the results are inherently limited because the data are restricted to historical *New York Times* articles. Below, in study 2.2, I expand the analysis by considering a more diverse set of news sources.

## Study 2.2: The Economic News Agenda, 2015–2020

The over-time analysis of newspaper transcripts in study 2.1 has shown that stock market coverage outpaces other economic indicators in journalists' coverage of the economic facts. In study 2.2, I examine whether further contextual factors—the ideology of news sources, region, and medium—influence the basic pattern seen above. Using identical data collection methods to those used in study 2.1, I obtained a large repository of daily newspaper and cable transcripts, including data from thirteen newspapers and two cable news networks.[10]

To test H3, I first present simple histograms that record the frequency of specific indicator mentions per day, from January 2015 to July 2020, across the thirteen newspapers included in the study. Because cable transcripts are much longer than the average news article, I analyze the two cable sources separately in a section to follow. Relying on the same lexicon of economic terms used to analyze the *New York Times* articles in study 2.1, I first summarize the economic news agenda of the thirteen newspapers in the sample.

Figure 2.4 provides an initial glimpse of the newspaper sample's economic news agenda from 2015 through 2020. We can immediately see that, consistent with the *New York Times* data, economic journalists across the contemporary period do not discuss all indicator types with equal frequency.

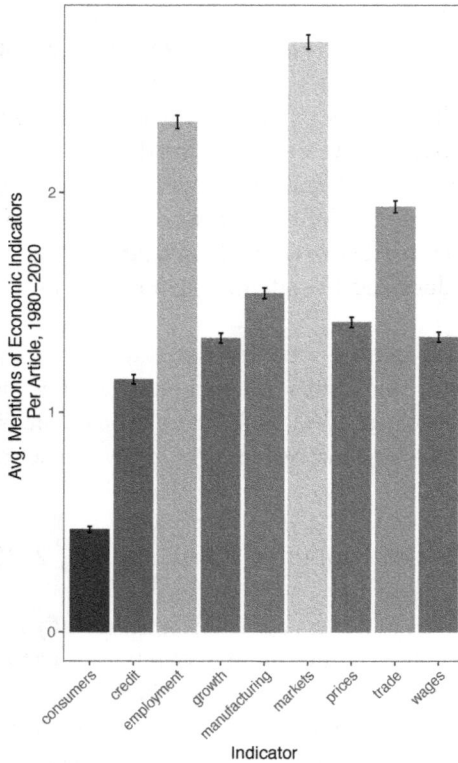

Figure 2.4. Mentions of economic news topics, thirteen newspapers, 2015–2020. *Source*: Author's own material.

Among the most frequently mentioned economic indicators in newspapers across the period under consideration were markets, trade, and unemployment. Both markets and unemployment were mentioned, on average, more than twice per article. Other very salient indicators, which are captured monthly or quarterly, are less frequently reported. For example, overall economic growth rates, manufacturing figures, and wages are all mentioned less than half as often as are market indicators. Much like the agenda-setting behavior of the *New York Times,* on average, newspapers in the sample tended to mention the stock market in their coverage more than other economic indicator types.

While figure 2.4 shows that diverse print sources appear to mention the stock market more than other indicators, this pattern could be an artifact of specific sources' coverage styles. While there is certainly some variation to be seen across source (the *Atlanta Journal-Constitution,* for example, is the sole source to mention unemployment more often than the stock market), I find it instructive to break the sources down across newspaper market type to better appraise the overall trend. Figure 2.5 shows

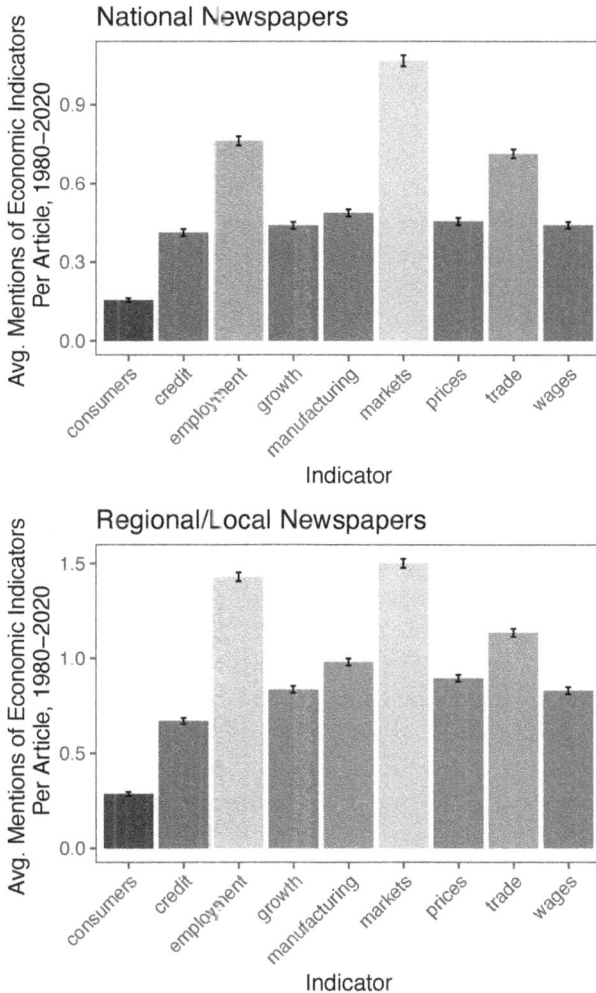

Figure 2.5. Mentions of economic news topics, national vs. local/regional newspapers, 2015–2020. *Source*: Author's own material.

the distribution of mentions of each economic indicator group among national newspaper sources (top panel) and local/regional newspapers (bottom panel) from 2015 through 2020. The results again show that both national and local newspapers tend to mention the stock market more than other indicators, though local newspapers mention unemployment, trade, and stock indices at similar rates.

This initial glimpse at the indicator-specific economic news agenda shows how a focus on the stock market seems to pervade indicator stories across a wide variety of sources in the modern era. National sources (and especially the *New York Times*) are more focused on the stock market than local newspapers, perhaps reflecting their need to describe the national economy instead of the local economy in their coverage. Among local papers, a balance of coverage between unemployment and the stock market may reflect the interests of local audiences, as well as a focus on the job market in the region. As we will soon see, it may also reflect the ideological preferences of audiences (Gentzkow and Shapiro 2011). Local audiences may be heavily pro-Republican or pro-Democratic relative to a national audience, meaning that local sources may cater to their audiences by publishing partisan-congenial facts more often than those that run counter to partisan talking points.

## A CLOSER LOOK AT ECONOMIC NEWS, 2015–2020

To examine the prevalence of stock market coverage across newspaper sources, I next examine the daily news agenda in the study 2.2 newspaper sample from 2015 through 2020. Results of this analysis are consistent with the patterns seen above. Figure 2.6 shows over-time trends in the daily mention of unemployment and the stock market in the thirteen newspaper sources under study, arranged by month. The figure again shows that economic news reacted to real-world shifts in the respective indicators. For example, we see peaks in the rate of market indicator mentions in December of 2015, when the market experienced an unexpected downturn; we see a similar peak again in June of 2016, when the Dow crossed the eighteen-thousand-point milestone before experiencing high levels of volatility. Similarly, the rate of mentions of employment-related figures peaks around the release of landmark BLS jobs reports, such as the highly optimistic reports of early 2019.

But overall, figure 2.6 corroborates figure 2.5's finding. Apart from the dramatic COVID-19 era of early 2020, economic news in daily newspapers

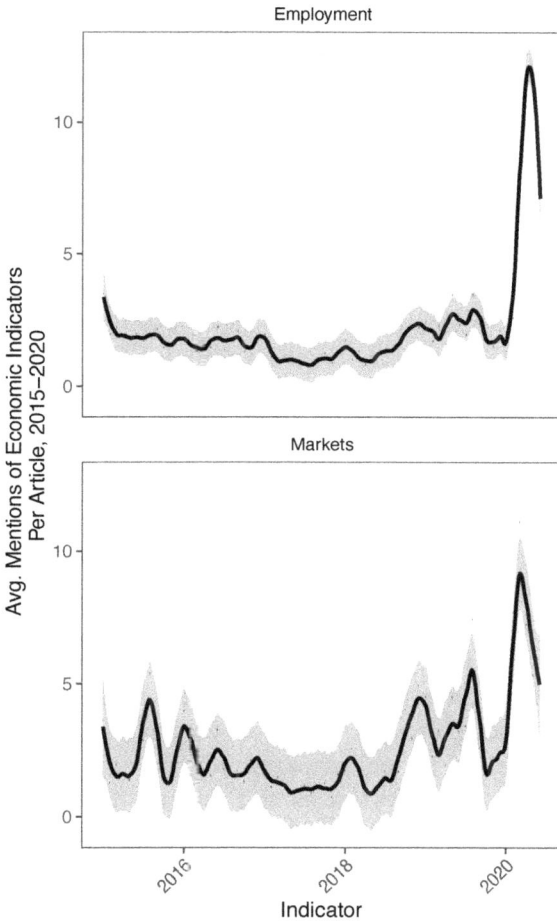

Figure 2.6. Mentions of stock market and unemployment indicators per day, 2015–2020. *Source*: Author's own material.

and cable transcripts tended to talk about the stock market more than jobs across the period. This is an important finding because smaller, regional newspapers often focus economic coverage on "personal issue" stories from the local area that involve mentions of employment. For example, the *Atlanta Journal-Constitution* often runs economic news stories featuring the experiences of local residents on the job market, such as a woman hoping to gain employment at Hartsfield-Jackson International Airport. However, even a focus on the local economy can draw attention to stock prices.

The *Atlanta Journal-Constitution* devotes coverage to Delta Airlines' share prices due to their importance as a regional employer. Despite varying coverage styles, newspapers across the country still find plentiful reasons to mention the stock market in their everyday economy coverage.

## Economics on Partisan TV: Comparing Cable Networks

While newspaper sources are heterogeneous in their coverage styles, we can also consider the motivations and news values of journalists on partisan-oriented cable television. Are there partisan-motivated differences in the economic agenda-setting behavior of Fox News Channel and MSNBC? As earlier hypothesized, we might expect cable journalists to mention the stock market as a matter of convenience: The need to fill the "news hole" with twenty-four hours of content means continuously updated economic data are in high demand. However, it is also possible that ideologically motivated cable networks will seek to provide *congenial* coverage that makes their favorite political party look good. This means that long-term fluctuations in the news agenda will be affected by the interaction between two conditions: which political party is in power, and whether an economic indicator is showing reason for optimism or pessimism. For example, when unemployment is very low, unemployment stories will look good for a presidential incumbent; a pro-incumbent network might boost their coverage of unemployment for this reason.

Figure 2.7 presents the rate of economic topic mentions over more than one thousand cable news show transcripts spanning from 2015 through 2020. Because these transcripts are generally much longer than a printed economic indicator story, with word counts sometimes reaching into the tens of thousands, we see that the number of mentions per transcript is higher than the number of mentions of indicators per newspaper article. But once again, a clear pattern presents itself.

In both the Fox News Channel and the MSNBC transcript samples, the most frequently discussed economic news topic is the stock market. While Fox News appears to discuss economic matters more often per transcript than MSNBC on average, viewers learn about the stock market relatively frequently on both networks. Fox viewers receive stock market references almost 4 times per transcript, while MSNBC viewers learn about stock markets around 1.5 times per transcript.

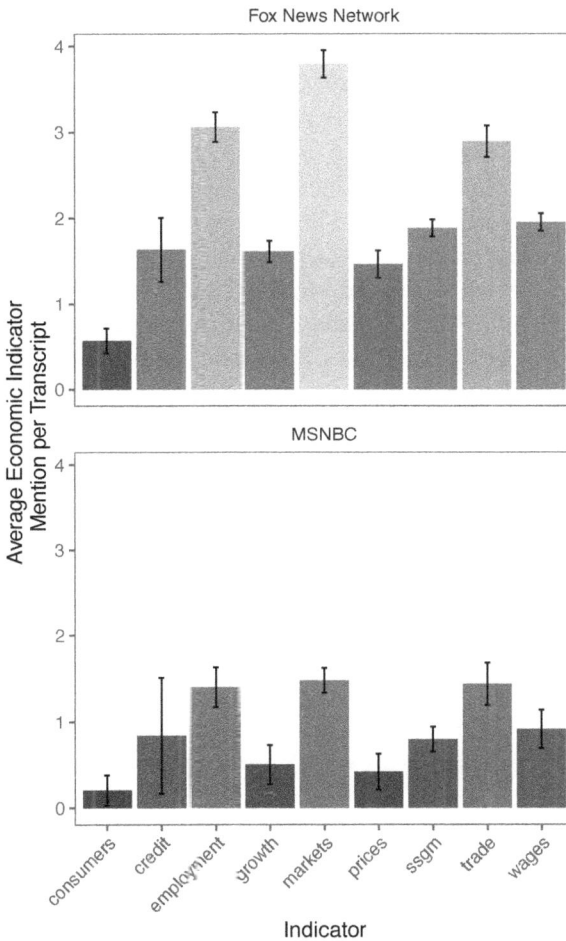

Figure 2.7. Mentions of economic news topics by cable tv channels, 2015–2020. *Source*: Author's own material.

While stock market information prevails over other data as the primary source of economic discussion on Fox, MSNBC's coverage is somewhat more balanced across economic topics. In the latter case, the rate of stock market mentions is indistinguishable from that of unemployment and trade. In fact, the same two indicators are discussed frequently on Fox, suggestive of the political nature of the networks' coverage. Trade and unemployment, as we will see in chapter 3, are favorite topics of partisan elites.

Because of this seemingly partisan-tinged agenda, we might also wonder if cable news networks like the Fox News Channel and MSNBC are especially sensitive to the *congeniality* of economic data. Because good news about the economy makes incumbent presidents look good, partisan guests and ideologically motivated producers might try to selectively discuss economic information that conforms to pre-existing partisan narratives. Thus, H4 implies that the agenda-setting behavior of partisan journalists will not always follow the expectations set out in H1–H3.

Figure 2.8, below, replicates the above figures showing the rate of indicator mentions per transcript. However, this time, the data have been separated into two time periods: cable transcripts recorded during the Obama administration, from January 3, 2015 through January 2, 2017, and those recorded during the Trump administration, from January 3, 2017, to the most recent data collected, on July 1, 2020. This clear break in the partisanship of the president represents a convenient way to test whether a very similar economy is discussed differently by these networks across different administrations.

Figure 2.8 shows a pattern that conforms to both H4 and the preceding expectations of H1. The biggest takeaway can be seen in the right side of the figure, in which Fox News's coverage of both unemployment and the stock market grows during the Trump administration. Fox transcripts discussed the stock market more than they did unemployment during the period of the Obama administration captured in the analysis, but this difference grows larger when the network engages in strongly congenial discourse since 2017. At that time, the stock market becomes increasingly congenial, and as a result, coverage imbalances become more pronounced.

The MSNBC transcripts, described in figure 2.9 below, are less definitive in this respect, partially also because of congeniality. During the Obama administration, unemployment improved over time, meaning that it only became an attractive indicator for the purposes of partisan credit claiming as the election grew nearer. Over much of the period, unemployment was not a prime target for partisan credit or blame. Instead, the default agenda-setting behavior on MSNBC, like the other news sources under study, was to discuss the stock market.

However, during the COVID-19 crisis of spring 2020, the Trump administration suddenly became susceptible to critiques related to unem-

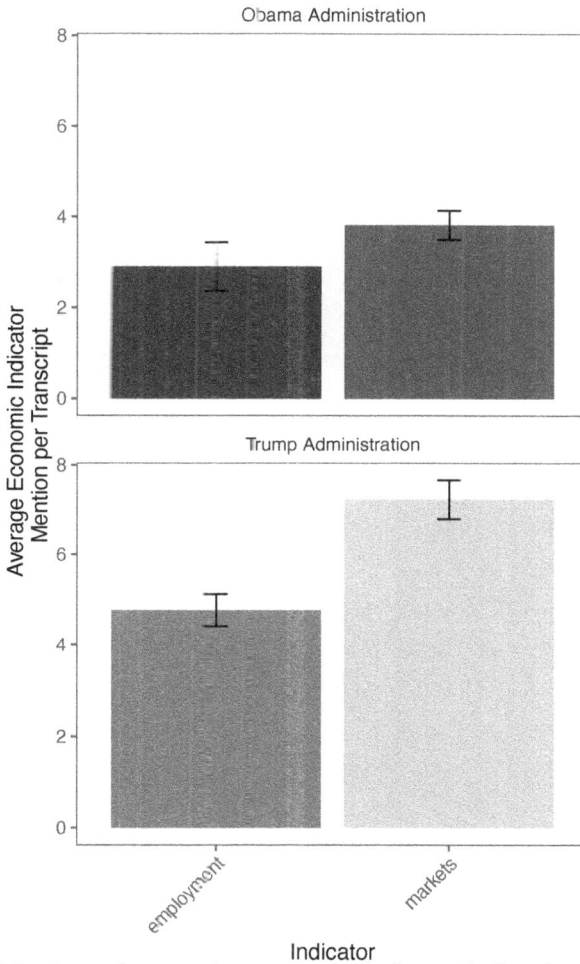

Figure 2.8. Mentions of economic news topics before and after Trump inauguration, FOX News Channel. *Source*: Author's own material.

ployment. Jobless numbers skyrocketed during this period, leading MSNBC hosts to critique Trump's handling of the crisis through the lens of unemployment data. Notable for the present theory, however, is the fact that this high level of coverage is still statistically indistinguishable from the increasing levels of stock market coverage witnessed at the same moment.

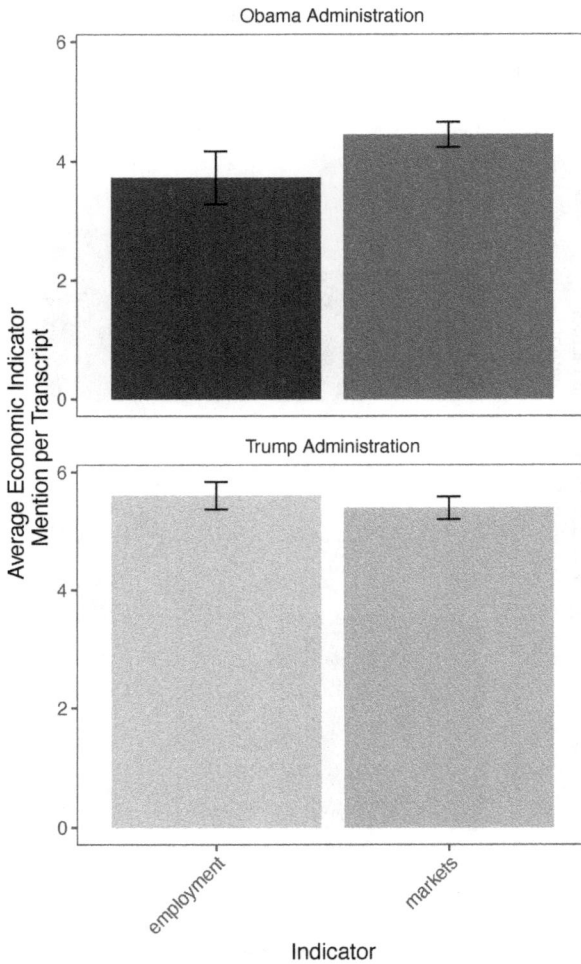

Figure 2.9. Mentions of economic news topics before and after Trump inauguration, MSNBC. *Source*: Author's own material.

## Summary: The Ubiquitous Stock Market Ticker

Taken together, the results of studies 2.1 and 2.2 confirm our expectations regarding the relative saturation of stock market coverage in media. It appears that the most frequently compiled indicators, regardless of the economic conditions at any given moment, are those that track market indices and stock prices on an up-to-the-minute basis. The second most frequently mentioned topic in economic news is unemployment. In the sections that follow, I summarize the meaning of these findings and look ahead to subsequent analyses.

The post–Great Recession period bore witness to an incredible stock market resurgence, peaking in 2020 as the Dow Jones Industrial average surged above twenty-five thousand points. Unemployment also fell slowly but steadily, eventually dipping below 5.0 percent and remaining near 4.0 percent for much of the period until the COVID-19 crisis. But other signs of economic progress, such as wage growth, depicted an economy with mostly meager returns for salaried workers. The economic indicators that claim center stage in journalists' reports can tell very different stories at the same time. However, their rates of mention do not always correspond with their performance levels. Instead, a major influence on their incorporation in news is the availability of new, relevant data from official sources.

At this point in the account, some readers might begin to feel that I am being unduly critical of economic journalists. I do not mean to suggest that economic journalists are doing a bad job—far from it, in fact. The difficulty of sifting through a massive volume of economic data to encapsulate the workings of the entire US economy is a staggering task. Because of the constraining nature of monthly and quarterly economic news reports, however, economic journalists are often forced to occupy space in the news cycle with stories about continuously aggregated indicators, causing unintentional (and as I asserted in chapter 1, largely subconscious) downstream effects on citizens' perceptions of the economy and political actors.

Early research on economic perceptions and economic voting asserted that citizens gather economic information much like insects might land on flypaper: mostly disinterested consumers float through their busy lives with little attention to the economy, occasionally picking up bits and pieces of information they might happen to hear (e.g., MacKuen, Erikson, and Stimson 1992). This method of passive acquisition squares with earlier assumptions about the low levels of attentiveness of the American public (e.g., Converse 1964). We rarely pay close attention to news stories on a quotidian basis, in part because it is rational not to. Only the most sophisticated and savvy Americans, high in the psychological attribute of "need for cognition," are likely to scour the headlines to obtain a full understanding of the economic data (Cacioppo and Petty 1982).

Taken together, the results presented thus far suggest that Americans' casual acquisition of economic information will lead them to internalize a narrow set of economic "facts." Importantly, even if American news consumers are aware of the notion that "the stock market is not the economy," they will still have the general impression that things are going better or worse in America based mostly upon what they hear about the stock market and unemployment. Priming means that their overall perceptions of the economy will be tinted by the valence of this coverage—whereas other knowledge, like that of wage growth, will have a more subdued effect.

The political implications of the stock market emphasis in American journalism, as we will see in later chapters, are far-reaching. This imbalance affects the factual perceptions of partisans, helping us to explain why partisans are heavily biased in their beliefs about *some*, but not all, of the economic facts. It affects the kinds of economic information that partisan elites are willing to discuss. And it has major consequences for the ways in which Americans make sense of the growing divide between the rich and the middle class in America.

In the next chapter I describe the *partisan* information environment more robustly, by examining the kinds of economic narratives used by partisans' trusted allies in Congress. As we will soon see, the finding that stock market information is widely available in news has an impact on elites' framing strategies. Perhaps unbeknownst to economic journalists, news values shift the willingness of political elites to take up economic matters in their discourse.

This leaves us with the question of intent, which is a difficult one to answer given the information we have at our disposal. Do journalists know that their economic agenda setting matters for politics? Herbert Gans (1979) reminds us that while journalists often see themselves as politically neutral, political proclivities can taint coverage styles. It may be that the editors of the *New York Times* or the bureau chiefs of the *Associated Press* have more of a vested interest in the stock market than the average American. It may also be that economic journalists are trained as economists or work at investment firms before reporting the facts to audiences.[11] And it is very reasonable to assume that the economists, businesspeople, and other experts that are often interviewed by journalists for economic news stories readily cast their focus on the stock market as well. Whatever the reason, we have seen evidence in this chapter that when accounting for a wide variety of the available economic data, American news coverage of the economy gives a disproportionate share of attention to stock markets.

Chapter 3

# Grappling with Bulls and Bears

## How Congress Discusses the Economy

As seen in the previous chapter, stock market information prevails in media discourse about the economy. Journalists work to set an economic agenda by writing stories about recent trends in familiar indicators. While this agenda-setting behavior holds across a variety of professional news sources, the information environment also includes many explicitly partisan agenda setters. In the present chapter, I consider the economic agendas of some of the most central partisan elites of all: incumbent US senators and members of the US House of Representatives.

How and when do these partisan incumbents signal economic performance to their constituencies? In the sections that follow, I develop a series of expectations related to these actors' willingness to talk about the stock market. Principally, I argue that partisan elites will seek to provide *congenial* (partisan-affirming) economic messages to their constituencies. However, because elites navigate the broader information environment when making these attempts to influence citizens, they often cite a different set of indicators than those relied upon most heavily by contemporary journalists. Partisan elites are strategic about what indicators will be easiest to use for the purposes of credit and blame. This means that members of Congress generally avoid using stock market performance as a vehicle for framing efforts. Because the stock market is rarely framed by political elites, reliable patterns of credit taking and blame giving are rarely evident in the aggregate.

This elite agenda is still responsive, however, to political context. In this chapter, I also trace the influence of President Donald Trump in shifting Republican narratives about the stock market from 2016 through 2020. While Democratic senators often discuss the stock market in service of policy discussions, stock market *performance* is rarely discussed on that side of the aisle. Among Republicans, however, the performance of the stock market increased in salience during the Trump administration. This shift in the strategic communications of elites foreshadows an increase in motivated reasoning behavior among rank-and-file Republican Party adherents, a phenomenon that I investigate in chapters 4 and 5.

Recent work in political science has paid a great deal of attention to biases in citizens' economic perceptions, but scholars have only infrequently scrutinized how partisan elite communications can drive divergent economic beliefs (Bisgaard and Slothuus 2018; Hart 2013; Pardos-Prado and Sagarzazu 2016). Studies in this vein have shown in specific cases that partisan elites can succeed in influencing the economic perceptions of citizens. In so doing, elites can cause partisans' opinions of the economic facts to diverge, such that adherents of a party in government might believe different things about the economy than adherents of an opposition party.

While these important contributions have shown strong evidence that elites *can* influence economic perceptions, we still know little about *how often* and under *what contexts* elite influence shapes economic perceptions. The existing evidence is primarily based upon scenarios where opinion change occurs due to focal events, such as a sudden and unexpected shift in a party's economic policy priorities (e.g., Bisgaard and Slothuus 2018). What are the limits of elite influence in the realm of economic perceptions?

I take up this investigation in the sections that follow, first by examining the "economic agenda" of US senators and representatives. This investigation does not provide us with information about citizens' *reactions* to elite economic messages—we will examine the effects of elite messages on public opinion in the next chapters. But for now, to develop expectations about the nature of these public reactions, we need to know what elites talk about when they try to influence citizens' economic perceptions through framing.

Earlier studies of partisan elite influence identify several reasons why elites might target a topic for persuasive communication. These accounts rely especially on a credit-blame framework that assumes electoral self-preservation as the primary motivation of office holders (e.g.,

Grimmer 2013; Grimmer, Westwood, and Messing 2014; Mayhew 1974). Elites are constantly seeking ways to curry their constituencies' favor by showing their involvement in good economic developments (and their opponents' responsibility for bad ones).

Building on this framework, I introduce a set of considerations that helps to explain variation in elite economic signaling. As discussed in chapter 1, I argue that the prevalence of economic information in media helps to explain whether elites deploy specific framing strategies. Most important, these assumptions help to explain why partisans traditionally leave stock market information by the wayside in their communications, resulting in less polarized and more accurate opinions of the stock market among partisans. Nevertheless, this story is changing in real time. Patterns of elite communication have evolved over the past decade, yielding the possibility for new and more subtle forms of partisan bias to emerge.

## Economic Discourse on
## Official Congressional Twitter Accounts

I examine congressional persuasion attempts in a relatively costless, but highly visible, environment: the social media platform of Twitter. Recent work has shown that members of Congress and their staffers work to stay "on message" in their Twitter communications, focusing on the same topics as those featured in traditional TV advertising (Kang et al. 2018). This is at least in part because Twitter is consumed by a wide audience in the United States.

Tweets have been studied in many recent examinations of elite communication. Official Twitter accounts are rapidly becoming standard tools for politicians, journalists, intellectuals, and commentators. Evans, Brown, and Wimberly (2018), for example, show that the 2016 election featured a surprisingly high density of political communication on Twitter among presidential candidates, sitting members of Congress, and congressional challengers alike. Twitter has had pervasive effects since that time, with more recent scholarship investigating the role of viral tweets in election results, misinformation, and shifting public attitudes (e.g., Chen et al. 2021).

Candidates signal issue positions, claim credit and direct blame, and advertise campaign events and constituency outreach opportunities in tweets and press releases. While members of Congress have many alternative forms of communication available to them, from the direct mail associated with franking privileges to press releases, Twitter is quickly coming to rival these options when it comes to incumbents' communication priorities (Conway, Kenski, and Wang 2013; Gross and Johnson 2016; Jungherr 2016). Such attention to Twitter as a platform for political discussion was further heightened by the election of Donald Trump, who claimed the moniker of "tweeter-in-chief" early in his presidency. Now that Trump is out of office, we still see the importance of social media communications for presidents, as the Biden administration also maintains an active presence on the platform.

By examining a comprehensive dataset of Congress's tweets from the 112th, 113th, and 114th Congresses, I measure the recent "economic agenda" of its members on Twitter from 2015 through 2020. Web scraping of the Twitter platform, performed in stages from 2018 to 2021, allows for a comprehensive dataset that dates to the start of the 114th Congress.[1] To analyze the economic content of these congressional tweets, I use the same dictionary-based coding scheme featured in chapter 2, in which I derive a lexicon of economic topic mentions from a large corpus of economic news articles.

In the sections that follow, I rely on this analysis to describe the overall congressional economic agenda. The large volume of unique congressional tweets that were captured (over 1.2 million since 2015) also allows for an examination of how Congress's economic agenda reacts to the economic news agenda and the signaling behavior of the incumbent president. Together, the results demonstrate that Congress's discussion of the stock market is rare. Due to its rarity, congressional stock market mentions are relatively insensitive to media and economic conditions, unlike other prominent economic data series like the unemployment rate.

Congressmembers consider whether to mention unemployment based on a variety of familiar strategic inputs, such as the current unemployment rate and the incumbent president's party. But while the stock market was occasionally brought up by Democrats in support of legislative actions, stock market *performance* was rarely mentioned by members of Congress until Donald Trump began cueing audiences (and congressional Republicans) in 2016. Since that time, we observe a steady increase in mentions of stock market prices among Republican senators and representatives. This shifting agenda runs contrary to other, more time-honored strategic considerations, and speaks to the power that prominent figures like the president hold over other elites' framing strategies.

## What Congress Talks About

Scholars have devoted much attention to the questions of how and when legislators frame current conditions.[2] In general, this literature has focused on several regularities that occur when elites communicate to audiences about developments in news. These patterns are most often associated with the logic of credit and blame (e.g., Grimmer, Westwood, and Messing 2014).

Partisan elites will almost always find ways to claim credit for positive developments in news, even when the causal link between the actions of these elites and economic performance is tenuous at best. In addition, congressional elites seek to deflect negative news by blaming others—usually members of the other party—to distance themselves from partisan-disconfirming developments. This basic pattern of credit and blame helps to explain why partisan elites target specific economic news stories for their framing efforts.

Existing work on congressional persuasion efforts has often studied legislators' press releases.[3] The work of Grimmer, Westwood, and Messing (2014) is especially relevant to the present analysis. This study reveals how members seek to engage in credit claiming for spending in the state or district. The authors demonstrate that legislators often seek to craft persuasive messages about appropriations, despite the opacity of the appropriations process. Legislators claim credit for appropriations even though it opens them to attacks from so-called "spending hawks."

These findings show that legislators' agendas are especially shaped by strategies of blame avoidance. Legislators seek to blame the out party for certain negative developments, highlighting news topics if they are certain that their partisan-congenial interpretations will be convincing. If successful, legislators can frame otherwise disconfirming developments as evidence of the superiority of the in party's management skills (Slothuus and De Vreese 2010; Druckman and Nelson 2003; Jerit 2008; Wagner 2007).

In the realm of the economy, these kinds of frames can take the form of *attributions of responsibility* for economic conditions (e.g., Iyengar 1990; Hobolt and Tilley 2014; Rudolph 2003; Rudolph 2016; Tilley and Hobolt 2011). They can also manifest as interpretations of major economic shifts and trends. Bisgaard (2015), for example, shows how the collapse of the British national economy from 2004 to 2010 resulted in polarized perceptions about the causes of the collapse. If legislators can convince their audiences to employ a partisan-congenial *causal interpretation* of economic indicators' performance through persistent framing of specific topics, they will have augmented their credit- and blame-shifting behavior with an additional layer of persuasion (e.g., Iyengar 1990).

Legislators are also sensitive to *issue ownership*—the perception among members of the public that one party will be more likely than the other to "handle" the issue with skill and care if elected (e.g., Petrocik 1996). Over time, Republicans and Democrats have variously "owned" the issue of economic performance. Majorities of surveyed Americans have signaled that one party is superior to the other at stimulating (and maintaining) good economic fortunes.

As a result, partisan communicators will feel constrained by a lack of ownership in certain circumstances. For instance, if an incumbent party "owns" the economy and is presiding over good times, the out party will downplay the issue in its campaigns. However, even if an incumbent has "owned" a record of good economic performance, a crisis can effectively strip them of this label and open the door for challenger attacks on the issue. Furthermore, Blount (2002) demonstrates that certain economic indicators—especially unemployment—can take on special political meanings and ownership characteristics as they relate to party platforms and prior performance on the issue.

In their important article on this subject, Pardos-Prado and Sagarzazu (2016) show that elites will affect citizens' economic perceptions only when recent economic performance is *ambiguous*. In this "middle zone" of economic conditions, signals coming from the economic news of the day are mixed, contradictory, and easy to frame. If overwhelmingly positive or negative conditions make headlines, the economic "facts" become difficult to spin. Mixed economic conditions are especially useful for out-party politicians, who often attack the incumbent party for wretched economic management using selective mentions of the economic facts.

Together, these studies imply that elites will only succeed in framing economic topics when the economy performs in ways that make framing easy. I next describe how the news agenda can serve as a further constraint on framing. When a notable economic event occurs, like a sharp jump in interest rates or a drop in the price of crude oil, partisan elites must decide whether this news provides a good opportunity for persuasion. This decision depends upon the continuing saturation of news about the topic in the news media and the ease with which that indicator's performance can be politicized.

## CRAFTING SUCCESSFUL FRAMING EFFORTS

When trying to create effective frames, strategic communicators are responsive to constantly changing conditions in media. Journalists' agenda-setting behavior, as we saw in chapter 2, affects the salience of different economic indicators. But these indicators also differ in terms of their clarity of responsibility. Clarity of responsibility is the degree to which the economic performance captured by an indicator can be easily and logically linked to the recent actions of a specific politician or party (e.g., Powell and Whitten 1993; Hellwig and Samuels 2008). Together, these factors can influence the effectiveness of a persuasive communication attempt.

Previous research shows that some economic performance signals are more *distal*, or conceptually removed from the actions of politicians, than others (Gomez and Wilson 2001; 2006). It is not immediately obvious to credit an incumbent governor when receiving a bonus check from a boss or to blame the president for an increase in the price of roast beef at the local diner. But reports of slow national GDP growth or high national unemployment can be more easily attributed to politicians' oversight of economic policy. While some recent scholarship has challenged the theory of "heterogeneous attribution" when it comes to voting behavior (Godbout and Bélanger 2007; Alt, Marshall, and Lassen 2016), the basic premise of distal attribution can be applied to the study of elite frames. Some economic narratives are simply a harder "sell" to partisan audiences than others.

This is because some features of economic performance are more closely linked to political actions than others. Stock prices are especially hard to attribute to politicians' actions because market futures are determined by an impossibly complex set of economic inputs. While political events and policies certainly do have an influence on short-term market values (e.g., Knight 2006; Snowberg, Wolfers, and Zitzewitz 2007), there is little evidence to suggest that incumbent presidents can boost stock prices using the tools at their disposal.[4]

In contrast, some indicators, like wage growth and unemployment, are more directly associated with political decisions. Policies like minimum wage laws or job-training programs can have direct effects on these indicators. However, the global economy, as well as the decisions of the nonpartisan (but increasingly pressured) Federal Reserve System, take many other economic decisions out of the hands of political actors (Ezrow and Hellwig 2014; Hellwig 2001; Stein 1990). It may be innately easier to justify pointing the finger at partisan actors for job losses, stagnant GDP growth, and other lagging economic indicators, than blaming partisan incumbents for the movement of the stock market.[5]

The present study tests these expectations by comparing Congress's Twitter mentions of unemployment and stock market performance. These two highly visible indicators differ in ways that allow for a strong test of the present theory. While stock market information is aggregated daily, unemployment figures are released monthly (Baumohl 2012). Unlike some indicators such as consumer confidence, though, unemployment is still discussed commonly in news reports. Unemployment is also more easily attributed to political actions than stock market performance. We can formalize this expectation in H1:

> H1. Members of Congress will mention the stock market less often than unemployment when making statements about the economy on Twitter.

Next, I consider how credit-blame communication strategies affect the timing of senators' mentions of economic indicators. I expect Congress to be sensitive to real economic conditions when making statements about unemployment and the stock market. However, this sensitivity is also contingent upon the party of the incumbent president. When an economic indicator is trending in a negative direction, members of the opposition party will seek to blame the president, boosting that party's mentions of the indicator. Members of the president's party, in contrast, will likely choose to either ignore the indicator or will press back against the opposition's claims by highlighting a different economic indicator that shows more favorable performance.

Regardless, mentions of a given economic indicator should increase under the following condition:

> H2. Members of Congress in the opposition party will be more likely to mention an economic indicator when that indicator's performance worsens.

We must also consider the role of the broader information environment in reshaping the agendas of senators and representatives on Twitter. As discussed above, the overall volume of economic news will have an influence on this behavior, as developments that capture many headlines (such as steep declines in stock prices) are expected to be "too tough to frame" for strategic elites. Instead, when economic news mentions of an indicator are at more moderate levels, we should expect to see a proliferation of framing attempts by members of Congress. This expectation can be captured by H3 below:

> H3. Members of Congress will mention an economic indicator less often when economic news mentions of that indicator increase.

It is also possible that legislators' economic mentions are strategically adaptive to the political environment. Specifically, in a follow-up analysis, I test whether there was an association between Donald Trump's mentions of stock market performance and the signaling behavior of senate Republicans during the Trump administration. Theories of elite cue taking and cue giving suggest that the president can reshape elites' communications through unilateral framing. This follow-the-leader behavior, though not influenced by the same strategic considerations seen in H1–H3, is likely due to the visibility of Trump on Twitter (prior to his eventual ban in 2021).

> H4. Congressional Republicans will increase their mentions of the stock market in response to the volume of Donald Trump's tweets about the stock market.

## Study 3.1: Analysis of Congressional Tweets

To assess these expectations, it was necessary to devise a text analytical strategy for studying the economic content of congressional tweets. From 2018 through 2021, I collected a total of 1,316,771 unique tweets from incumbent senators (444,798 tweets) and members of the House of Representatives (871,973 tweets) using specialized tools.[6] This data collection sought to include any message sent by members' official Twitter accounts from January 3, 2015, to the start of Q3 2020 (July 1).[7] The corpus was filtered to ensure that data collection only captured tweets posted during Congressmembers' terms in office. For example, while former Senator Jeff Flake continued to tweet from his account in later years, the dataset only records tweets posted prior to his retirement from the Senate in 2018.

As tweets were limited to 140 characters or less during most of the period of study, many tweets in the dataset are quite brief. Nevertheless, a cursory reading of the corpus shows many instances when senators mention economic developments or current conditions on Twitter (around 180,000 mentions total, 53,000 of which were posted by senators and 127,000 of which were posted by representatives). To systematically analyze this economic tweet agenda, I turned to the same strategy featured in chapter 2: the application of a specialized lexicon of economy-related terms in news media.

As we saw before, these terms were grouped into nine economic issue areas, each corresponding to a large variety of specific indicators reported by government agencies, private research groups, and stock markets. Of these nine economic topic areas, I engage in a structured comparison of mentions of stock markets and unemployment in the sections that follow.

It is certainly possible that members of Congress use different terminology than professional journalists when referring to economic developments. However, the diversity of terminology captured by the lexicon, which includes statements within articles made by professional economists, affected citizens, and politicians themselves, helps to assuage these concerns. Applying the identical terminology may mean that we miss out on some elites' discussion of the economy. But there is no reason to believe a priori that such differences in terminology (if any exist) might pertain specifically to one aspect of the economy more so than others. As a result, searching the tweets using the economic lexicon can provide us with an important, if necessarily limited, understanding of the economic agenda of members of Congress.

## PROCESSING AND ANALYZING TWEETS

Once tweets were collected, I next processed the corpus using canonical methods.[8] Armed with the dictionary of economic indicator-specific terminology derived from news reports developed in chapter 2, I next used a simple text comparison method to count the presence of relevant N-grams (phrases) in congressional tweets. Tweets were associated with metadata such as the name of the legislator, the date, the legislator's partisanship,[9] and national economic conditions at the time of the tweet (including the monthly change in national unemployment and the monthly change in the Wilshire 5000 Index of stock prices). Some N-grams were also recorded for the purposes of filtering recurring false positives (for example, mentions of "bump stocks," a firearm accessory, were excluded through this filtering method).[10]

The resulting dataset shows roughly 13.6 percent of congressional tweets mention at least one of the nine economic indicators included in the dictionary from 2015 through 2020. Perhaps unsurprisingly due to the Senate's role in foreign policy, the most-mentioned set of indicators among senators was trade (mentioned in roughly 3.3 percent of tweets), whereas among members of the House, the most mentioned topic was unemployment (3.4 percent of tweets). Already, we have some indication that economic matters make up a fair portion of the congressional Twitter agenda. This is again consistent with theories of responsibility attribution, credit, and blame for valence issues.

RESULTS: DESCRIBING CONGRESS'S TWITTER ACTIVITY

The first step in the process of examining Congress's economic twitter discourse is to compare the proportion of tweets that discuss unemployment and the stock market among Republicans and Democrats (H1). To establish these preliminaries, figure 3.1 shows the overall rates of mention of these indicators across the period under study. To assess H1, I visualize yearly rates of mention of economic indicators by legislator party. In this and all successive figures in the chapter, the vertical bars represent 95 percent confidence intervals around the point estimates.

Figure 3.1 shows clear initial evidence that members of Congress frequently use unemployment as a vehicle for framing, while the stock market is rarely mentioned. In comparing this figure to figure 2.1 in the preceding chapter, we become aware that Congress talks about the economy on Twitter in ways which substantially depart from the habits of news media. Not only is unemployment a much more frequently discussed indicator in the dataset, but both parties seem to have been keen on mentioning it from 2015 through 2020. Senate Democrats, for example, mentioned jobs and unemployment roughly once in every seventy tweets since 2015, whereas Senate Republicans mentioned jobs and unemployment at a rate of roughly once in every sixty-five tweets.

This attention to unemployment in the Twitter data stands in contrast to the rate of mention of financial markets. Consistent with the theory advanced in sections above, we see evidence that Senate Republicans and Democrats mentioned financial markets only 0.2 percent and 0.28 percent of the time, respectively. Compared to news media sources, the lack of discussion of markets is especially striking. Republican senators, for instance, only mentioned financial markets in one out of every 500 tweets since 2015. A similar ratio is observed for Republican members

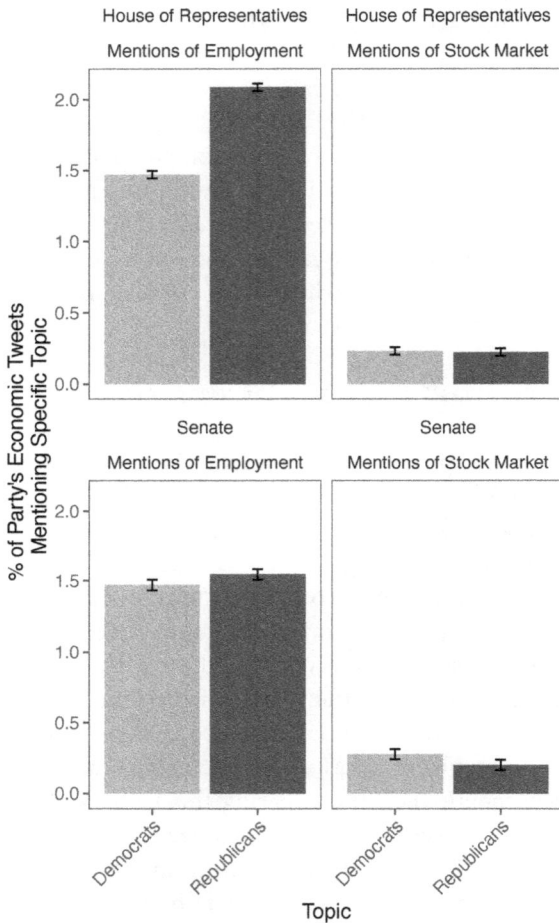

Figure 3.1. Percent of party's tweets mentioning selected economic topics, 2015–2020. *Source*: Author's own material.

of the House, who mention markets about once every 450 tweets. The intensity of news coverage of these indicators seems at first glance to be inversely related to the attention given to them by members of Congress. Though not shown in the above Figure, the same holds true for other indicators such as wage growth and manufacturing.

Looking across time and across party lines, however, reveals that these topics are mentioned for different strategic reasons. I next present figure 3.2, which shows Republican and Democratic legislators' rates of mention of jobs and employment since 2015.

As we can see from this second figure, Republicans and Democrats mentioned jobs at different rates, and in response to different political and economic contexts, across the period under study. The graphic aggregates unemployment mentions on a yearly basis, showing Republicans' rates of mention in dark grey and Democrats' rates of mention in a lighter hue. In most cases, Republicans and Democrats' mentions differed significantly, based on two-tailed t-tests of the sample proportion.

In 2015, during the Obama administration, Democrats outpaced Republicans in their mentions of unemployment in both the House and

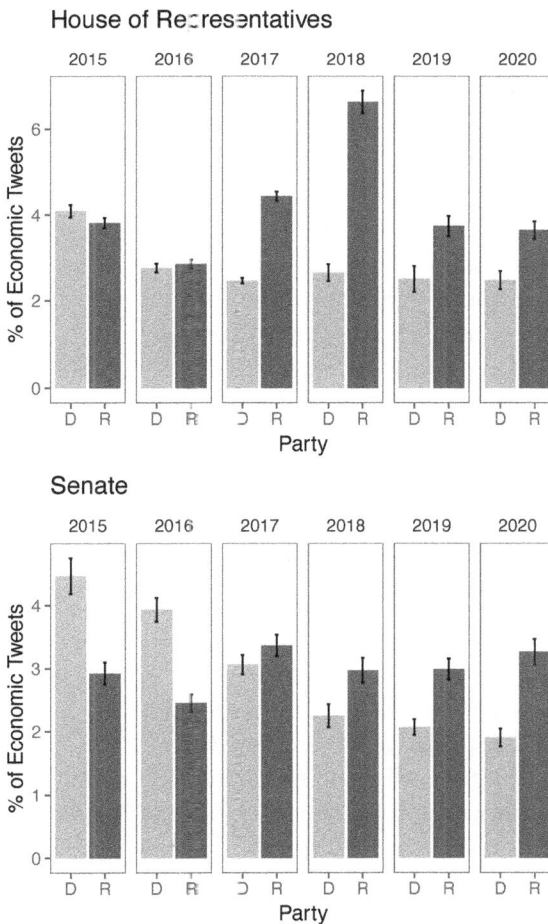

Figure 3.2. Percent of party's tweets mentioning jobs and unemployment, Senate and House of Representatives, 2015–2020. *Source*: Author's own material.

the Senate, perhaps to take credit for the falling unemployment rate at the time. However, by the time Donald Trump was inaugurated in 2017, Republicans increased their mentions of the strengthening labor market, outpacing Democrats from 2018 through 2020 to a statistically significant degree (p < 0.05, based on t-test comparisons for both the House and the Senate). In these later years, Democrats likely found it more difficult to frame unemployment as bad news for Republicans. Conditions in the labor market were too good to contradict using conventional framing techniques (at least until the tail end of the dataset, April of 2020, at which point the unemployment rate exploded to a staggering 14.8 percent).[11]

A qualitative reading of these mentions shows that one of the most important moments for job mentions came in late January of 2018. This was when Congress initiated debate over the Tax Cuts and Jobs Act, a Trump-sponsored bill that substantially overhauled the tax code. It was at this moment that Republicans begin to massively increase their discussion of jobs—even though the present analytical method filters out mentions of the name of the bill itself. While the bill was expected to have major effects across many aspects of the economy, Republican framing of the bill centered on hiring and unemployment during the debate. That we did not see a similar uptick in jobs mentions on Twitter in the spring of 2020 speaks to the power of partisanship in driving these strategic considerations. The Tax Cuts and Jobs Act stands as a prominent example of the fact that when members of Congress are hoping to persuade Americans to support a new policy with economic consequences, a tried-and-true strategy is to rely upon discussions of jobs and employment.

*Stock Market Mentions, 2015–2020*

While jobs are a priority in Senators' and Representatives' communications, historically, the stock market is rarely discussed. Below, figure 3.3 shows the rate of partisan mentions across time for market indicators among senators (top panel) and representatives (bottom panel).

Figure 3.3 provides an initial assessment of H2–H4. It helps us answer the question of whether legislators use conventional communication strategies when making references to stock market performance.

It appears from figure 3.3 that the biggest trend in stock market mentions is an over-time increase in Republicans' mentions of the indicator. A qualitative reading of the tweets shows that Republicans also mention the stock market for different reasons than Democrats. While Democrats spent much of the period of analysis discussing the stock market as it

## House of Representatives

## Senate

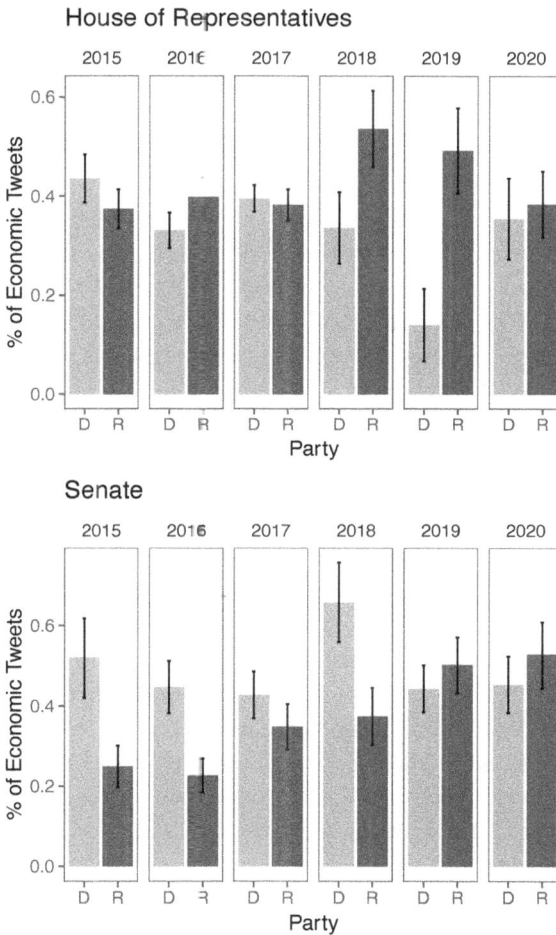

Figure 3.3. Percent of party's economic tweets mentioning stock market indicators, 2015–2020. *Source*: Author's own material.

related to various legislative initiatives, Republicans' stock market discourse became more performance focused over time. Representatives like Paul Gosar, Kevin Yoder, Louie Gohmert, Clay Higgins, John Rutherford, and Jim Renacci began mentioning the Dow Jones Industrial Average in their tweets by 2018, but never prior. Only recently have Republican senators begun using stock market mentions as a vehicle for economic credit taking and blame giving, perhaps in response to Donald Trump's overt and highly visible habit of doing the same since 2016. Jim Renacci (R-OH), for example, tweeted in August of 2018, "Thanks to confidence in our economy [*sic*] & progress with Mexico, the Nasdaq crested above the 8,000 mark for the first time . . . We must continue to push for pro-growth policies like we did with #TaxReform which ushered our economy into a new prosperous era."[12] Renacci had never mentioned the stock market on Twitter prior to Trump's inauguration.

Senate Democrats talked about the stock market more often than usual in 2018 (roughly once in every 150 tweets), in part due to the Senate Economic Growth, Regulatory Relief, and Consumer Protection Act, which reformed earlier Dodd-Frank Wall Street regulations. Note that the same increase in mentions was not visible among House Democrats, in part because the majority of the debate did not take place in the House. This partial repeal was staunchly opposed by Democrats, who took to Twitter to voice their concern about unregulated stock market activities. Policy discussions made up much of Democratic mentions of stock market indicators.

In comparison, Democrats rarely sought to claim credit or give blame for the actual performance of the stock market. The phenomenon is especially visible in 2019, when House Democrats only discussed the stock market a handful of times across the entire year's corpus of tweets (in part because of a dearth of legislation in that year targeting Wall Street). Framing stock market performance is something that did not become commonplace until after Trump's inauguration. Later in the dataset, stock market mentions are made more frequently in service of credit claiming among Republicans, especially in the Senate from 2019 through 2020 and the House from 2018 through 2019. Senator Mike Braun of Indiana, for example, retweeted a *Wall Street Journal* article on July 1, 2020, celebrating "U.S. Stocks' . . . Best Quarter in More Than 20 Years." This type of mention is intended to tout the Trump administration's role in boosting stock market performance. Congenial stock market mentions were rare in preceding years' data, and virtually nonexistent before 2017.

*Modeling Economic Indicator Mentions*

To assess H2–H4, I next model economic indicator mentions in a regression context. Using negative binomial regression models that take monthly counts of Twitter mentions as their dependent variable, I simultaneously assess the expectations outlined in the hypotheses above.[13] The results of these investigations are presented together in table 3.1 below. The models demonstrate a variety of significant effects for the relevant variables in the study, including the overall volume of MCs' tweets, the partisanship of an MC, the presidential administration, media mentions of economic indicators, and movement in the real economy. However, these baseline effects are very difficult to interpret because they are only meaningful when multiple interactions are included in the models as well. For instance, the baseline effect of being a Republican MC is not meaningful unless we take account of the incumbent president's party and real economic conditions. The multiple strategic implications of the political and economic context make for a complex modeling exercise.

The models therefore yield quite complex tabular results, as seen in table 3.1. The results can be more easily understood through visualizations of the models' predictions. In the discussion below, I show predicted counts of individual congressmembers' mentions, based on model predictions that manipulate key independent variables while holding other variables at their mean values. First, I examine H2, the partisan congeniality hypothesis, using this analytical strategy. I do this by modeling the interactive effects of presidential incumbent party and member's party on monthly counts of unemployment and stock market mentions. Figure 3.4 first shows this pattern of predicted mentions for MCs' mentions of unemployment.

Figure 3.4 shows a pattern that aligns closely with the expectations of existing theories of elite strategic framing. With unemployment held at its mean value (around 4 percent), mentions of unemployment should generally accord with a credit-taking, rather than a blame-giving, framing objective. The facets of the figure show Democratic (left) and Republican (right) congressmembers' willingness to mention unemployment during the Obama administration (left bar in each facet) and the Trump administration (right bar in each facet).

These comparisons show meaningful differences across the administrations for both Republicans and Democrats. Consistent with expectations, under conditions of objectively low unemployment rates, Democrats' mentions of unemployment are higher under the Obama administration than the Trump administration. During Obama's tenure, Democrats in Congress sought to engage in credit taking for low unemployment (in this case, a predicted value of 4 percent). Under these party-congenial conditions, Democratic members of Congress mentioned unemployment around 1.5 times per month. Had they witnessed an identical labor market with 4 percent unemployment under the Trump administration, the model predicts that such mentions would have declined to around 1.1 mentions per month.

We see evidence of the same pattern of credit claiming for Republicans. The right facet of figure 3.4 shows that discussion of jobs and

Table 3.1. Negative Binomial Regression Models Predicting MC Tweets about the Stock Market and Unemployment, 2015–2020

| | Dependent variable: | | | | | | | |
|---|---|---|---|---|---|---|---|---|
| | Employment | | | | Stock Market | | | |
| | (1) | (2) | (3) | (4) | (5) | (6) | (7) | (8) |
| MC Tweet Volume | 0.013*** (0.0001) | 0.013*** (0.0001) | 0.013*** (0.0001) | 0.005*** (0.0001) | 0.013*** (0.0003) | 0.012*** (0.0003) | 0.012*** (0.0003) | 0.005*** (0.0001) |
| Republican MC | -0.153*** (0.027) | -0.086 (0.056) | -0.404 (0.505) | -0.169** (0.082) | -0.205*** (0.065) | -0.211*** (0.065) | -0.197*** (0.066) | -0.235 (0.199) |
| Trump Admin. | -0.402*** (0.028) | -0.384*** (0.028) | 2.800*** (0.382) | -0.661*** (0.177) | -0.064 (0.064) | -0.043 (0.064) | -0.017 (0.065) | -0.907*** (0.216) |
| Unemployment Rate | | 0.016** (0.008) | 0.638*** (0.075) | | | | | |
| Media Mentions | | | | -0.188 (0.115) | | | | -0.220*** (0.069) |
| Wilshire 5000 Index | | | | | | -0.014 (0.009) | 0.014 (0.017) | |
| Repub. MC * Trump Admin. | 0.610*** (0.036) | 0.602*** (0.036) | 0.918* (0.507) | 0.629*** (0.047) | 0.213** (0.086) | 0.196** (0.086) | 0.172* (0.088) | 0.218** (0.096) |
| Repub. MC * Unemployment Rate | | -0.013 (0.010) | 0.046 (0.099) | | | | | |

|  | (1) | (2) | (3) | (4) | (5) | (6) | (7) | (8) |
|---|---|---|---|---|---|---|---|---|
| Trump Admin. * Unemployment Rate | | | -0.629*** | | | | | |
| | | | (0.075) | | | | | |
| Repub. MC * Unem. * Trump | | | -0.059 | | | | | |
| | | | (0.100) | | | | | |
| Repub. MC * Media Mentions | | | | 0.014 | | | | 0.018 |
| | | | | (0.050) | | | | (0.063) |
| Trump Admin. * Media Mentions | | | | 0.164 | | | | 0.275*** |
| | | | | (0.115) | | | | (0.070) |
| Repub. MC * Wilshire 5000 | | | | | | 0.008 | -0.017 | |
| | | | | | | (0.011) | (0.023) | |
| Trump Admin. * Wilshire 5000 | | | | | | | -0.037* | |
| | | | | | | | (0.020) | |
| Repub. MC * Wilshire 5000 * Trump | | | | | | | 0.034 | |
| | | | | | | | (0.026) | |
| Constant | -0.279*** | -0.349*** | -3.504*** | 1.003*** | -2.389*** | -2.374*** | -2.388*** | -0.746*** |
| | (0.022) | (0.044) | (0.380) | (0.174) | (0.051) | (0.051) | (0.052) | (0.210) |
| Observations | 22,233 | 21,954 | 21,954 | 7,805 | 22,233 | 21,954 | 21,954 | 7,805 |
| Log Likelihood | -37,862.750 | -37,626.990 | -37,534.240 | -19,876.520 | -11,590.990 | -11,520.300 | -11,518.570 | -7,719.416 |
| Akaike Inf. Crit. | 1.034*** | 1.039*** | 1.057*** | 1.502*** | 0.251*** | 0.253*** | 0.253*** | 0.470*** |
| | (0.018) | (0.018) | (0.019) | (0.035) | (0.009) | (0.009) | (0.009) | (0.019) |

Note: *$p < 0.05$; **$p < 0.01$; ***$p < 0.01$

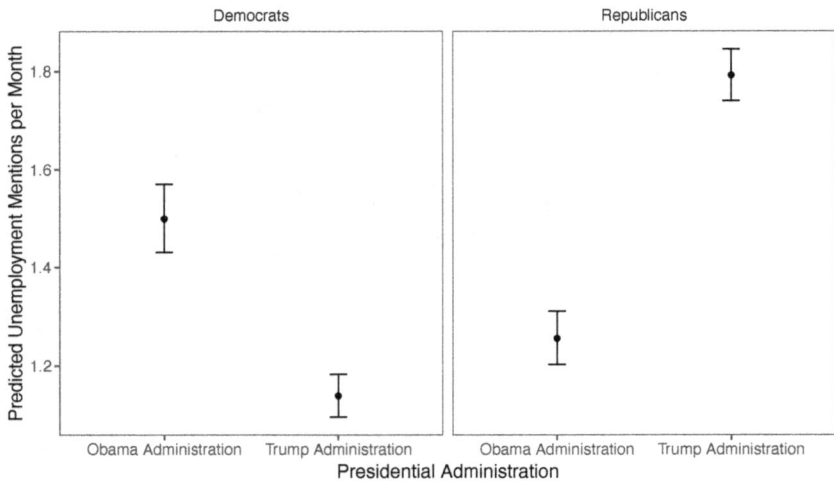

Figure 3.4. Expected monthly mentions of unemployment by party and incumbent, Congress members' tweets, 2015–2020. *Source*: Author's own material.

unemployment is much higher among Republican members of Congress in the Trump era compared to the Obama administration (again assuming a constant unemployment rate of around 4 percent). Republicans' unemployment mentions increase in this context from a predicted rate of about 1.3 mentions per month to an impressive 1.8 mentions per month. Congress's mentions of unemployment on Twitter seem to reflect long-standing assumptions about partisan elite signaling.

Next, we can examine the same pattern of credit claiming when it comes to the stock market. Figure 3.5 depicts partisan mentions of the stock market in the same manner as figure 3.4. Democrats' mentions of stock market indicators are presented on the left half of the figure, while Republicans' mentions are captured on the right half; the leftmost bar in each facet reflects a prediction for the Obama administration, and the rightmost reflects a prediction for the Trump administration. These predictions show us what happens to Congress's tweeting behavior when the stock market grows at a modest rate of about 1 percent over the prior month.

Unlike the case of unemployment, figure 3.5 shows a pattern that does not fully accord with conventional theories of blame avoidance. Instead, we see a pattern in which Republicans increase their stock market mentions during the Trump administration, while Democrats fail to decrease their

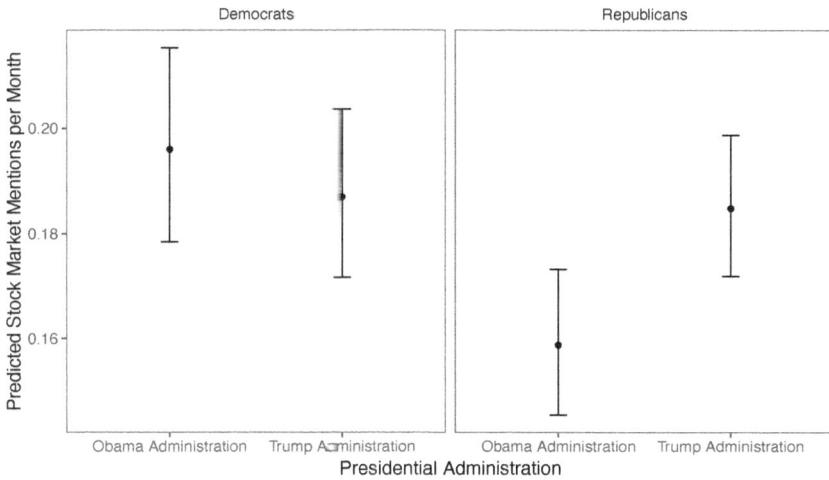

Figure 3.5. Expected monthly mentions of stock market by party and incumbent, Congress members' tweets, 2015–2020. *Source*: Author's own material.

mentions by a statistically significant margin. Republicans increase their mentions of the stock market from 1 in every 625 tweets to about 1 in every 500. Altogether, the pattern is one in which we cannot statistically distinguish between Republican and Democratic mentions of the stock market during the Trump administration.

This pattern does not show consistent evidence of strategic behavior in response to current conditions. Instead, we see an overall increase in attention to the stock market among political elites during the Trump administration. While still not as attentive to these indicators as unemployment, MCs appear not to conform to classic strategies of blame avoidance in the case of the stock market. Instead, the Trump administration witnessed an increase in Congressmembers' willingness to "follow the ticker" as Republicans latched on to the indicator as a source of economic pride, while Democrats chose to engage with this discourse instead of shifting their attention to other topics.

## Do Economic Tweets Respond to Media Saturation?

Next, I take up H3, which examines whether legislators' communications are responsive to over-time shifts in the media environment. We saw above that Congressmembers reflect on incumbency and partisan congeniality when selecting which indicator to discuss in their communications (H1). But as discussed in chapter 1 and above, we might additionally expect MCs to adjust their mentions of economic indicators in response to spikes in media saturation. When journalists focus on an economic indicator in their coverage, what effect might it have on elite strategy?

Figure 3.6 shows the results of additional negative binomial regression models that incorporate media mentions as predictor variables. These are the same variables developed, measured, and analyzed in chapter 2's study 2.1, which identified the rate at which the *New York Times* discussed nine economic indicators from 2015 through 2020. Because this variable is a quarterly series, the resultant negative binomial models must also predict Congressmembers' quarterly (rather than monthly) mentions of economic indicators. To facilitate comparisons, I once again show results pertaining to stock market mentions alongside unemployment mentions.

Figure 3.6 shows the predicted quarterly count of congressional unemployment Twitter mentions for Democrats (left panel) and Republicans (right panel). The figure also breaks these estimates down across two levels of media saturation. In the left bar of each panel, we see the predicted count of mentions when unemployment is one standard deviation more salient in media than average. In the right bar, we see what happens when unemployment is one standard deviation less salient in media than average.

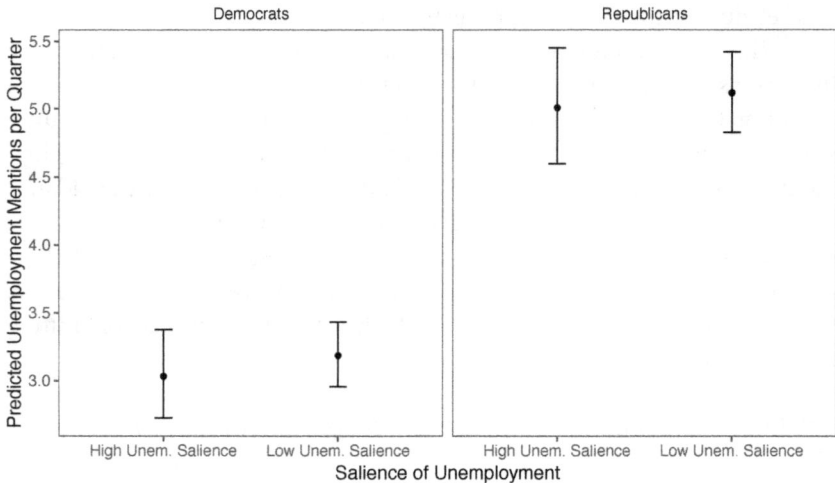

Figure 3.6. Predicted quarterly mentions of unemployment by party, Senators' tweets, 2015–2020. *Source*: Author's own material.

The results show that for both Republicans and Democrats, Twitter mentions of unemployment decrease when media mentions become highly salient, though these differences are statistically indistinguishable from zero. Instead, the much larger source of variation in the model's predictions come from partisanship alone, in response to Republican incentives to claim credit for low unemployment during the Trump administration. Among Democrats, unemployment mentions fall slightly in response to media saturation, from about 3.2 per quarter to about 3.1 per quarter; among Republicans the decline is similar, from around 5.1 per quarter to around 5 per quarter. The direction of this shift accords with the expectation that strategic framing will become difficult when Congressmembers face a saturated media environment. However, the small size of these shifts indicates that senators and representatives choose to emphasize unemployment based on the real economy and the party of the president more so than the relative newsworthiness of the indicator.

Next, I test H3 in the case of stock market mentions. In figure 3.7, below, we see the predicted quarterly rate of mentions of the stock market for Democrats (left panel) and Republicans (right panel) since 2015. In this case, I examine stock market mentions when quarterly media mentions of the stock market are one standard deviation higher than average (the left bar within each panel), and when stock market mentions are one standard deviation lower than average (the right bar within each panel).

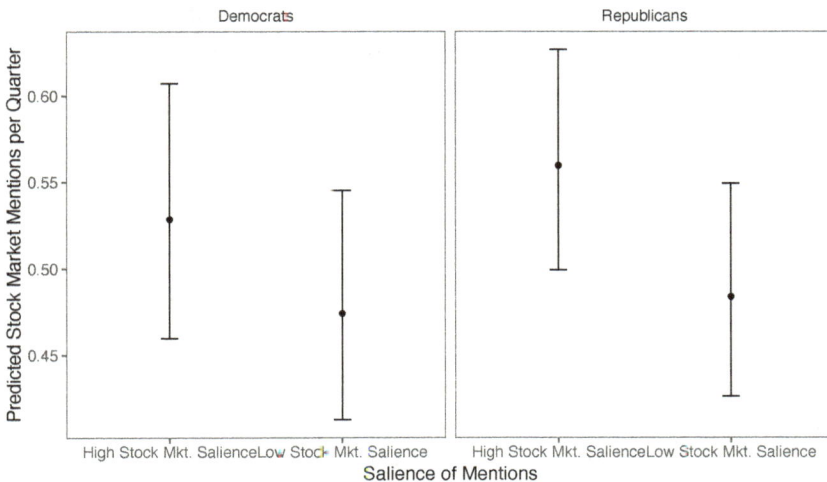

Figure 3.7. Predicted quarterly mentions of stock market by party, Congress members' tweets, 2015–2020. Source: Author's own material.

The results show that Democrats and Republicans do not decrease their mentions of the stock market when media mentions are higher than average. Instead, Twitter mentions *increase* when media mentions of the stock market increase, for both Republicans and Democrats. Attempts to frame stock market developments when they capture more headlines runs contrary to the expectations set out by existing research on strategic framing. We likely observe these findings because even a below-average quarter for stock market mentions still reflects a highly saturated media environment (as seen in chapter 2). Because stock markets are mentioned so often in media, the present analysis again reveals Congress's relative inability to deploy strategic considerations in reaction to stock market news. Instead, an increasing reliance on stock market coverage in news has yielded increasing attentiveness to stock market developments as a source for credit claiming, especially among Republicans.

But there is an alternative strategic consideration, captured by H4, to which we must attend. Perhaps legislators' mentions of the stock market are responsive to another source of strategic cueing: the president of the United States. In figure 3.8, I present the results of a regression model that predicts congressional Republicans' (top panel) and Democrats' (bottom panel) monthly Twitter mentions of stock markets. In this model, I include a variable measuring how many times President Donald Trump has tweeted about the stock market in each month.[14] To generate this variable, I scraped all of Trump's tweets since his inauguration and then applied the algorithm presented in chapter 2 to identify the economic content therein.[15] The variable ranges from a low of 0 to a high of 9 stock market mentions per month by the @realDonaldTrump Twitter account.

Figure 3.8 shows, consistent with expectations, that Senate Republicans "follow the ticker" in part because they follow the leader. All else equal, Trump sending five additional stock market tweets yields a significant ($p < 0.05$) increase in Republicans' mentions of stocks (0.182 mentions per month, 95% CI = [0.172, 0.194]), compared to a month in which he did not tweet at all (0.159 mentions per month, 95% CI = [0.152, 0.167]). Interestingly, no such increase is visible for Democratic legislators, whose mentions of the stock market are virtually the same during the Trump administration regardless of how many times Trump tweets about stocks in each month.

While the magnitude of these shifts is small when compared with the results for an indicator like unemployment, these cueing effects are heretofore undiscovered. The increasing willingness of Republicans to talk

Republican Members of Congress

Democratic Members of Congress

Trump's Monthly Stock Market Tweet Activity

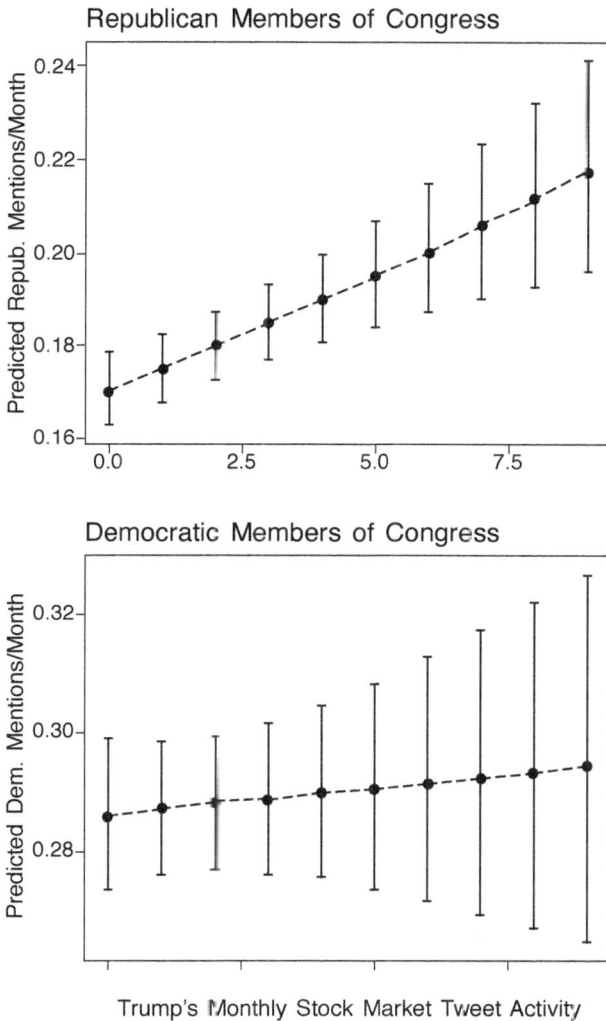

Figure 3.8. Predicted monthly mentions of stock market among Republicans, Congress members' tweets, 2015–2020. *Source*: Author's own material.

about stock market *performance* with their constituencies has unexplored effects on perceptions of the economy and its representative indicators. In the next chapter, I begin to take up this investigation by exploring citizens' economic perceptions over time and across party lines. Critically, we will see that interpretations of the *meaning* of economic developments are rapidly changing in the contemporary information environment. The development presented in figure 3.8 above is one reason why we might expect ongoing shifts in public attitudes about the economy since 2016.

## Conclusions

The present study is not without many substantial limitations. Twitter is only one medium for the dissemination of economic framing efforts, and the time-bound nature of the exploration limits our ability to evaluate further survey evidence that might strengthen the case for the hypotheses under study.

Nevertheless, to this point, we have mapped several important features of the economic information environment. In the chapters that follow, the investigation shifts from the study of the information environment to a study of economic perceptions. Principally, I seek to understand how the patterns uncovered in chapters 2 and 3 influence the formation and maintenance of biased economic beliefs. As we will see in chapters 4 and 5, these seemingly unassuming patterns bear important consequences for Americans' economic and political judgments.

Chapter 4

# The Politicization of
# Stock Market Perceptions

In the past several chapters, we have seen how the economic information environment is shaped by the agenda setting of journalists and the
framing attempts of politicians. While economic news tends to favor the
discussion of the stock market over other economic indicators, partisan
elites often avoid this economic indicator for strategic reasons. The next
step in the present empirical investigation is to link these information
flows to the perceptions of citizens. In this chapter, I explore the effects
of the stock market on Americans' beliefs about politics and the broader
economy. In addition to gaining a baseline understanding of stock market perceptions, my goal is to better understand how partisans use stock
market information to interpret the political world, especially given their
well-known tendency towards party-biased judgments in the economic
realm (e.g., Bartels 2002).

   While many earlier studies have examined bias in partisans' overall
economic perceptions (e.g., Evans and Andersen 2006), in this chapter,
I study Americans' perceptions of the stock market alongside other economic indicators. By studying partisans' beliefs about the performance
of the stock market, unemployment, wage growth, and inflation, I can
better understand how agenda setting and framing affect stock market
perceptions relative to beliefs about other core economic data. In addition, this comparative examination allows for an improved understanding of the *downstream* effects of these perceptions on other beliefs and
judgments.

In the first study in this chapter, I examine the contours of partisan bias in Americans' beliefs about the stock market. The results of this study support the idea that the information environment conditions partisan bias. Looking across indicators, we see that partisans disagree most about unemployment, an often-politicized issue with only occasional bursts of media saturation. In contrast, Republicans' beliefs about stock market performance are mostly indistinguishable from those of Democrats over the past forty years. The persistent saturation of stock market information in news, combined with relatively rare historical framing efforts from partisan elites, has constrained partisan bias most of the time. In study 4.1, a closer examination of these media effects using specialized regression techniques supports these initial expectations.

Nevertheless, when it comes to stock market perceptions, a "second face" of bias is emerging. In study 4.2, I show that Republicans have recently become more likely than Democrats to argue that stock market performance is *important* for the broader economy. When partisan elites drew their attention to this highly salient economic indicator during the Trump administration, Republicans responded by altering their interpretations of the facts. Such an effect is likely a unique consequence of the persuasive appeals of Republicans and would likely not have occurred had the stock market hit record highs during a hypothetical Democratic administration. This finding supports the idea that political elites can have powerful effects on partisans' economic "narratives" (Anson 2017). It offers a pessimistic revision to earlier assumptions about the role of media saturation in staving off partisan bias. Though professional economists assert that "the stock market is not the economy," Republicans' efforts to cheerlead are increasingly convincing them of the opposite.

Finally, in study 4.3, I examine the effects of the stock market on Americans' attitudes about the job performance of the president of the United States. Any effects that stock market judgments might have on these presidential performance evaluations are important for our understanding of economic voting. The results of study 4.3 show that Americans do use stock market information to inform their view of recent presidential performance—even when accounting for other economic indicators canonically used in prior studies. The relatively unbiased nature of partisans' stock market perceptions helps to explain why stock market performance exerts an independent, and increasingly substantial, effect on Americans' perceptions of incumbent presidential job performance. While other, biased perceptions have little independent impact on partisans' appraisals, the stock market causes partisans to strengthen or waver in their approval of in-party politicians. Altogether, the results in chapter 4 support the central premise of this volume: namely, that the modern information environment has made the stock market increasingly politically consequential for Americans across the political and economic spectrum.

## Studying Perceptions of Economic Indicators

Political scientists have only occasionally examined Americans' beliefs about specific economic indicators (e.g., Conover et al. 1986; Matthews and Pickup 2018). Across the decades, however, there exist numerous instances where survey firms have asked respondents about the economic specifics. Moving beyond overall "economic retrospection" items, these questions have asked Americans to think carefully about topics like the stock market, unemployment, gasoline prices, and other basic indicators of economic progress. By studying these granular perceptions systematically, we can take advantage of survey firms' historical efforts, gaining a far more nuanced, comparative understanding of Americans' thoughts about the economy in the process.

The results of the preceding chapters inform a variety of expectations about Americans' stock market beliefs, as well as their downstream consequences. We know from chapters 2 and 3 that the "economic information environment" possesses several surprising features. Journalists prioritize stock market data over other topics; partisan elites favor other indicators as targets for framing efforts; and credit-claiming about the stock market is increasing since Trump took office in 2017. How have partisans reacted to these trends? Do these environmental characteristics constrain or exacerbate partisans' cognitive biases?

By assembling survey evidence from a wide variety of polling sources from the 1980s to the 2010s, I compile the most comprehensive available dataset of partisans' detailed economic perceptions, including 185 different survey items comprising more than 500,000 individual responses. This survey repository allows for the simultaneous exploration of both individual-level and contextual-level determinants of Americans' beliefs about the economy. We can begin to discern whether media mentions of indicators, or the real economy, can constrain partisan motivated reasoning (following the results of chapter 2). The dataset also allows us to understand how partisan elite communication influences the gap between Republicans' and Democrats' economic beliefs, as speculated in chapter 3. Finally, we can use a subset of this data to discern whether stock market perceptions influence support for incumbent presidents.

We already know much about the psychological origins of partisan perceptions, as we have seen especially in chapter 1. But studies of the subject have not yet fully accommodated the framing and agenda-setting characteristics of the information environment.[1] Many researchers have devoted substantial effort to cross-sectional explanations of partisan bias— that is, to examinations of why some people express greater partisan bias than others in certain situations (e.g., Druckman, Peterson, and Slothuus 2013). In later chapters, I use experimental methods to trace the causal pathways supporting the initial evidence presented below. But for now, the study presents descriptive patterns over time.

## Biased Economic Perceptions

Early research on economic perceptions was primarily concerned with demonstrating that partisan perceptual gaps were real and difficult to attenuate (e.g., Bartels 2002; Sanders and Gavin 2004; Wilcox and Wlezien 1993). These studies often relied upon public opinion data spanning the 1990s, which showed that partisans update their economic beliefs in systematically biased ways.

Since that time, Gerber and Huber (2010) have corroborated the idea that partisans engage in biased assessments of incumbent economic performance. A panel survey designed to coincide with the 2006 midterm elections allowed the authors to tap the economic perceptions of the same individuals at a narrow time interval. This helped the study compensate for many rival explanations for biased perceptions, such as the effects of selective exposure or over-time differences in the economic experience of partisans.

The results showed that Democrats roughly doubled their chances of believing that the economy would get better in the postelection context. This study, and related literature, shows that when the winners and losers of elections are determined, partisan update their perceptions in reliably biased directions.[2] These observations lead to a well-established initial expectation:

H1. Partisans' perceptions of economic indicators will be warmer when their co-partisan occupies the White House, and colder when the out party is in office.

Despite the expectation that partisans' perceptions will be predictably biased along the lines of H1, we also know that these biases are attenuated by certain environmental factors. When the national, local, or regional economy is performing very well or very poorly, even the most biased partisans can struggle to rationalize conflicting information (Chzhen, Evans, and Pickup 2014; De Vries, Hobolt, and Tilley 2018; Dickerson and Ondercin 2017; Evans and Pickup 2010; Gerber and Huber 2010; Parker-Stephen 2013).[3] Most of the time, partisans are expected to moderate their biases when economic data swing heavily in one direction. Unlike in the context of the 2006 election studied by Gerber and Huber (2010), in which economic performance was ambiguous, studies showing substantial bias corrections often focus on cases in which disconfirming information becomes essentially unavoidable.

Learning disconfirming facts causes partisans to experience *ambivalence*. Groenendyk (2013), for example, studies how accuracy motivations increase partisans' ambivalence. This research shows that partisans can be dissuaded from cheering for the "home team" if their cognitive resources are depleted.[4] When arguing against the tide of economic information becomes too effortful, some partisans' accuracy motivations will win out over their desire to maintain biased beliefs.

Taken together, these ideas mean that partisans' perceptions, though often biased, will still track the performance of economic indicators across time. When economic signals trend in unambiguous positive or negative directions, some partisans will give up on their biased positions to admit the truth. The challenge of maintaining biased perceptions will increase when the observed economy runs counter to a congenial worldview.

H2. All else equal, partisans' perceptions of economic indicators will grow warmer when an economic indicator's performance improves, and colder when that indicator's performance worsens.

## BIAS AND THE INFORMATION ENVIRONMENT

While economic conditions can constrain the extent of bias in partisans' judgments, we must also take media effects into consideration. When news about an economic indicator is omnipresent (regardless of the overall state of the economy), partisans are expected to have a harder time rationalizing biased judgments. Republicans and Democrats will disagree more intensely about the performance of economic indicators when they are absent from news coverage. The long-term agenda-setting behavior described in chapter 2 suggests that partisans' beliefs about the stock market will usually be less biased than other indicators due to that indicator's consistent media saturation. Perceptions of unemployment, prices, and other indicators are expected to yield stronger partisan biases most of the time as monthly and quarterly aggregated indicators are less reliably covered in the long timespans between data releases.

> H3a. Partisans' perceptions will be more highly polarized when economic indicators receive scant news coverage, and less polarized when they receive robust coverage.

> H3b. Partisans' perceptions of the stock market will be less polarized on average than perceptions of monthly and quarterly aggregated indicators.

While these expectations conform to the broader theory advanced in chapter 1, they deserve some continued discussion. This is because, when taken together, they require us to think carefully about the effects of the *congeniality* of economic news on partisan bias. Some economic indicators' performance will align with Republicans' preexisting assumptions, whereas others will align with those of the Democrats—at the exact same moment in time. Consider the situation in April of 2018. The Consumer Price Index, a measure of inflation, was measured at 250.01 index points at that time. This reflected a nearly 2.5 percent increase relative to April of 2017, providing modestly worrying (but not entirely surprising) news for investors and consumers alike (Bureau of Labor Statistics 2018a). The same month showed an unambiguous decline in the nation's unemployment rate, down to 3.9 percent from 4.1 percent in April and 4.4 percent in March (Bureau of Labor Statistics 2018b). In addition, we witnessed unambiguously strong stock market performance in the Spring of 2018, as the S&P 500 closed at $2,604.47 on April 1, up nearly 10.6 percent in value since the same day in 2017. Of those three indicators, the unemployment rate, CPI, and the S&P 500, which would we expect partisans to disagree about the most?

Extant theories, like the cognitive resources account described above, suggest that the starkest, most unambiguous changes to the economy should be the hardest for partisans to rationalize. This means that the unemployment situation (unambiguously improving) and stock market perceptions (also unambiguously improving) should be less biased than views on inflation (which exhibited more muddled performance). Nevertheless, the expectations of H3 suggest that media coverage of the stock market will outpace discussion of these other topics in April of 2017, yielding widespread (and irrefutable) awareness of the stock market's performance. In this case we would expect to see relatively unbiased partisan perceptions of the stock market. Perceptions of unemployment and inflation, however, would be characterized by greater disagreement among Republicans and Democrats. All three indicators capture elements of the same observed economy, but the extent of partisan bias in public perceptions is expected to reliably vary depending upon the economic topic.

## THE ROLE OF PARTISAN ELITES

While the real economy and the news media are central drivers of partisan bias in the present account, the previous chapter suggested that political elites have a role to play as well. The analyses contained in chapter 3 show that elites are strategic in their willingness to frame economic content, resulting in heavily imbalanced mentions of different economic indicators. Do these elites have a collective impact upon the perceptions of partisans, after compensating for the effects of news and the current economic conditions?

While some framing studies show strong effects on citizens' perceptions (e.g., Druckman 2001), recent work suggests that partisan elites' framing efforts can lead to subtler forms of bias in the realm of economic perceptions. In one study, Bisgaard and Slothuus (2018) show that Danish partisan elites can lead adherents to change their views on the importance of the national debt as a priority for policy making. And Bisgaard (2015) shows that partisan discourse during the Great Recession dissuaded British in-party adherents from blaming the Labour party for their economic struggles. These studies show that partisans' views are complex and powerfully mutable when it comes to the economy.

Another salient example of this framing behavior came in the lead-up to the 2012 election. President Obama was campaigning for re-election, and the economy was doing him few favors. While the depths of the

Great Recession were far in the rearview mirror, the recovery had been tepid, featuring quarter after quarter of high unemployment and GDP growth rates ranging between 1.6 percent and 2.5 percent. When in early November the official jobs report was released by the Bureau of Labor Statistics, partisan elites pounced upon the much-improved official rate of 7.8 percent as a target for framing. Many Republican elites went so far as to question whether the BLS had "cooked the books." Some even suggested that Obama supporters had lied on the BLS's surveys in a concerted effort to help buoy the president's reelection chances (Yakabuski and Carmichael 2012).

What happens when these intense framing efforts come in conflict with media saturation? As I showed in a paper in 2016, it is possible that overt partisan messaging about the economy will have less of an influence on baseline economic perceptions that we might expect (Anson 2016). Taken in conjunction with the findings above, these results suggest that partisan bias can reemerge in the *interpretation* of economic developments rather than in basic economic performance evaluations. Even topics that receive large amounts of news coverage, and that feature unambiguous positive or negative performance, can yield biased partisan interpretations.

We might therefore hypothesize that Republicans' and Democrats' "economic narratives" will differ under varying conditions. When Republicans occupy the White House, Republican identifiers will strengthen their belief in the stock market's importance—but only if stock prices go up, in accordance with their partisan preferred world state. If stock prices crash, Democrats might suddenly find reason to claim the stock market's importance, while Republicans might deny the same. With Democrats in power, the pattern should reverse: Republicans would then *diminish* their belief in the importance of a booming stock market, while Democrats would assign greater importance to bullish NASDAQ and Dow Jones Industrial indices.

As we maintained in chapter 3, though, such economic narratives are only likely to flourish when elite frames reach the public. Republicans have recently increased their efforts to frame stock market performance during the Trump administration. As a result, during the Trump administration we should expect the following:

H4: Republicans will strengthen their beliefs that the stock market matters for the overall economy when subjected to congenial co-partisan framing efforts during the Trump administration.

H4 offers an important test for theories of partisan motivated reasoning. In earlier accounts such as those of Parker-Stephen (2013) and Redlawsk, Civettini, and Emmerson (2010), media saturation can blunt the effects of partisan motivated reasoning. Enough information about a topic can push partisans beyond a psychological "tipping point," exhausting their ability to maintain biased beliefs. Here, I suggest that media saturation can cause Americans to give up their biased positions on the *facts* (that is, whether the stock market is performing well or poorly). But economic narratives of cause and effect, though complex, can help committed partisans use their accurate perceptions of the economic facts to retain partisan-biased worldviews.

## Stock Market Perceptions: Downstream Effects

While the preceding expectations contend with the *determinants* of stock market perceptions, I now consider what *effects* these judgments might have on citizens' broader views. H3 predicts that media attention will yield relatively bias-free perceptions of the stock market among partisans. Republicans, Democrats, and independents alike will have a great deal of stock market information stored in their memory when performing an "information search" to form economic retrospections. Critically, this unbiased information search likely occurs *regardless* of whether Americans believe the stock market matters for the broader economy (H4). The automaticity of the information search process means that mere exposure to stock market information will be enough to link these judgments to other attitudes, even among those who believe the stock market has a weak impact on the overall fortunes of average Americans (e.g., Bargh and Ferguson 2000; Gomes, Brainerd, and Stein 2013; Lau and Redlawsk 2006).

This means that stock market fluctuations likely have an exogenous influence on political judgments because of their impact on the valence of citizens' overall economic perceptions. Many earlier studies have shown that the macroeconomy predicts presidential approval (e.g., Clarke and Stewart 1994; Dickerson 2016; Donovan et al. 2020; MacKuen, Erikson, and Stimson 1992). However, most of these studies use a standard set of economic indicators to represent the effect of the "real economy" on presidential approval, including change in unemployment, GDP growth, and leading indicators of consumer sentiment. The studies' findings have bolstered the economic voting hypothesis despite the strong motivated reasoning effects observed in other studies (e.g., Hansford and Gomez

2015). By reconciling these two branches of research, scholars now believe the "economic vote" is thought to have exogenous and endogenous components. On one hand, economic and political judgments are intertwined because of the inherent bias in partisans' economic evaluations; on the other, partisans automatically internalize some of the economic facts and automatically apply some of this knowledge to inform their presidential support (Pickup and Evans 2013).

The correlation between stock market performance and presidential performance evaluations likely reflects the latter, exogenous economic voting relationship. This is because of the relatively bias-free nature of stock market perceptions, which are accurately and automatically updated thanks to the high degree of media saturation described in chapter 2. Perceptions of the stock market are therefore expected to exert an *independent* effect on presidential support, even when compensating for other, more partisan-biased economic judgments. Together, these observations lead to a final hypothesis:

> H5. Even when compensating for the movement of other economic indicators, increasing stock prices are associated with increasing public approval of the incumbent president.

## Study 4.1: Exploring Bias in Partisan Perceptions

In study 4.1, I take up H1–H3 in a large-scale study of partisans' perceptions of economic indicators. To identify these patterns, I compile cross-sectional survey evidence from 1980 to 2018. In that time, the economy experienced a wide variety of conditions, from booms to freefalls to volatile eras of mixed and unpredictable performance. This lengthy data collection process yielded evidence about partisans' economic beliefs dating back to the Carter administration.

While Americans' perceptions of specific economic indicators are rarely featured in the academic literature, they are common in survey repositories (Alt 1979). Studies of US economic perceptions often rely upon the Michigan Index of Consumer Sentiment (ICS), a major source of data on consumer confidence and business conditions. However, studying *partisans'* economic perceptions substantially limits the availability of polling data on the economy, eliminating sources like the ICS from use.

This is because surprisingly few tracking polls include both economic perceptions questions and reliable measures of partisan identification.

Modern political scientists generally agree that partisanship, as a social identity, is best measured by asking respondents whether they identify with one of the two major political parties (Campbell et al. 1960; Levendusky 2009). Party identification questions are consistently included on omnibus political science surveys like the American National Election Studies (ANES) or the Cooperative Election Studies (CES). However, these gold-standard surveys rarely measure economic perceptions at the granular level of economic indicators.

Due to survey space constraints, economic perceptions are generally confined to standard "national retrospection" and "national prospection" items, which ask whether the economy has gotten or will get "much better," "better," "the same," "worse," or "much worse." These "sociotropic" economy questions help us to understand the contours of biased economic perceptions. However, they do not afford the more detailed view of partisans' beliefs discussed in previous chapters.

## THE ECONOMIC INDICATOR SURVEY REPOSITORY

To address the hypotheses described above, it was necessary to compile evidence from nationally representative surveys conducted by professional polling firms. National tracking polls that tap respondents' beliefs about economic indicators like the unemployment rate, commodity prices, inflation, and the stock market are especially valuable in this regard. Many polls, such as those produced by CBS, the Associated Press, Gallup, and the Pew Research Center, are stored in large searchable data repositories for academic use. Across this wide variety of historical polls, economics items are commonplace. But to find *partisans'* perceptions, a specialized search was required.

I used the Roper iPoll database, along with the Inter-University Consortium for Political Science Research (ICPSR) dataverse and the Pew Research Center database, to assemble the largest possible combined repository of partisan economic perceptions. The resulting dataset spans four decades (1980–2018) and contains 187 unique economic perception questions. All in all, the repository contains nearly 635,000 individual records of Americans' economic perceptions. For more information on these data sources, including the dates of survey administration, the topics covered, and each survey's overall number of respondents, see the appendix.

## Criteria for Inclusion

The repository includes several different kinds of questions about the economy. One consideration is the question's temporal nature–that is, whether the question asks respondents to reflect on the past, present, or future. Some polls ask respondents to compare current economic conditions to those witnessed at the time of the incumbent president's inauguration. These questions are poorly suited to our purposes because they are likely fraught with partisan cues, making a faithful judgment of the contemporary economy difficult to disentangle from partisan sentiments.

Instead, the most useful items for the present purposes are those tapping recent economic progress *sans* overt partisan cues. These questions might ask about general ("in recent times"; "recently") or specific ("in the past year") timespans. Some others might ask about the immediate economic circumstances ("in your view, is the economy currently getting better, . . . worse?") or even the future ("in the near future, do you think the US economy will get better?"). It is important to keep track of these temporal differences. Questions about the past may be more prone to biases because they ask partisans to consider what they remember over the long term, which might allow them to engage in patterns of motivated recall (Krosnick 1991). Despite their differences, all these questions are useful for the analysis of partisan bias. Consider the following examples, the first from the December 2008 edition of the CBS News monthly poll, and the second from the January 2014 edition:

> "In the next year or so, do you think the stock market will go up or down?" [Up/Down/Same/Don't Know]

> "Do you think the stock market is getting better, getting worse, or staying about the same?"

> [Better/Worse/Same/Don't Know]

These economic indicator perception questions can have different response options. The classic economic retrospection battery asks respondents whether the economy has gotten "better, worse, or stayed about the same" in the recent past. A follow-up question might ask those who said "better" whether they might be willing to extend their optimism to "much better," while those who said "worse" are asked whether "much worse" is a more appropriate description. Those questions yield a five-point scale that captures intensity as well as direction.

Other measures have less useful response options. Some questions quiz respondents on the observed performance of an indicator, by asking, for example, "What is the current unemployment rate, to the nearest tenth of a percent?" This kind of question is not well-suited to the present investigation, though the results are often interesting. This is because we cannot easily distinguish between a rating of "better" or "worse" and a partisan's report of "3.9%" as a guess at the unemployment rate. Partisans might have far different interpretations as to the meaning of the number they have guessed.

Overall, then, the present survey repository captures any available survey about the economy (and its constituent indicators in the databases described above) that satisfy the following criteria: they include an acceptable measure of partisanship; they are nationally representative; they are large-N (800+); they ask a retrospective, current, or prospective question; they ask if an indicator is getting, or has gotten, better, worse, or the same; and they do not make explicit or implicit reference to a political figure or party.

These criteria are surprisingly restrictive, given the thousands of professional surveys that have been administered in the United States over the past four decades. But together, they help guide the construction of a comprehensive and specialized dataset of economic perceptions.

## STUDY 4.1: RESULTS

The first step in examining the survey repository is to depict partisans' perceptions over time. In table 4.1, below, I show the difference between the average Republican's and the average Democrat's perceptions of various economic indicators in each presidential administration dating back to 1982. Where enough observations were available, the table includes average perceptions of the stock market, unemployment, prices, and evaluations of the overall economy. In the left column of each section of the table, we see the percentage of Republicans who reported that the economy was "the same" or "better" (relative to "worse"). In the center column we see the same percentage for Democrats; the rightmost column in each section

Table 4.1. Extent of Republican-Democratic Difference in Four Economic Perceptions, 1980–2018

| Administration | Stock Market Perceptions | | | Perceptions of Unemployment | | |
|---|---|---|---|---|---|---|
| | Republicans | Democrats | Difference | Republicans | Democrats | Difference |
| **Reagan** | | | | 85.50% | 60.76% | **24.74%** |
| **G. H. W. Bush** | | | | 34.48% | 11.47% | **23.01%** |
| **Clinton** | 78.72% | 78.01% | **0.71%** | | | |
| **G. W. Bush** | 67.51% | 47.41% | **20.10%** | 42.64% | 22.30% | **20.35%** |
| **Obama** | 74.37% | 78.27% | **-3.89%** | 52.66% | 70.68% | **-18.01%** |
| **Trump** | 54.02% | 36.92% | **17.10%** | | | |

| Administration | Perceptions of Prices | | | Perceptions of Overall Economy | | |
|---|---|---|---|---|---|---|
| | Republicans | Democrats | Difference | Republicans | Democrats | Difference |
| **Reagan** | 75.80% | 54.63% | **21.18%** | 79.21% | 53.71% | **25.49%** |
| **G. H. W. Bush** | 63.36% | 35.14% | **28.21%** | 36.35% | 22.37% | **13.98%** |
| **Clinton** | | | | 80.10% | 85.66% | **-5.56%** |
| **G. W. Bush** | 51.50% | 39.07% | **12.44%** | 56.14% | 21.11% | **35.03%** |
| **Obama** | 59.72% | 68.19% | **-8.47%** | 34.34% | 79.30% | **-44.95%** |
| **Trump** | | | | 93.19% | 63.01% | **30.18%** |

reports the absolute difference between these two partisan groups. A 10 percent absolute difference, for example, might correspond to 50 percent of Republicans thinking the economy was doing "the same" or "better," relative to 60 percent of Democrats thinking the same. While we might see such a pattern during a Democratic administration, this optimism gap would almost certainly reverse once a Republican took office.

Table 4.1 shows us several things that we might have already suspected about partisans' perceptions. First, looking at the columns of differences reported in each section of the table, we see that partisans rarely agree on the economic facts. During the Clinton administration, Republicans and Democrats were quite similar in their views that the economy was doing well (86 percent of Democrats rated the economy in the "same" or "better" categories, compared to around 80 percent of Republicans). But this seeming consensus proves the exception rather than the rule. Co-partisans of the presidential incumbent almost always have much more positive economic evaluations than members of the out-party on average; when the out-party assumes office, opponents' perceptions trend downward. The Obama administration, for example, witnessed a whopping 44 percent discrepancy between the average overall economic evaluations of Republicans and Democrats. Recent studies have charted this over-time increase in partisan bias using other data, finding that the gaps in partisan economic evaluations have grown steadily wider since the Clinton administration (Brady et al. 2022).

Nevertheless, we also see that perceptions of different economic *indicators* are not identically biased, even at the same moment. The average magnitude of partisan bias for the stock market items is the lowest in the data, whereas the unemployment and overall economy measures are often far higher. We can see this borne out in the individual polls in the dataset just as well as in the aggregated columns of table 4.1. Consider, for instance, a CBS News poll conducted in February of 2015, which showed 33.5 percent of Republicans believing the economy had recently improved or stayed the same, compared to 72.6 percent of Democrats—a difference of around 41.1 percent. Other, more specific evaluations measured by the same poll, however, show evidence of greater similarity across the two parties. Republicans (60.5 percent were only around 13.6 percent less likely than Democrats (74.1 percent to suggest that *housing prices* were good or getting better, a partisan gap that is roughly three times smaller than the overall economy item. In addition, Republicans were only 9.7 percent more likely than Democrats to say the *stock market* had gotten worse, reflecting a difference that is more than four times smaller than the economy item, again measured by the exact same survey. In the aggregate, the survey data show that these kinds of differences are the rule more so than the exception.

To further examine these differences, figure 4.1 shows the absolute magnitude of Republicans' and Democrats' disagreement across surveys and indicators, aggregated across the entire timespan of the study.

As opposed to table 4.1, which shows us the direction and quantity of partisan bias across time, this figure can only show overall rates of partisan disagreement. We should not necessarily take this view of the data without a grain of salt, given that the surveys captured in the dataset do not always reflect an even balance of indicator questions across time. Stock market perceptions, for example, are mostly limited to the 2000's and beyond in the data, meaning these data are captured during a period when overall economic perceptions are more strongly biased. These imbalances in the series can affect the overall amount of partisan bias in the aggregate, in part because temporal trends in the real economy can work against partisans' biases.

But figure 4.1 does help us to identify which of the four indicators in this data most reliably exhibit large amounts of partisan bias and which

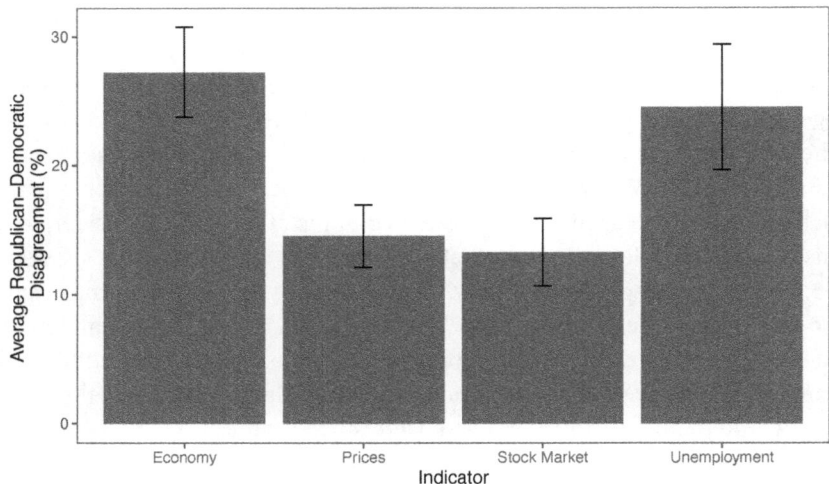

Figure 4.1. Average rate of Republican-Democratic disagreement across four economic perceptions, 1980–2018. *Source*: Author's own material.

indicators exhibit little divergence in Republicans' and Democrats' perceptions. The pattern conforms to our initial expectations. Overall economic retrospections once again clearly show the most bias, with an average deviation between Republicans and Democrats of 27.5 percent across the period (95 percent CI: 23.8%, 30.8%). Perceptions of unemployment also show major differences in partisans' perceptions, represented by an average over-time deviation of 24.5 percent (95 percent, CI: 19.6 percent, 29.4 percent.

Perceptions of the stock market stand in contrast to these figures. Whereas partisan biases in these perceptions are by no means nonexistent, they are much smaller in magnitude compared to some of the other topics queried by survey administrators across the period. On average, partisans disagreed by a margin of around 13.3 percent (95 percent CI: 10.7 percent 15.9 percent in terms of their beliefs about whether the stock market was getting better or worse. And beliefs about prices, which include estimates of inflation, are similarly immune to major partisan disagreement, with average evaluations differing by a more modest 14.5 percent (95 percent CI: 12.1 percent, 16.9 percent).

While these figures present initial evidence in favor of H1–H3, as discussed above, these snapshots do not consider the simultaneous influence of the many potential determinants of economic perceptions reviewed above. To more robustly examine whether these differences are meaningful, I next model perceptions using hierarchical linear regression techniques.

MODELING ECONOMIC PERCEPTIONS

To evaluate the hypotheses presented earlier in the chapter, I construct a hierarchical linear model (HLM) of economic indicator perceptions that simultaneously accounts for economic and political context, the information environment, and individual respondents' demographic and perceptual differences. I limit this analysis to the three specific indicator groups under study, removing the overall economy items due to their broader evaluative nature. While a formal, tabular presentation of this hierarchical model can be seen in the appendix, for the time being I depict relevant tests of H1-H3 graphically.

Hierarchical models account for the fact that each individual survey contained in the dataset reflects a unique context for the respondents who answered it (Gelman and Hill 2006). Much like a researcher wishing to predict student performance might assume that students who attend the same school draw similarities from their shared context, the model improves its estimates by clustering the respondents by survey. This basic assumption helps to improve overall model fit. It also avoids bias in estimates of group-level coefficients.

It is important to accurately estimate these contextual-level effects, as our tests of H2 and H3 draw on contextual-level data from chapters 2 and 3. Because we know the dates of each survey's deployment, we know from these series what aspects of the economy the media were discussing at that time. I use the *New York Times* data series from study 2.1 to match economic media mentions to the survey items from 1980 to the present. I also use a measure of congressional framing of the economy gleaned from study 3.1. By aggregating the mentions of economic topics made by MCs on Twitter, quarterly from 2015 through 2018, I next study the effects of Republican and Democratic credit-claiming attempts on the economic perceptions of co-partisans. Finally, I also link respondents' perceptions with the real economic performance of a variety of economic indicators, drawing on data from the St. Louis Federal Reserve's FRED database.

Contextual-level variables aside, the models also include standard controls such as party identification, age, race, income, and sex. Ultimately, the models are designed to study the *contingent* relationships between party ID and the contextual-level variables of media saturation, twitter discourse, and economic performance. HLM models are well-suited to this task.

Interaction effects from these models can tell us whether partisans become polarized under certain conditions. For instance, we might expect the partisan perceptual "gap" to decline when media mentions of an economic subject increase. In general, these coefficients are hard to interpret by themselves, meaning that the results of the models are best assessed by graphing the models' predictions under specific conditions, as seen in chapter 3.[5]

In the figures that follow, we must nevertheless remain aware of certain interpretive limitations. The figures plot predicted probabilities with most of the variables held at their mean values. This means that the predictions faithfully report outcomes for a very particular area in the data space, and not others. Thus, the baseline values of the predictions are not always as informative as the contrasts between Republicans and Democrats. It also means that tests of statistical significance should be reported from the model coefficients themselves, alongside appraisals of the 95 percent confidence intervals seen in the visualizations. When significant interactive model coefficients are identified, alongside visualizations that depict non-overlapping confidence intervals, we can be sure that the hypothesized effects are reliable in general (due to the coefficients) and in the specific data space captured by the graphics. For this reason, I find it useful to include tabular model results alongside the more intuitive visuals.

First, I test the effects of economic performance on Republicans' and Democrats' perceptions across eras of presidential incumbency (H1–H2). In table 4.2, we see that all coefficients in the HLM model are significant (in part because the number of observations in the model is in the hundreds of thousands, yielding significance for even the smallest effects). Critical for H1 and H2 are the significant interactive effects, however. While Republicans have more negative economic appraisals than Democrats during Democratic administrations (the baseline condition), the large positive interaction effect indicates that the effect reverses when Republican incumbents take power.

To visualize this pattern, which is anticipated by H1, I present figure 4.2. In the left panels, I show the relationship between partisanship and economic indicator perceptions when a Democrat is in office; in the right panels, we see the relationship under Republican administrations. The visuals also account for the state of the economy, by varying the performance

Table 4.2. Mixed-Effects Logistic Regression Predicting Positive/ Neutral Economic Evaluation from Presidential Incumbency

| Predictor | Est | SE | 95% CI | |
|---|---|---|---|---|
| Intercept | 1.524 | 0.122*** | 1.285 | 1.763 |
| Republican | −1.754 | 0.010*** | −1.775 | −1.734 |
| Age | −0.065 | 0.004*** | −0.073 | −0.057 |
| Nonwhite | −0.040 | 0.010*** | −0.059 | −0.022 |
| Income | 0.381 | 0.008*** | 0.366 | 0.397 |
| Female | −0.273 | 0.008*** | −0.288 | −0.258 |
| Real Indicator Performance | 0.279 | 0.082*** | 0.118 | 0.439 |
| Republican Pres. Incumbent | −2.120 | 0.169*** | −2.451 | −1.789 |
| Republican x Republican Incumbent | 3.270 | 0.016*** | 3.238 | 3.302 |
| Survey Random Effect SD | 1.097 | | | |
| AIC | 420852.300 | | | |
| BIC | 420961.300 | | | |
| Log Likelihood | −210416.1 | | | |

Note: ***p < 0.001; **p < 0.01; *p < 0.05.

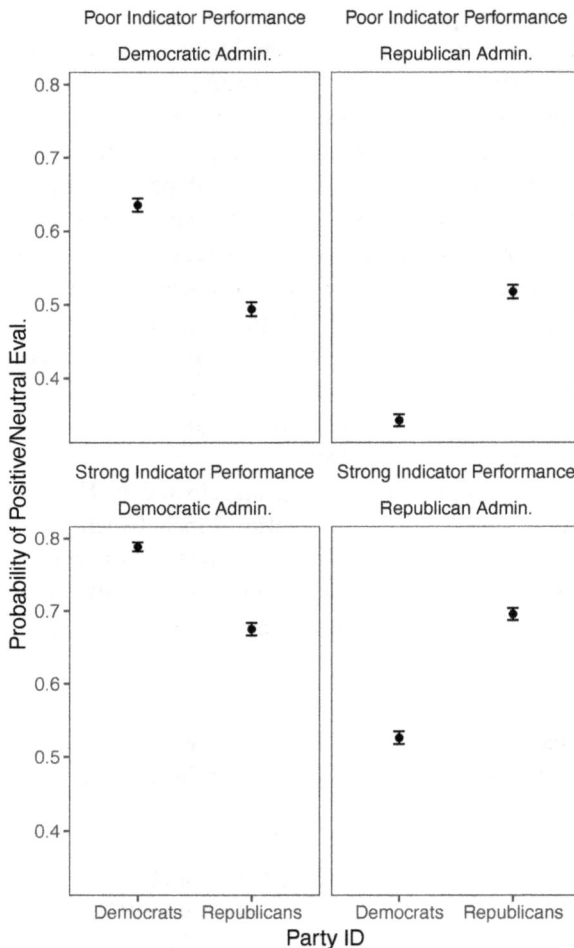

Figure 4.2. Effects of the real economy on partisan evaluations across incumbent partisanship. *Source*: Author's own material.

of the economic indicators in question. The top row of panels shows the relationship when a given economic indicator is performing one standard deviation worse than its average for the timespan from 1980 through 2018; the bottom row shows predictions when economic performance is one standard deviation better than average (a test of H2).

Figure 4.2 shows us a pattern that conforms to the expectations of both H1 and H2. Despite the complexity of the underlying model, as seen in table 4.2, these predictive results line up with what we might expect from a more traditional model of overall economic perceptions.

Within each panel, we see a substantial partisan gap in economic indicator perceptions. Looking left to right across the figure's panels, however, we see that Republicans are more positive than Democrats (and vice versa) at different moments in time. When Democrats are in office, they are always more positive than Republicans about the economy; when Republicans are in office, they are more positive than Democrats regardless of economic conditions (H1). These differences are all highly statistically significant (p < 0.01).

During periods of weak economic performance (top row), both Republicans and Democrats exhibit worse evaluations in all conditions compared to periods of strong economic performance (bottom row). Thus, we also have evidence in support of H2's proposition that partisans are still responsive to real changes in economic indicator performance, despite their biases. This "intercept shift" is about 10 percent of the scale in every condition. To interpret this finding, we can say that when real economic conditions worsen by two standard deviations, about 10 percent of Republicans and Democrats adjust their perceptions from "better/the same" to "worse," regardless of who is in office.

## MEDIA SATURATION AND ECONOMIC PERCEPTIONS

Next, I examine the effects of news media mentions (H3) on the "partisan gap" in economic indicator perceptions. To study H3 I present table 4.3, which models economic indicator perceptions using multiple interaction effects. In addition to the standard individual-level control variables included in table 4.2 (age, sex, race, income, and party ID), the model includes three contextual variables: economic performance, presidential incumbent party, and the normalized density of news mentions of the economic indicator in question. The model also includes cross-level interactions between a respondent's party ID and each of the three contextual variables. Finally, I include two three-way interactions: one between party ID, economic performance, and news mention density; and the other between party ID, incumbent partisanship, and news mention density.

The model's complexity means that interpretation of the main and interactive effects in the table is difficult. Figure 4.3 eases this interpretation by distilling the interactive effects of interest for H3. It shows Republican and Democratic economic perceptions as the volume of news coverage varies, across Republican and Democratic administrations. All

Table 4.3. Mixed Effects Logistic Regression Predicting Positive/
Neutral Economic Evaluation from Media Agenda Setting
Characteristics

| Predictor | Est | SE | 95% CI | |
|---|---|---|---|---|
| Intercept | 1.034 | 0.158*** | 0.724 | 1.344 |
| Republican | −0.622 | 0.026*** | −0.674 | −0.570 |
| Age | 0.038 | 0.008*** | 0.023 | 0.053 |
| Nonwhite | −0.065 | 0.021** | −0.105 | −0.025 |
| Income | 0.349 | 0.016*** | 0.318 | 0.381 |
| Female | −0.230 | 0.015*** | −0.259 | −0.201 |
| Real Indicator Performance | 0.339 | 0.109*** | 0.126 | 0.552 |
| News Mention Density | −0.099 | 0.048* | −0.194 | −0.004 |
| Republican Pres. Incumbent | −1.425 | 0.227*** | −1.870 | −0.979 |
| Republican x Republican Incumbent | 1.555 | 0.033*** | 1.491 | 1.620 |
| Republican x News Mention Density | 0.234 | 0.031*** | 0.173 | 0.295 |
| Republican x Real Indicator Performance | −0.077 | 0.021** | −0.118 | −0.036 |
| Real Perf. x News Mention Density | −0.076 | 0.039 | −0.152 | 0.001 |
| News Mention Density x Repub. Incumbent | 0.214 | 0.068*** | 0.080 | 0.347 |
| Republican x Real Perf. x News Mentions | 0.160 | 0.021*** | 0.119 | 0.201 |
| Repub. x Repub. Inc. x News Mentions | −0.463 | 0.036*** | −0.535 | −0.392 |
| Survey Random Effect SD | 1.034 | | | |
| AIC | 110788.0 | | | |
| BIC | 110949.9 | | | |
| Log Likelihood | −55377.0 | | | |

Note: ***p < 0.001; **p < 0.01; *p < 0.05.

other variables in the model are held at their mean values in this plot of predicted probabilities.

Like in figure 4.2, we see that Democrats (left bar in each panel) and Republicans (right bar in each panel) generally disagree about the state of economic indicators. Significant differences emerge between average Republican and Democratic economic evaluations in each panel. However, the size of that partisan "gap" differs substantially depending upon the context described in each panel. In the top row of panels, we see what

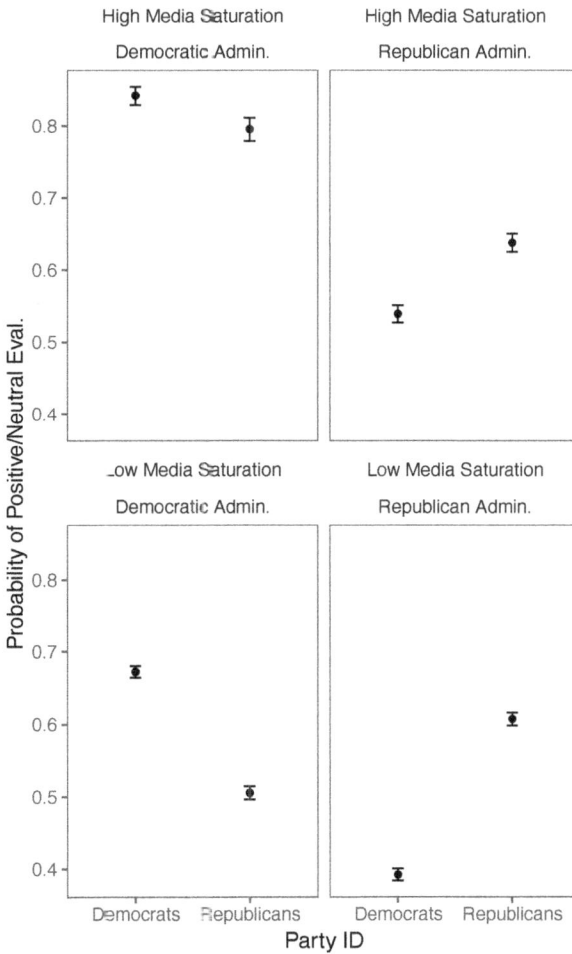

Figure 4.3. Effect of news mentions on partisan evaluations across incumbent partisanship. *Source*: Author's own material.

happens when economic indicators are mentioned more frequently than normal in media (in the high media saturation condition, mentions are one standard deviation higher than average, with other variables held at their mean values). In the bottom panels, we see what happens when media mentions of a given indicator are one standard deviation lower than average.

The contrast between the top and bottom panels in the figure show us the effect of news media saturation on partisans' perceptions. In the top left panel, we see that this gap is quite small. Under Democratic presidents, periods of high media saturation witness a partisan perceptual gap of only $\delta = 0.05$, meaning that roughly 5 percent of partisans said contradictory things about the economy under these circumstances. Under Republican presidents, this gap is somewhat larger in the high media saturation condition (top right panel; $\delta = 0.10$).

However, comparing these panels with those directly below them shows what happens when media saturation diminishes. The result in both conditions is accelerating partisan bias. Under Democratic administrations, this gap grows from $\delta = 0.05$ to $\delta = 0.16$ (p < 0.01 for the interactive contrast). Under Republican administrations the gap also grows from $\delta = 0.10$ to $\delta = 0.21$ (p < 0.01). This symmetrical predicted probability shift of 0.11 in each condition suggests that heightened media saturation reduces partisan disagreement about the economy by roughly 11 percent. This reduction is roughly the same size as the effect of the real economy, as seen in figure 4.2. These patterns accord with the significant (p < 0.001) interaction between incumbent partisanship, respondent partisanship, and news mention density in model 4.3, and provide further evidence in support of H3.

## TWITTER AND ECONOMIC PERCEPTIONS

Next, I consider what happens when economic indicators become the target of partisan framing efforts. In a model that includes observations from 2015 through 2018 (spanning the late Obama administration through the early Trump administration), I measure the effects of two sources of congressional framing activity. The first is a measure of how many times Democratic congressional Twitter accounts mentioned an economic topic in each quarter since 2015. The second series is the same quarterly count of economic topics, but this time among Republican MCs.[6] These measures are derived from the Twitter dataset described in Chapter 3. Both series include tweets gathered from the accounts of both Senators and members of the House of Representatives. In the model, I also include interactive terms between an individual's partisanship and the Twitter behavior of Republican and Democratic members of Congress. The results of this mixed-effects logistic regression, presented in table 4.4, show that Twitter mentions are associated with meaningful shifts in partisans' economic indicator perceptions.

Table 4.4. Mixed Effects Logistic Regression Predicting Positive/
Neutral Economic Evaluation from Congress' Twitter Activity

| Predictor | Est | SE | 95% CI | |
|---|---|---|---|---|
| Intercept | 0.788 | 0.256*** | 0.286 | 1.290 |
| Republican | 0.389 | 0.025*** | 0.341 | 0.438 |
| Age | 0.016 | 0.007* | 0.001 | 0.030 |
| Nonwhite | −0.135 | 0.017*** | −0.168 | −0.101 |
| Income | 0.509 | 0.015*** | 0.480 | 0.538 |
| Female | −0.378 | 0.015*** | −0.408 | −0.348 |
| Republican Incumbent | −0.358 | 0.473 | −1.285 | 0.568 |
| R Congressional Tweets | −0.171 | 0.150 | −0.465 | 0.124 |
| D Congressional Tweets | 0.229 | 0.186 | −0.135 | 0.593 |
| Repub. x R Cong. Tweets | 0.641 | 0.012*** | 0.618 | 0.664 |
| Dem. x D Cong. Tweets | 0.992 | 0.011*** | 1.013 | 0.970 |
| Survey Random Effect SD | 0.898 | | | |
| AIC | 113749.65 | | | |
| BIC | 113864.71 | | | |
| Log Likelihood | −56862.8 | | | |

Note: ***p < 0.001; **p < 0.01; *p < 0.05.

While the tabular results (especially the significant interactive effects; p <0.001 for both interactions) are promising for H4, the magnitude of these effects is once again difficult to interpret from the table alone. To better understand these effects, I next calculate and visualize partisans' predicted probability of positive economic evaluations when Republican tweet density (top panels) and Democratic tweet density (bottom panels) varies. In these predictions, I hold all other variables at their means. With a strong economy observed throughout the period of the study, the effects presented here are those of increasing partisan *credit-claiming* behavior for both parties. That is, in the left-hand side of the figure, we see what happens when Republicans (top left panel) and then Democrats (bottom left panel) become increasingly willing to tweet positive things about the economy, in an effort to take credit for the prevailing positive economic conditions spanning the late Obama administration and early Trump administration.

The results contained in figure 4.4 show us that the divergence between Republican and Democratic economic perceptions grows as Twitter mentions increase. Republicans become more optimistic about economic performance in the top panel when their co-partisans engage in economic

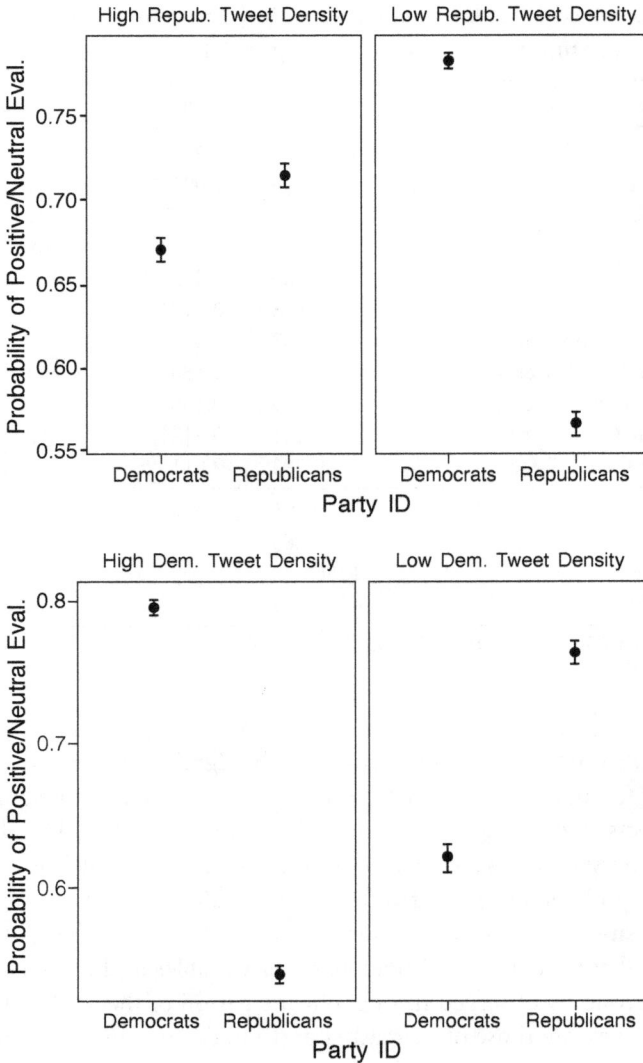

Figure 4.4. Effect of Senate Twitter activity on partisan evaluations, 2015–2018. *Source*: Author's own material.

credit-claiming on Twitter. Democratic respondents are less enthusiastic about the economy in these moments, reducing their likelihood of a positive evaluation relative to Republicans (though not dramatically; all groups remain more likely than not to report a positive economic perception). The net result is a gap of 19 percent during periods when Republicans engage in intense tweeting about an economic indicator. In those periods where Republican credit-claiming is reduced (top right panel), Republicans' perceptions become slightly *less* enthusiastic than Democrats', with a gap of only around 5 percent separating the two groups. While again, both panels show a significant ($p < 0.05$) divergence in partisans' economic perceptions, the size of that gap appears to vary along with the Twitter environment (H4). We see the same pattern for Democratic credit-claiming in the lower panels: Democratic tweets increase the gap between Democrats and Republicans (to around 31 percent); when Democratic tweets subside, the gap shrinks to only around 8 percent.

Overall, these results show that during moments when party elites take up discussion of a specific economic indicator on Twitter, partisans' perceptions of economic indicators tend to polarize. Partisan framing efforts ramp up when partisans disagree most about the economy (and vice versa), while the news saturation variable in figure 4.3 is associated with reduced partisan disagreement. Overall, while this preliminary view of "factual polarization" in economic perceptions cannot establish causality, the results accord with the view that economic perceptions are sensitive to context. Some of these contextual elements are grounded in economic reality: economic performance can move partisans' beliefs despite their inherent biases. But large shifts in party adherents' economic perceptions can still be witnessed when partisan framing efforts are strong, and in moments when media mentions do not saturate the information environment.

## Study 4.2: Partisan Economic Narratives

The preceding study examined the "first face" of economic perceptions: citizens' basic appraisals of the facts of economic performance. That is, study 4.1 tested claims related to partisans' beliefs about whether a specific indicator was performing "better," "the same," or "worse" in recent times. The results showed that media saturation and partisan framing efforts were associated with shrinking and growing partisan "gaps" in economic perceptions, respectively.

These results help us to understand why stock market perceptions are the most accurate and unbiased perceptions in the dataset on average, as seen in figure 4.1. Taken side-by-side with the results from chapters 2 and 3, it appears that partisans reduce the strength of their motivated reasoning when media saturation is high and when partisan framing efforts are low. Together, the results give us optimism for the accuracy of partisans' stock market perceptions: these conditions are ideal for broad partisan agreement on the facts.

In study 4.2, however, I next examine a "second face" of stock market beliefs. Specifically, I study a subset of more recent surveys from the repository that included questions asking *whether the stock market matters for the broader economy.* These questions, detailed in the appendix, were not posed to respondents often. Nevertheless, the repository contains eleven surveys since the 2000s that asked partisans about the importance of the stock market across time.

These questions allow partisans to express their beliefs in the form of an "economic narrative" (Anson 2017). As we have seen in chapter 1, these narratives allow partisans to express biased opinions even in cases when economic conditions are incontrovertibly good or bad (e.g., Bisgaard 2015). Does this phenomenon extend to the realm of stock market perceptions? Given that stock market coverage often showcases such high media saturation, biased economic narratives (rather than biased appraisals of stock market performance) are likely to emerge in response to elite framing. This line of reasoning leads to H5:

> H5. All else equal, Republicans and Democrats will differ in the degree to which they believe the stock market matters for the broader economy.

I take up this investigation by modeling a three-point "stock market importance" item that was asked in each of the eleven surveys under study. These items ask whether a respondent believes the stock market is important for the performance of the broader US economy. The surveys containing these items derive from a variety of polling firms and result in an overall N of around ten thousand. The most common sources are Pew Research Center, CNN/ORC, and CBS News. See the appendix for additional details, including question wording.

For ease of interpretation, I model stock market importance using OLS regression.[7] The model accounts for a variety of individual-level variables, including party ID, age, race, income level, gender, and education. The model also accounts for the monthly percent change in the price of the S&P 500 during survey deployment, to control for observed stock market performance. Because good stock market performance is congenial to Republicans' and Democrats' priors depending upon the party of the incumbent, I also include a dummy variable capturing whether survey deployment occurred during a Republican or a Democratic administration.

STUDY 4.2: RESULTS

The results of the model described above are included in table 4.5. This table reports OLS coefficients, which are far more interpretable than the

Table 4.5. OLS Regression Predicting Perceived Stock Market Importance

| | |
|---|---|
| Independent | 0.054** |
| | (0.025) |
| Republican | 0.019 |
| | (0.020) |
| Female | 0.008 |
| | (0.015) |
| White | 0.027 |
| | (0.018) |
| Not College Grad | −0.116*** |
| | (0.017) |
| Age | 0.004*** |
| | (0.0005) |
| Income $50k–$99k | −0.080*** |
| | (0.020) |
| Income Less than $50k | −0.223*** |
| | (0.020) |
| S&P 500 | 0.054*** |
| | (0.003) |
| Trump Administration | −0.034 |
| | (0.026) |
| Independent x Trump Admin | −0.156** |
| | (0.062) |
| Repub. x Trump Admin | 0.058* |
| | (0.035) |
| Constant | 1.980*** |
| | (0.039) |
| Observations | 10,098 |
| $R^2$ | 0.073 |
| Adjusted $R^2$ | 0.072 |
| Residual Std. Error | 0.758 (df = 10085) |
| F Statistic | 65.973*** (df = 12; 10085) |

*Note:* $^{*}p < 0.05$; $^{**}p < 0.01$; $^{***}p < 0.01$.

logistic regression coefficients presented in earlier tables in the chapter. The dependent variable is measured on a 3-point scale, with 3 indicating that the stock market is "very" important for the overall economy, 2 indicating that it is "important," and 1 indicating that it is "not important." We see from these results that while it appears that party ID has little effect on perceived stock market importance (due to the nonsignificant effects of Republican party ID relative to the baseline of Democratic party ID), the significant interactive effect for Republican x Trump administration ($\beta = 0.058$, $p < 0.05$) reveals that the magnitude of the partisan gap in "economic narratives" depends upon context. Specifically, while the partisan gap may not be substantial during the Obama administration (the model's baseline), during the Trump administration, the gap appears to increase in a statistically reliable fashion.

In figure 4.5, below, I provide a more descriptive view of H5 by examining the interaction between party ID and presidential administration on the outcome. The left panel shows partisans' average response to this item during the Obama administration. The right panel shows this pattern during the Trump administration. All other variables are held at their mean values within the dataset, though the S&P 500 variable is held at the more appropriate long-term average value of 3 percent.

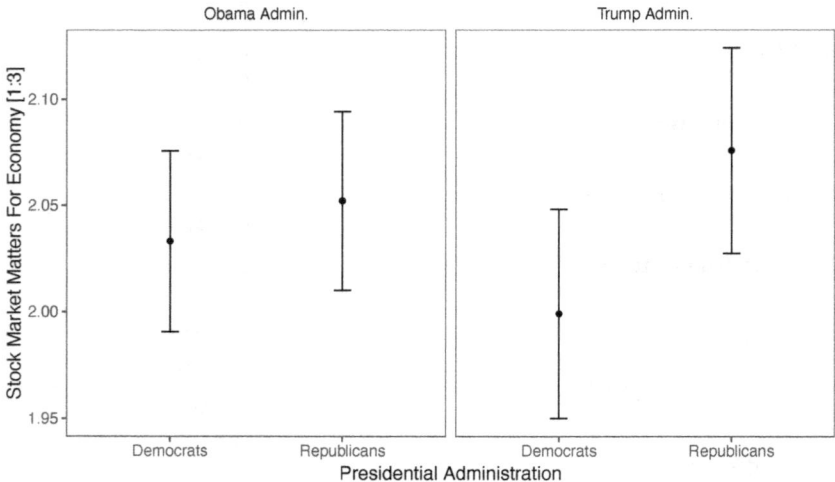

Figure 4.5. Belief in stock market importance by party ID and incumbency. *Source*: Author's own material.

Figure 4.5 shows that while the Obama administration witnessed both Republicans and Democrats holding moderate views on whether the stock market matters for the economy, partisan narratives diverge during the Trump administration. While the left panel shows little partisan divergence, the right panel shows that Republicans become around 2.5 percent more supportive of the idea that stocks matter for the economy than Democrats. While H5 does not find any support during the Obama administration, the more recent Trump era shows a growing gap in economic narratives. While the partially overlapping confidence intervals in the figure are challenging to interpret, this increase in partisan disagreement corresponds with a significant ($p < 0.05$) interactive effect in table 4.5. Together, these findings provide substantive and statistical evidence in support of H5.

Partisan-fueled narratives about the meaning of the stock market are especially surprising given that relatively few Americans have large investments in the stock market. However, perhaps due to the framing effects described in earlier chapters, some partisans are beginning to contest these economic narratives to reinforce their overall partisan worldviews. While these effects are likely still nascent, they call into question the broader impact of the stock market on Americans' political appraisals. Do Americans react to the stock market by updating their judgments of incumbent presidents?

## Study 4.3: Presidential Approval and Salient Economic Signals

In study 4.3, I consider the downstream effects of stock market performance on political attitudes. While scholars have long charted the effects of indicators like unemployment, GDP growth, and consumer sentiment on aggregate presidential approval, the stock market is a rarely examined determinant (c.f. Fauvelle-Aymar and Stegmaier 2013). In addition, scholars who examine these links use a handful of standard economic indicators as proxies for a broader conceptualization of the "overall economy." This makes sense if one is studying topics like partisan bias in the economic vote, or negativity bias in economic news: The goal in these cases is to compare some highly accurate composite of the objective economy to the (biased) outcome of interest (e.g., Chzhen, Evans, and Pickup 2014; Soroka et al. 2015).

But in this account, I examine how the stock market *rivals* other standard economic indicators in its effects on presidential approval. That is, I ask if there exists an *independent* effect for the movement of the stock market on presidential approval, in the presence of signals that usually stand in for the "objective economy" in other analyses. In the context of linear regression, when a model includes multiple independent variables, that model successfully accounts for covariance (overlapping influence) between the variables. The regression's model coefficients therefore report each variable's unique, independent effects on an outcome, even if those variables were initially correlated with one another. In plainer terms, multiple regression can help us sort out whether the stock market exerts an effect on presidential approval that stands apart from the rest of the "objective economy" as it is normally measured. According to the logic of H5, presented above, we might expect to see this independent effect if Americans react to the large volume of daily stock market coverage documented in chapter 2 by automatically updating their economic beliefs. If so, most people would maintain accurate opinions of the stock market's performance despite the influence of partisan bias in other economic topics. They would use their accurate stock market knowledge to revise their presidential appraisals, while the movement of other economic indicators would serve to reinforce their preexisting party-congenial assumptions about incumbents.

To evaluate this hypothesis, I gathered data on presidential approval from a large repository of survey toplines administered by the American Presidency Project at UC-Santa Barbara. This data source compiles survey data from the Gallup Poll and contains thousands of observations across time. I combined these polling toplines, which span the George H. W. Bush, Bill Clinton, George W. Bush, Barack Obama, and Donald Trump presidencies (up to July, 2020). While some imbalances exist in the frequency of the polling toplines (more were available for the Obama and Trump presidencies than any others), the dataset provides a large-N over-time measure of what Americans thought of the president since the 1980s.

To model approval, I gathered data on the real economy from the St. Louis Federal Reserve's FRED database. In the OLS regression models presented below, I include the monthly percent change in GDP and the monthly unemployment rate as standard measures of economic progress (e.g., Anderson 2020). In addition, I measure the quarterly percent change in the Wilshire 5000 Index, a large index of listed stocks that roughly captures shifts in the entire stock market.

## Results

To assess H5, I include the results of a pooled OLS regression model predicting the effect of quarterly stock market performance on presidential approval rating. Controlling for unemployment and GDP growth and their lagged values, the results demonstrate variation in the strength of this signal across time. Following Fauvelle-Aymar and Stegmaier (2013), I control for lagged values of approval in addition to the economic predictors mentioned above.

The left column of table 4.6 depicts a positive and significant independent effect for stock market shifts on presidential approval, all else equal—an important initial finding in support of H5. We can say from this model that a 1 percent increase in the quarterly Wilshire 5000 index appears to boost presidential approval by a small but statistically signifi-

Table 4.6. OLS Regression Predicting Presidential Approval, 1980–2020

| | | |
|---|---|---|
| Approval$_{t-1}$ | 0.944*** | 0.943*** |
| | (0.005) | (0.005) |
| ΔUnemployment (%) | −0.296** | −0.297** |
| | (0.144) | (0.143) |
| ΔUnemployment$_{t-1}$ (%) | 0.251* | 0.248* |
| | (0.143) | (0.143) |
| ΔGDP (%) | 0.208*** | 0.221*** |
| | (0.064) | (0.064) |
| ΔGDP$_{t-1}$ (%) | 0.200*** | 0.207*** |
| | (0.056) | (0.056) |
| ΔWilshire 5000 (%) | 0.115*** | −0.080 |
| | (0.041) | (0.120) |
| Year Since 1980 | −0.025*** | −0.025*** |
| | (0.005) | (0.005) |
| ΔWilshire 5000 (%) x Year | | 0.008* |
| | | (0.004) |
| Constant | 53.127*** | 53.907*** |
| | (10.432) | (10.439) |
| Observations | 3,748 | 3,748 |
| R² | 0.921 | 0.921 |
| Adjusted R² | 0.921 | 0.921 |
| Residual Std. Error | 2.334 (df = 3740) | 2.333 (df = 3739) |
| F Statistic | 6,232.365*** (df = 7; 3740) | 5,456.548*** (df = 8; 3739) |

Note: *p < 0.05; **p < 0.01; ***p < 0.01.

cant (p < 0.001) 0.115 points, meaning that a larger stock market gain of 10 percent moves presidential approval, on average, by more than a full percent—again, compensating for the effects of unemployment and GDP growth, and their lagged values.

More interesting for the present analysis is what happens when we introduce a temporal component to the analysis. In the right-hand column of table 4.5, I include a year coefficient that ranges from 1980 to 2020. An interaction term between the Wilshire 5000 index and the year variable renders a statistically significant (p < 0.05) result—and a nonsignificant baseline effect for the original Wilshire 5000 index variable. Ultimately, this result tells us that while the effect of the stock market on presidential approval was unreliable in 1980, the effect has since strengthened. In figure 4.6, I generate predictions for the model in 1990, 2000, 2010, and 2020, to determine whether and how the stock market's effect on presidential approval has changed over time.

Each facet of figure 4.6 shows the predicted approval rating (percent of Americans who "approve" of the incumbent president) across a wide range of stock market performance. On the left-hand side of each facet, the stock market is charted at a –30 percent quarterly change in value—a

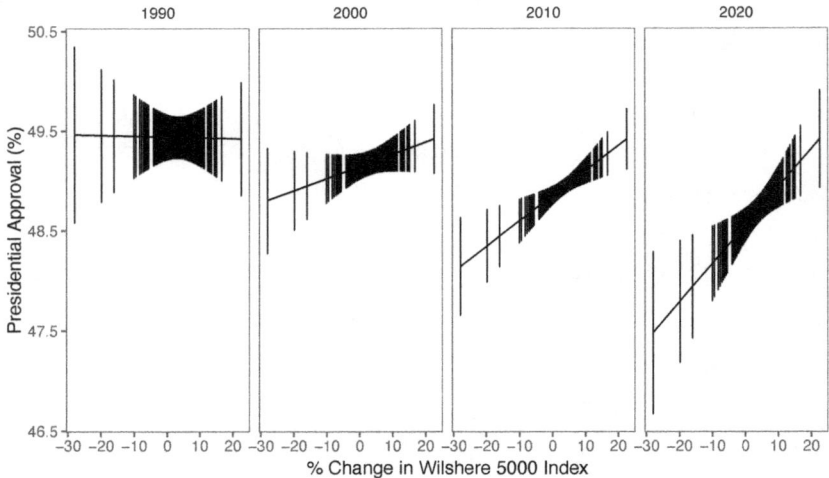

Figure 4.6. Predicted presidential approval by percent change in Wilshire 5000 Index, 1990–2020. *Source*: Author's own material.

major crash of the same order of magnitude as the Coronavirus crash of 2020 or the onset of the Great Recession. On the right-hand side we see what might happen during ebullient market conditions (30 percent quarterly gains). In between, we see more modest domains of gains and losses.

The results show that stock market performance exerts an increasingly large and significant effect on presidential approval in later decades. Despite the relatively small magnitude of these shifts, study 4.3 does provide suggestive evidence that the stock market matters more for politics today than it did in previous eras. While previous studies have confirmed that presidential approval–and by proxy, accountability–are shaped by real economic conditions, it is becoming increasingly clear that today's citizens are beginning to focus their attention on the movement of the stock market ticker when evaluating presidents, even when compensating for other features of the real economy.

Despite the results of study 4.3, there still exists the potential for new media practices to renovate Americans' economic beliefs. As discussed above, subtle changes in the behavior of economic journalists could dramatically improve the accuracy of our perceptions of core economic indicators. It remains to be seen how economic perceptions will evolve as Americans brace themselves against the political turbulence following the 2020 election and the subsequent events of January 6, 2021. But despite our rancorous political climate, the potential for objectivity in economic perceptions still lies within our reach.

## Conclusions

Together, the tests performed in this chapter have shown us that partisans' views of the economy are contingent upon several factors, including the information environment, elite messages, and the real economy. They show us that partisan identities are powerful determinants of Americans' beliefs about the facts—until circumstances and informational content rein in the ability of partisans to rationalize performance. However, "bias finds a way" when elite cues signal the importance of the stock market. During the Trump administration, Republicans' economic narratives are evolving towards a new infatuation with stock market performance as a source of political credit and blame.

The findings presented in this chapter are limited in several respects. First is the fact that observational, over-time correlations in Americans' economic perceptions and the broader information environment cannot eliminate all rival explanations. For example, we might wonder about the role of partisans' willingness to seek out different kinds of information on their own—a self-selection mechanism that thus far has received little attention. I take up these issues in the next chapter by studying economic perceptions using experimental research designs.

Partisan bias in economic perceptions matters for political outcomes. Unless partisans work hard to recall the exact specifics of whatever information was presented to them, their economic perceptions will yield more general positive or negative feeling towards an incumbent (Arceneaux and Vander Wielen 2017). The present results speak to the power of media mentions as a determinant of accuracy in these broader economic perceptions. They also suggest that the *specifics* of media agenda setting (that is, the choice of economic topics presented to audiences) can help to determine what topics will ultimately form the basis of economic performance voting.

But a pressing question remains outstanding. Tables 4.3 and 4.4 showed evidence that media agenda setting and partisan framing can work in opposition to grow and shrink biases in partisans' perceptions. What happens when we contend with both effects simultaneously? Can we find similar effects using a causally identified experimental test? Can partisan frames succeed in shifting stock market perceptions, or the economic narratives that underlie them? In chapter 5, I take up these questions using survey experimental methods.

Chapter 5

# Framing the Stock Market

## Experimental Evidence

The preceding chapters have shown that Americans' perceptions of economic indicators are shaped by the contemporary media environment. Among such influences, the mainstream news agenda and the messages of partisan elites are powerful forces. These agenda-setting effects not only influence Americans' economic sentiments; they also influence what aspects of the economy are salient to the public. So too are these information flows consequential in driving the degree of bias in partisans' assessments of the American economy.

Presently, though, it is still unclear whether economic perceptions are *causally* influenced by such messages. The observational patterns in chapter 4 could be subject to a variety of sources of spuriousness, meaning that the true magnitude of these effects is difficult to ascertain. Polarized economic perceptions and media attention may be simultaneously driven by many features of the political environment, complicating efforts to single out specific effects. Recent studies, for example, show that media tone may be biased in favor of incumbents under certain circumstances (Larcinese, Puglisi, and Snyder 2011; Merkley 2019). Studies 4.1 and 4.2 help us evaluate correlational evidence in the available data, but they cannot compensate for unobserved variables.

Thankfully, scholars of economic voting possess strategies for causal identification. One of these methods is the survey experiment. Survey experiments can subtly manipulate the economic information environment of respondents in a way that is unrelated to any outcome measured later in the study (e.g., Anson 2016; Simonovits 2015). This type of randomized controlled trial is especially useful when seeking to understand how and when survey respondents change their perceptions in response to messages conveyed to them through media. While survey experiments often examine message effects in settings that lack external validity, when combined with observational assessments like those in chapter 4, experiments can help us causally link the features of the media environment to shifts in public perceptions.[1]

Earlier chapters also point to another benefit of survey experiments. Thus far we have examined rival causes of bias in partisans' beliefs about the economy. Returning to the central question posed by chapter 1—Why do partisans agree on the facts when it comes to the stock market, relative to other indicators?—we have discovered two potentially conflicting circumstances. In addition to the long-term coverage volume of economic indicators, we have also seen evidence that partisan elites play a role in shifting beliefs about economic perceptions.

What we have not causally verified, however, is whether long-term agenda setting can limit partisan motivated reasoning when partisan persuasive efforts intensify. This question is increasingly relevant, as partisan elites such as Donald Trump have recently taken up the stock market as a new source of economic credit claiming. Because of these developments, stock market perceptions are now a critical case in the study of motivated reasoning and elite cue receptivity.

Perhaps partisan persuasion *must* remain absent for partisans to hold accurate economic perceptions on average. If partisan elites were to suddenly direct their framing efforts towards a new economic topic, would partisans necessarily polarize? For example, rising prices in durable goods such as lumber caught the attention of partisan critics during the COVID-19 lockdowns of 2020. Partisan framing of this new pricing issue could result in Republicans and Democrats disagreeing about the severity of the price increases. This type of effect has been observed in some recent experimental work (e.g., Bisgaard and Slothuus 2018; Slothuus, Leeper, and Druckman 2018).

Nevertheless, by virtue of their overwhelming, consistent media saturation, some economic topics could be relatively immune to this "factual polarization" phenomenon. In particular, the stock market may be an economic topic that is relatively impervious to elite framing. Over the past several years, this theory has been put to the test by Donald Trump. Trump began to tweet more often about the stock market after Congress passed the Tax Cuts & Jobs Act of 2017.[2] However, unlike the Twitter activity of members of Congress, who are noticeably unwilling to mention indicators like the stock market and prices (see chapter 3), Trump's mentions of the economy seemed to constantly draw upon the stock market as a valuable source of congenial information. Consider the following @realDonaldTrump tweet sent in January of 2018: "The Fake News Media barely mentions the fact that the Stock Market just hit another New Record and that business in the U.S. is booming . . . but the people know! Can you imagine if 'O' was [sic] president and had these numbers—would be biggest story on earth! Dow now over 25,000."[3] Over the span of 2017, Trump would tweet about the stock market forty-one times, each time receiving hundreds of thousands, if not millions, of likes and retweets.

The pressing question is whether viral partisan cues like these can reorient partisan perceptions in biased directions or whether media saturation of stock market information prevents Republican and Democratic identifiers from factually disagreeing about its performance in the wake of such persuasive messages. Thus far, we have considered elite messaging and the information environment as *congruent* influences on the broader pattern of economic beliefs. That is, we have thought about elite framing as a process that increases partisan bias and that normally occurs when the media agenda is *not* saturated with information about an economic topic. The present study is instead designed to examine what happens when elite framing and the valence of economic information in the news environment come into direct conflict.

## Source Cues and Congeniality

Existing research proposes a series of expectations related to this conflict. When economic news reaches viewers, it is often accompanied by a variety of cues. Cues help news consumers understand how to think and feel about the things they are currently learning (e.g., Bullock 2011). While the *source* of information is doubtlessly among the most important cues available to partisans, other cues also serve this function as well. We might consider the effects of cues stemming from the popularity of a news story, as informed by the number of likes, shares, tweets, Facebook posts, or other user-generated information that accompanies the story in an online environment. These "endorsement" cues help consumers figure out whether a story is worthy of their attention. How many peers have chosen to pay attention to (or ignore) an item? The answer can help consumers figure out what is worth their attention, across diverse platforms like Facebook, Twitter, and Instagram (Messing and Westwood 2014).

Another type of cue derives from the *content* of information itself. *Credibility* cues can stem from a reader's judgment of the quality of writing of an article, or in the case of multimedia, from the production quality of a video or audio recording. For example, Druckman (2001) examines credibility cues by manipulating the source of a political argument, and Baum and Groeling (2009) study the credibility of messages about national security and war. Many websites (sometimes unintentionally) provide users with clear credibility cues through design elements: the look and feel of a site can enhance or dissuade users' willingness to learn from its content (Xu 2013).

These cues can help consumers decide whether to accept the contents of a news story as true or false. But as discussed previously, when it comes to economic news, we know the partisan *congeniality* of a story can be just as important as credibility, source, and endorsement cues. This is because the positive or negative nature of news developments can be interpreted by partisans through the lens of a "preferred-world state," resulting in acceptance or rejection of the information by its contents alone.[4] Any examination of partisans' perceptions must simultaneously contend with these conflicting features of the information environment.

## Two Cueing Experiments

To better understand how cues and the information environment interact to influence partisans, I conducted two survey experiments. These experiments exposed survey participants to "vignettes:" short stories containing news about the economy. By randomly varying small parts of these vignettes' content, the experiments isolate the effects of cues in ways which shed light upon the broader theory advanced in chapter 1.

We have already introduced and analyzed several kinds of cues in previous chapters, but we have not yet tested the simultaneous influence of content cues and source cues on perceptual updating across economic topics. This is the central goal of study 5.1. In study 5.2, I take up the question of informational self-selection, an aspect of public opinion formation that is especially important when dealing with partisan motivations (e.g., Arceneaux and Johnson 2013; Guess 2015; Messing and Westwood 2014).

We have good reason to expect the positive-negative valence of an economic message will influence Republicans' and Democrats' willingness to update their economic perceptions. At the time of this writing, with Joe Biden in the White House and a slim Democratic majority in Congress, we might expect Democratic identifiers to feel eager to consume positive economic news stories. Republicans, however, are amenable to any stories that provide evidence against the narrative that Biden is successfully managing the economy. Thus, our first baseline expectation is that in general, exposure to positive economic information will cause Democrats to update their perceptions in a positive direction, whereas Republicans will be less likely to do the same. Exposure to negative economic information, conversely, would cause Republicans to adjust their perceptions downward, while Democrats will exhibit no such movement. In early 2016, when study 5.2 was administered, these patterns should be similar due to the incumbency of the Obama administration.

> H1. When exposed to congenial information from an official source, the incumbent's co-partisans will update their perceptions in a direction that is congenial to the incumbent.

Because these directional expectations are well-established (e.g., Anson 2017), in study 5.1 I *exclusively* study the effects of congenial information on partisans' perceptions, ignoring the effects of disconfirming information exposure. Previous experimental work has shown that disconfirming information, as we might expect, has a weak impact on partisans' views.[5] By examining the conditions under which congenial information *does* have an impact on beliefs, we can more closely attend to considerations of relevance to the present line of inquiry.

In addition to a vignette's congeniality, we must also consider what happens when this information is paired with a co-partisan source cue. Partisan-sourced congenial messages, which have been attributed to trusted and visible party elites, are even more likely to be accepted by co-partisans than otherwise. In turn, these messages are more likely to be rejected by members of the opposite party.

> H2. When exposed to congenial information from a co-partisan source, partisans will update their perceptions in a congenial direction.

H1 and H2 provide a set of expectations that are familiar to students of public opinion and economic perceptions. Congeniality and partisan source cues have been found to influence a wide array of perceptions, from overall economic evaluations to perceptions of public health crises (e.g., Guay and Johnston 2022). Republicans and Democrats learn from cues and often reach opposing conclusions about factual developments as a result.

## WHY CONGENIAL STOCK MARKET INFORMATION WILL NOT CHANGE OPINIONS

But what might happen when we manipulate the economic *topics* that partisans learn about, by creating fictional narratives focusing on different economic indicators? In both study 5.1 and study 5.2, a key feature of the experimental design is the manipulation of the economic topic of the vignettes, in addition to the message's congeniality. This topic variation is expected to influence the degree to which partisans update their economic beliefs in response to the treatments. Specifically, I expect congenial stock market information to have weak influence on respondents' economic perceptions relative to other economic indicators.

This is not because stock market information is uninformative for Americans seeking to adjust their economic perceptions, or that survey respondents are not expected to value stock market information (as we will see, they do value this information). Rather, new economic information will have smaller effects if an audience has already learned everything there is to know about that topic. This phenomenon is known as *pre-treatment exposure*. Experimental respondents are not living in a vacuum; they are sensitive to the framing and agenda-setting behavior they experience in real life, prior to experimental treatment exposure (Druckman and Leeper 2012; Linos and Twist 2018). Pretreatment exposure is often conceptualized in the experimental literature as a methodological concern.[6] However, it can also become a relevant substantive consideration if we have clear theoretical reasons to *expect* strong pretreatment effects will reduce the impact of experimental treatments in some cases and not others.

Based on what we have learned in chapters 2 through 4, pretreatment exposure should vary based upon the long-term agenda-setting behavior of economic journalists. High levels of media saturation should attenuate the effects of experimental treatments, all else equal. This is because partisans already possess large reservoirs of information about very ubiquitous economic topics. For instance, reading a single news item about stock prices during a crash would not do much to change the reader's views on whether the stock market is doing well or poorly. For a rarely mentioned economic topic, however, a one-shot experimental treatment should yield bigger shifts in respondents' economic perceptions.

Consider beliefs about gasoline prices, which are easily updated every time someone goes to the pump. Following modern approaches to the study of public opinion (e.g., Bartels 2002; Leeper and Slothuus 2014). experimental exposure to a story about gas prices would not be expected to strongly influence attitudes. Respondents' perceptions of gas prices may be previously well-informed, thanks to their quotidian encounters with gas price data. During every weekly fill-up, every segment on the morning radio show, and every glance at a gas station sign on the way to work, people learn about gas prices. Even an experimental treatment designed to make this information more available to respondents in memory would be outweighed by their prior knowledge. Respondents will have already accounted for this information in their judgments about the overall economy, meaning that further information will yield little updating.

Only when partisans have had relatively *few* chances to gather economic news about a topic will a single-shot message have the capacity to substantially move economic perceptions. This might be especially likely if economic news is accompanied by a partisan source cue. In a situation analogous to reading a partisan leader's tweet or hearing an interview segment with a member of Congress on NPR, a salient mention of an indicator could have a short-term polarizing effect. We have seen evidence in chapter 3 that MCs craft their framing efforts with this phenomenon in mind. Rarely will framing efforts target the stock market due to its overwhelming media saturation. But if elites do seek to frame the stock market using congenial cues, will pretreatment effects render these efforts ineffective?

## PRETREATMENT EFFECTS ACROSS ECONOMIC TOPICS

In the studies that follow, I randomly expose treated groups to congenial information about the stock market, wage growth, and in study 5.2, unemployment. These indicators have been chosen on the basis of study 4.1's findings: each indicator is reported to the public at a different time interval. Up-to-the-minute stock market data are reported to the public more than twice as often as monthly or quarterly wage-growth data; the BLS' unemployment reports are reported on a monthly basis.

Americans often view these three indicators as important signals of the health of the broader economy. While unemployment statistics, wage-growth indicators, and stock prices are all quite different in their ability to describe the economic situation of the average American, surveys have shown that respondents across the economic spectrum value these data as important (e.g., Poterba 2000). Later, we will see that all three perceptions are strongly correlated with overall economic perceptions among participants in the present studies.

Partisans may value these economic topics as important, but they are limited in their daily exposure to information like wage growth. This pattern informs our priors about the strength of pre-treatment exposure in the experiments that follow. When exposed to new wage-growth information, Republicans and Democrats are expected to update their beliefs about the overall economy. During the Trump administration, Republicans should become more positive as they learn about rising wages, while Democrats are similarly expected to become more negative in their evaluations of wage growth if they learn that wages have stagnated.

However, when it comes to the stock market, we expect Republicans not to increase their optimism about the broader economy when hearing good news during the Trump administration; Democrats will also fail to update their perceptions in a negative direction upon hearing negative news about stocks. Critically, *even though the information is just as congenial in all cases*, a feature that should engage partisans to universally update their beliefs, we expect partisans to be pretreated by their exposure to economic news about stock markets—rendering the treatments far less effective.

The same situation applies in study 5.2, which reverses the congeniality of the economic stories due to Barack Obama's tenure in the White House. Topic-based differences in treatment effects are instead expected to endure regardless of the presence of cues or the congeniality of information. Even co-partisan sources will be unable to move partisans' perceptions when the news concerns the stock market. Ultimately, we can capture this expectation in H3:

> H3. Regardless of congeniality or the source, partisans will fail to update their economic perceptions in a congenial direction when the topic of the story is the stock market.

## CUEING, PRETREATMENT, AND SELECTIVE EXPOSURE

In study 5.2, I take up another dimension of the information environment: the phenomenon of selective exposure. Because partisan sources are prevalent in today's media environment, and because Americans increasingly seek out news in a high-choice online environment, study 5.1 lacks realism.[7] Study 5.2 adds the element of choice to the online experimental environment by allowing respondents to identify the subject that most interests them, among the stock market, wage growth, or unemployment. In some cases, respondents receive a positive vignette about the topic they identified as interesting to them. In other cases, respondents do not receive an experimental vignette. In this way, study 5.2 allows us to evaluate the effects of treatment exposure in a second experimental setting: one in which preferences for news topics are accounted for.

While this second design is still quite artificial in nature, it allows us to assess whether pretreatment effects persist even when respondents are afforded a degree of choice over their information diet. In this setting, the effects of vignette exposure on partisans' economic judgments are still expected to be most evident when the economic topic has not received as much coverage in news. Respondents are likely to select an economic news topic for one of two reasons. They might seek out the information because, as partisans, they want to be reminded of information they already know to be congenial to their worldviews. In this case, pre-exposure is expected to drive news selection. Second, they might seek out the information because they believe it is important for the broader economy. Following study 4.2, we might expect Republicans and Democrats to differ in their willingness to support the "economic narrative" that stock markets matter for the broader economy.

We should therefore observe two patterns if a theory of persistent agenda setting is to find support. The first pattern is related to the topics that partisans seek to learn about. We should expect Republicans and Democrats to seek out pre-exposed information like the stock market at much different rates because they will be able to anticipate the congeniality of the story they will read. Because less ubiquitous indicators prohibit partisans' ability to develop expectations about the feel-good nature of the story, partisans should not differ in their levels of interest. In January 2016, Republicans should seek out information about the stock market more so than Democrats. Major volatility in the indicator caused the indicator to become increasingly congenial to Republicans at the time: a news article published during the administration of Study 5.2 described the market climate as "gut-wrenching drama" (Egan 2016). While other indicators were also congenial to one party and disconfirming to the other, most partisans will not know this *a priori*. This expectation can be captured by H4:

> H4. Republicans are expected to demand stock market data more than Democrats, whereas partisans should not differ in their demand for other economic data.

Finally, Republicans and Democrats who received the treatments are again expected to update their economic perceptions on the basis of less frequently reported information, whereas they are not expected to shift their beliefs when exposed to ubiquitous information. This means that the effects of long-term agenda setting are expected to supersede the effects of self-selection, allowing us to extend the credibility of the present theory to a more realistic experimental environment:

> H5. Even when accounting for topic self-selection, respondents will update their economic beliefs in response to information about economic stories other than stock market coverage.

## Study 5.1: Experimental Design

To assess these expectations, it was necessary to design a series of studies that expose partisans to new information about the economy. I first assess H1–H3 through a survey experiment administered in August 2018. This survey reached 1,560 anonymous online participants through the Amazon MTurk platform. While this convenience sample is not representative of the US population, modern social scientists frequently rely on this kind of low-cost sample to learn important things about public perceptions and attitudes (Clifford, Jewell, and Waggoner 2015; Huff and Tingley 2015). Evidence also continues to mount that MTurk samples are remarkably well-suited to survey experimental research relative to other kinds of online and in-person samples (Anson 2018; Krupnikov and Levine 2014). They often allow researchers to examine public perceptions of rarely studied topics due to their comparatively low cost.[8]

The greatest benefit of MTurk samples is that researchers can efficiently and precisely manipulate the things that different groups of respondents see when they participate in an online survey. To conduct an experiment like the one described above, I randomly presented treatment groups with vignettes. Below, I describe how these treatments were constructed.

## EXPERIMENTAL TREATMENTS

The experiment randomly sorted respondents into one of five groups. The experiment is based upon a "2x2" design in that it manipulates two different aspects of a news story that partisans read before answering questions about the economy (the presence or absence of a partisan source cue, and the topic of the article). Four of the groups received one of these stories; the fifth received no news before the economy questions were presented.

These treatments contain an added wrinkle, however. They contain different language depending on whether the recipient of the story is a Republican or a Democrat. As described above, to maximize the relevance of each treatment, the experiment always exposes partisans to congenial news. This means that when respondents were randomly assigned to one of the four treatments, they would have read a version of the story that conformed to their preferred world state. In table 5.1, we see how these split treatments are worded. Altogether, then, Republican and Democratic respondents randomly received stories that varied in terms of the topic of the article (wages or the stock market) and the presence or absence of a partisan source cue that was always partisan-congenial.

Table 5.1 shows the design of the experimental treatments presented to respondents who took the survey. As we can see from the table, the treatments are designed to be as similar as possible, regardless of the valence that Republicans or Democrats experienced. In each case, the vignette includes a message about either stocks or wages that included a large amount of congenial language. Consider terms like "stocks up," "strong gains," "rallied," "solid" in the Republican-congenial version of Treatment 1 to the language seen in the Democrats' version of the treatment: "dipped sharply," "growing concerns," "unsteady." In addition, we also see variation in the treatments in terms of the source: either a fictional economist named Bruce Sittenfeld is responsible for the quote in the document, or the text is attributable to Nancy Pelosi among Democrats and Paul Ryan among Republicans.

## QUESTIONNAIRE DESIGN

After treatment exposure, partisans were next shown a questionnaire designed to measure the impact of the treatments on respondents' perceptions of multiple economic performance indicators.[9] These included overall economic retrospections, which asked whether the economy

Table 5.1. Experimental Treatment Conditions, Study 5.1

**Treatment 1 (Stocks, No Party Cue):**
NEW YORK—Stocks [were up/dipped sharply] last week, [lending further evidence/adding to growing concerns] that the markets are headed for [even stronger gains/even bigger losses] in the near future. The Dow Jones [rallied substantially/experienced volatility] in the past quarter, as investors displayed a growing [appetite for/aversion to] risk and a striking [disregard/amount of concern] towards potential reversals. "Today's report continues to signal [a solid/ an unsteady] investing environment," said Bruce Sittenfeld, senior economist at RBS in Stamford, Connecticut.

**Treatment 2 (Wages, No Party Cue):**
NEW YORK—Last week's income report showed [strengthening/weakening] wage growth, lending mounting evidence to the view that American incomes will continue to [gain steadily/fall] across a number of sectors this year. The median salary among nonfarm employees [increased/decreased] 3 percent in the past quarter, and the rate was even higher among those working in service industries, the Labor Department said on Thursday. "Today's report continues to signal [solid/ faltering] middle-class wage growth," said Bruce Sittenfeld, senior economist at RBS in Stamford, Connecticut.

**Treatment 3 (Stocks, Party Cue):**
WASHINGTON—Congressional [Republicans/Democrats] are [enthusiastic/ worried] about the stock market. "Stocks [were up/dipped sharply] last week, [lending further evidence/adding to growing concerns] that the markets are headed for even [stronger gains/bigger losses] in the near future," [Speaker of the House Paul Ryan/House Minority Leader Nancy Pelosi] said in a prepared statement. "The Dow Jones [rallied substantially/has experienced worrying volatility] in the past quarter, as investors displayed a growing [appetite for/aversion to] risk and [a disregard/concern] towards potential reversals of fortune. Today's report continues to signal a [solid/unsteady] investing environment."

**Treatment 4 (Wages, Party Cue):**
WASHINGTON—Congressional [Republicans/Democrats] are [enthusiastic/ worried] about wages. "Last week's income report showed [strengthening/ weakening] wage growth, lending mounting evidence to the view that American incomes will continue to [gain steadily/fall] across a number of sectors this year," [Speaker of the House Paul Ryan/House Minority Leader Nancy Pelosi] said in a prepared statement. "The median salary among nonfarm employees [increased/ decreased] 3% in the past quarter, and the rate was even higher among those working in service industries. Today's report continues to signal [solid/faltering] middle-class wage growth."

had gotten "much better," "better," "worse," "much worse," or had stayed "about the same" over the past year. They also included measures tapping respondents' perceptions of the stock market and wages. These items were measured on the same five-point scale, generally written as "much worse" ranging to "much better."[10] The questions were presented in random order to prevent some indicators from receiving less attention than others due to the phenomenon known as satisficing (Krosnick 1991).

The questions asked of the respondents therefore constitute a broader array of economic perceptions than what is included on most national surveys. In addition to these dependent variable items, in a pretreatment battery, I asked respondents to provide demographic and perceptual information that helps us to describe the sample more accurately.[11] These measures include relevant political information, such as respondents' partisanship (and its strength) and their left-right ideology (measured on a seven-point scale).

RESULTS

The first goal of the present analysis is to examine the extent of partisan bias in the perceptions of untreated (control-group) respondents. This helps us to accomplish two things. First, it allows us to compare the pattern observed in chapter 4 to the present data, to ensure that the observational results replicate in the MTurk sample. Second, the analysis helps us to evaluate the pretreatment effects of the information environment on the stock market perceptions of partisans.

We should not expect the control group in the sample to be free of bias, even though they have not been exposed to congenial economic information as in the case of the other treatments. Figure 5.1 shows the percent of Republicans and Democrats in the study who thought each indicator had performed "better" or "the same" (as opposed to "worse").

The control-group-only comparison in figure 5.1 shows us that across the economic topics included in the question battery, partisans' rates of disagreement varied substantially. On the left side of the figure, we see that Democrats and Republicans were both far more than 50 percent likely to say the overall economy had gotten better, indicating optimism on average for both groups. But the "gap" between Republican and Democrat respondents was substantial, with more than 90 percent of Republicans looking forward to "morning in America" compared to only 74 percent of Democrats.

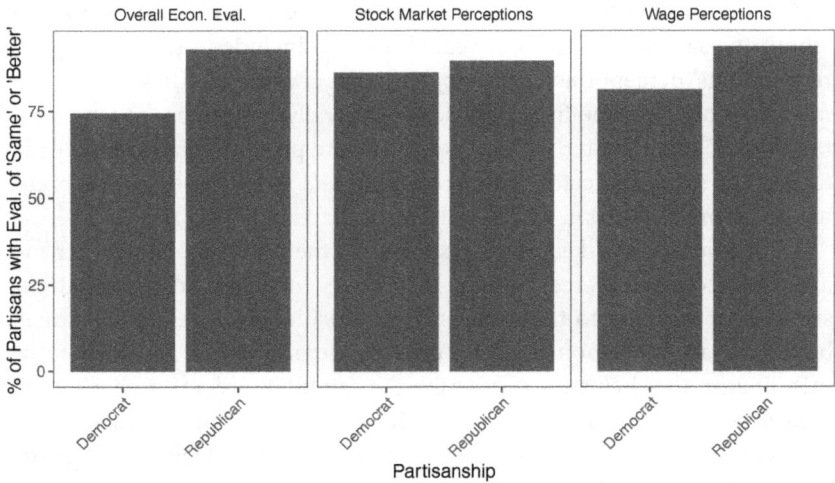

Figure 5.1. Partisan disagreement in three economic topics, control group only. *Source*: Author's own material.

In comparison, views on the stock market (in the center panel of figure 5.1) were quite similar for both partisan groups. Eighty-nine percent of Republicans thought the stock market was performing well in 2018, compared to 86 percent of Democrats. This 3 percent gap was not statistically significant in a t-test comparison. However, wage growth (seen in the rightmost panel) showed a statistically significant gap ($p < 0.05$) that resembled that seen for the overall economy measure. Around 93 percent of Republicans thought wage growth had improved or stayed the same, compared to about 80 percent of Democrats.

In addition to lending additional support for the patterns seen in chapter 4, figure 5.1 also assuages a potential methodological concern. The fact that partisan bias differed from one economic perception to the next tells us that respondents considered each economic item as a separate concept. Rather than "straight-lining" their way through this economic perceptions battery, Republicans and Democrats asked themselves whether each facet of the economy was truly improving or not.

TREATMENT EFFECTS

Next, we can assess the effects of experimental treatment exposure on perceptions of wage growth and stock market performance. To do this,

I divide Republican and Democratic respondents into separate groups. This is because the experimental treatment effects are expected to run in opposite directions for the two parties.

Among Republicans in the control group, we would expect mostly positive economic evaluations because of the combined effects of pre-exposure and motivated reasoning. These evaluations should then become even *more* positive among Republicans in treated groups.[12] Among Democrats, we should see less enthusiasm in the control group, and even more negativity among those in the treatment groups. In figure 5.2, I show these partisan treatment effects for Republicans (seen in the right panel) and Democrats (seen in the left panel). For ease of interpretation, I rescale the economic evaluation variable to a continuous scale ranging from 0 (most negative) to 1 (most positive). On both sides of the figure, the control group estimate is seen in the leftmost bar. The vertical lines for each treatment group show 90 percent (black) and 95 percent (grey) confidence intervals surrounding the point estimates. Please see the appendix for tabular model results.

While H1 and H2 might lead us to expect significant upward (downward) shifts among Republicans (Democrats) in each treatment group, the rival expectation summarized by H3 finds greater support. Figure 5.2 demonstrates that relative to the control groups for both parties, only

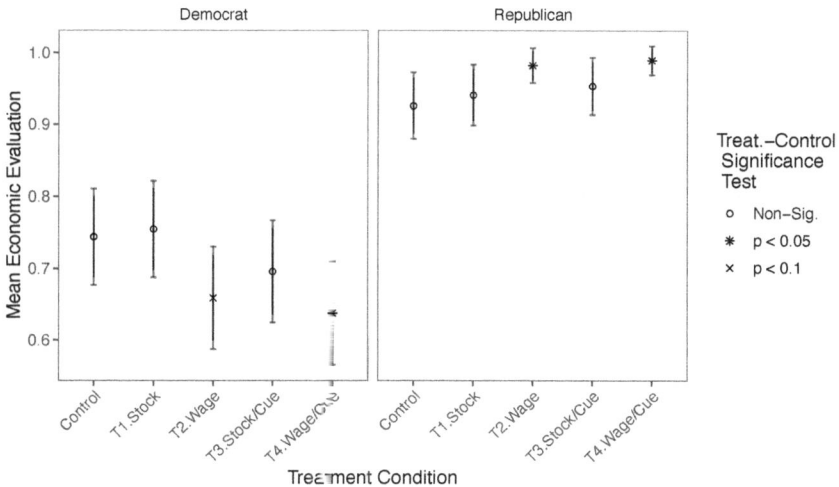

Figure 5.2. Effect of treatment conditions on partisans' economic evaluations. *Source*: Author's own material.

certain treatments yielded increasingly polarized economic perceptions. Consistent with H3's assumptions about experimental pretreatment, stories that focus on wage growth are far more influential on overall economic perceptions than those focusing on stock performance.

Interestingly, this pattern prevailed *regardless* of the source cue. No matter whether the story was attributed to Nancy Pelosi, Paul Ryan, or an economist, wage-growth stories produced treatment effects, while stock market stories did not. Among Democrats, wage-growth news from professional economists yielded around 8 percent more negativity (p = 0.09), whereas partisan sources increased the negativity of evaluations by around 11 percent (p = 0.03). Among Republicans, wage-growth news drove evaluations in a more positive direction in both nonpartisan and partisan cueing conditions ($\delta$ = 0.056, p = 0.03; $\delta$ = 0.063, p = 0.02, respectively). Because respondents already had access to a large amount of information about stock prices, these treatments (which were otherwise identical to those in the wage-growth condition) had little additional influence on economic perceptions. According to these results, partisans may have already factored their knowledge of the stock market in to their broader economic judgments, resulting in no significant differences between the treatment groups and the control group.

Figure 5.3 also allows us to assess the degree of *polarization* that occurs in response to economic news exposure. This figure shows the

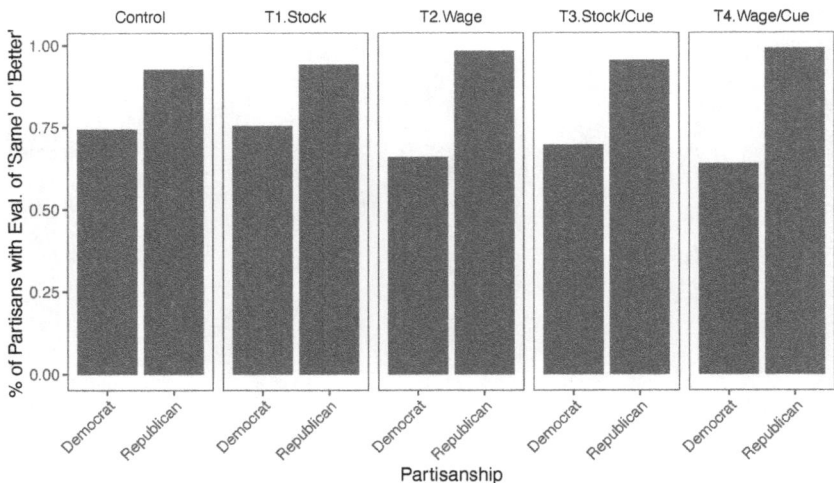

Figure 5.3. Effect of treatment conditions on partisans' economic evaluations. *Source*: Author's own material.

pattern of partisan bias across treatment groups when partisans reflect on overall economic retrospections. Each pair of bars in the figure shows the distance between the average Republican and the average Democratic economic evaluation in the treatment conditions. The control group's economic perceptions are biased, as seen in figure 5.1 above, with a difference of roughly 16 percentage points. However, relative to the control group, the partisan bias expressed by all the treatment groups is greater. In response to all the treatments, Republicans move towards the positive end of the scale in each treatment (almost reaching the maximum possible value of 100 percent), whereas Democrats move in a negative direction.

However, it is only in T2 and T4 (the wage-growth conditions) that these partisan gaps become *significantly* greater than under the control condition ($p < 0.05$ in both instances based on $\chi^2$ tests for significance). Much like we saw in chapter 4, it is only after exposure to seldom-reported economic data that partisans can turn up the bias. When it comes to the stock market, pretreatment effects attenuate the effect of treatment exposure. Since partisans have already heard much about the stock market in news—some of it disconfirming—the effects of a vignette-style treatment on partisans' evaluations are relatively small.

## THE IMPORTANCE OF ECONOMIC DATA

While study 5.1's main results seem to indicate the presence (and absence) of pretreatment effects across economic topics, one additional possibility is that stock market information does not impact perceptions because people do not think its movement matters for the broader economy. Study 4.2 shows using observational evidence that many Americans *do* think the stock market is an important signal for economic performance. But the question remains unexamined in these data. Are stories about wage growth more influential on economic perceptions because people ascribe greater importance to this type of information?

Study 5.1, consistent with study 4.2, shows evidence to the contrary. Partisans do trust the stock market as a source of valuable economic data—but their pre-exposure limits the degree to which they can use this information for cheerleading purposes. First, we can consider the correlations between respondents' overall economic perceptions and the specific indicators they were asked to evaluate. Table 5.2 reports the correlations between all economic perceptions captured in the data, among members of the control group only. An analysis of this group helps us understand the nature of experimental pre-exposure because these respondents were never exposed

Table 5.2. Correlation Matrix, Three Economic Perceptions

|  | Overall Evaluations | Wage Perceptions | Stock Market Perceptions |
|---|---|---|---|
| Overall Evaluations | 1.00 | 0.35 | 0.59 |
| Wage Perceptions | 0.35 | 1.00 | 0.36 |
| Stock Market Perceptions | 0.59 | 0.36 | 1.00 |

to a treatment. Strong correlations between overall economic retrospections (the top-leftmost item) and other economic perceptions among members of the control group would tell us that Americans associate these economic topics in their minds. Low correlations would suggest that the economic topics are unrelated in respondents' understanding of economic reality.

Perhaps unsurprisingly given what we know from study 4.2, we see that wage-growth perceptions are strongly correlated with overall economic perceptions. With a correlation coefficient of 0.35, there is a very good chance that a respondent who thought wage growth was getting "much better" also thought the overall economy was getting "much better." But when it comes to the stock market, we see an even higher correlation coefficient ($r = 0.59$). Consistent with the results of study 4.2, this correlation coefficient is higher still among the Republicans in the sample. A correlation does not definitively prove that Americans value stock market information more than all other economic information when they reflect upon the overall economy. But it does show that to a greater extent than wage growth, the two items are associated in respondents' (and especially Republicans') minds.

BIAS WILL FIND A WAY? THE RELATIVE IMPORTANCE OF ECONOMIC TOPICS

A second way we can assess whether respondents care about the indicators in study 5.1 is to ask them. After exposure to the treatments and the collection of the eight economic perceptions listed above in figure 5.1, respondents were asked, "How important is [the stock market/wage growth] for the economic well-being of ordinary Americans?" The item was measured on a 0–100 scale. The results not only afford us a basic measure of the perceived importance of the two topics; they also show us the effects of treatment exposure on beliefs about the *meaning* of economic data. Following study 4.2, I expect exposure to partisan-congenial information to shift these beliefs.

Figure 5.4 shows the effects of treatment exposure on partisans' beliefs about the importance of the stock market for the broader economy. The first major pattern to emerge from this figure is the wide gap between Republicans' and Democrats' beliefs about this topic. Republicans in the control group, who were not exposed to any new economic information, were significantly more likely than Democrats to believe the stock market matters for the well-being of "ordinary Americans" ($\delta = 12.99$, $p < 0.001$). This control-group gap, much like the gap witnessed in chapter 4, may reflect the effects of recent framing efforts described in chapter 3.

For the moment, the more valuable insight to emerge from figure 5.4 is the lack of discernible treatment effects. Republicans and Democrats across the treatment conditions rate the stock market above fifty on the one-hundred-point importance thermometer in all conditions, both experimental and control; any shifts in the pattern are very small. While some of these treatment effects are in the expected direction (Republicans exposed to a cue-free stock market story in treatment 1, for example, increase their importance score by 3.7 points on average; $p = 0.19$) the effects are statistically indistinguishable from zero. Thus, it seems that

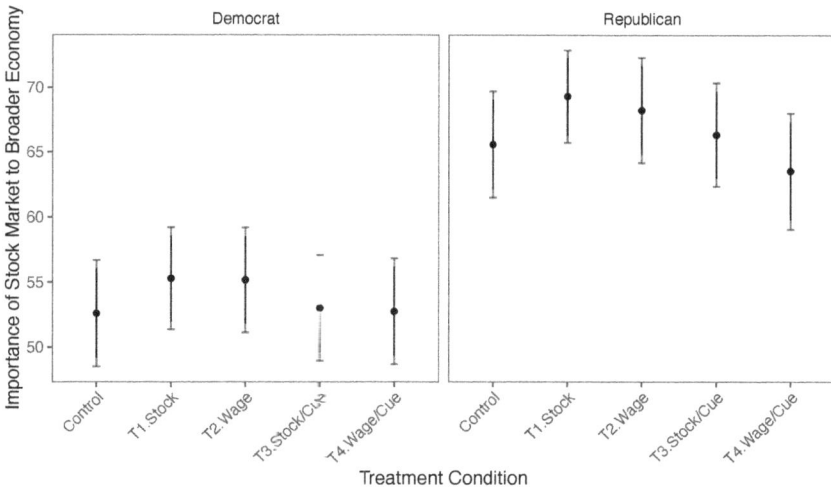

Figure 5.4. Effect of treatment conditions on partisans' beliefs about the importance of the stock market. *Source*: Author's own material.

exposure to congenial information has little influence on respondents' already-strong beliefs about the importance of stock market information. Respondents across the partisan spectrum hold the stock market in high regard as a meaningful indicator of economic performance.

Figure 5.5 next shows the effects of the treatments on partisans' beliefs about the importance of wage growth. Once again, we see that these effects are statistically indistinguishable from zero in all cases. Interestingly, it appears that many respondents highly value wage growth as an indicator of broader economic performance. Control-group Democrats ($\mu = 82.33$) and Republicans ($\mu = 77.36$) exhibited a small but significant difference in the average importance score ($\delta = 4.96$, p = 0.03), also in the expected direction given that recent trends in wage growth were not as congenial to Republicans as other economic information at the time of the study. But the broader pattern is one of relative consensus that wage growth is a meaningful indicator for the overall economy.

Despite these beliefs, it appears that the treatments did little to convince Republicans and Democrats to shift their beliefs about the subject's importance. No treatment effect achieved significance, though Republicans exposed to treatment 4 (positive wage-growth news with a party cue) did experience a slight increase in their belief that wage growth matters for ordinary people ($\delta = 4.04$, p = 0.07).

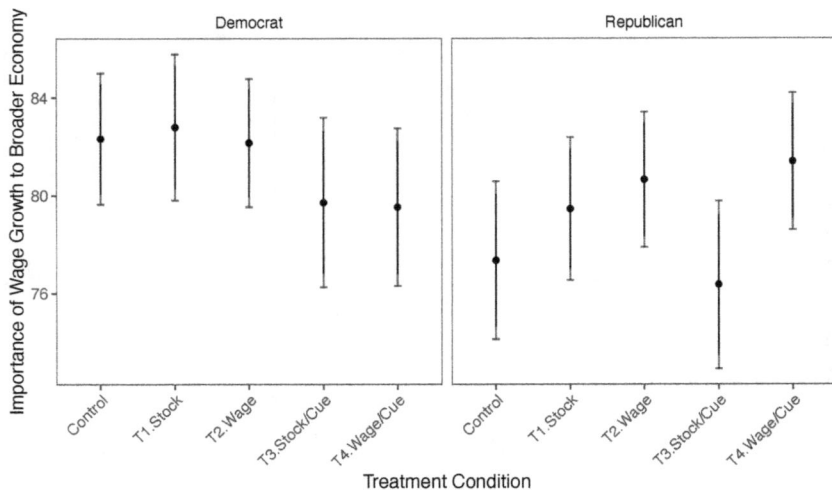

Figure 5.5. Effect of treatment conditions on partisans' beliefs about the importance of wage growth. *Source*: Author's own material.

Taken together, these results show that partisans' "economic narratives" are less flexible than overall economic perceptions. In the absence of pretreatment effects, persuasive economic cues can powerfully shape partisans' beliefs about the economy. However, when it comes to beliefs about the importance of economic data, even these kinds of cues may have also been the subject of powerful pretreatment exposure. Regardless of whether Republicans and Democrats receive congenial economic information, Republicans seem to always value the stock market more than Democrats as an economic indicator, at least during the Trump administration when this study was conducted.

STUDY 5.1: SUMMARY

Our exploration of experimental evidence has lent support to a variety of proposals contained in chapter 1. We have seen how the effectiveness of economic cues vary due to the persistent agenda-setting of economic topics. We have shown that Americans' assessments of the importance of different types of economic data are resistant to new information exposure. And we have suggestive evidence in favor of the idea that stock market perceptions are meaningfully correlated with overall economic perceptions—at least among the unrepresentative sample of respondents in our study.

However, this line of inquiry can only take us so far. While we know more about the effects of persistent agenda setting in shaping the limits of partisan bias, we have seen this effect in a highly artificial survey environment. Next, I examine economic news exposure under a more realistic setting, in which partisans can "choose their news" when learning new facts about the economy. Specifically, in a highly competitive online news environment, partisans might select stories that are expected to provide them with a congenial economic narrative.

## Study 5.2: Self-Selection and Economic News

In study 5.2, a nationally representative sample of GfK (formerly KnowledgePanel) respondents were contacted between January 21 and 31 of 2016 (N = 2,030).[13] The survey experiment was designed to measure the effects of exposure to news coverage of three different economic indicators (the stock market, wages and income, and unemployment) on the economic perceptions of citizens.

Subjects were first presented with a question asking them to indicate which of the three economic indicators they would be most interested in reading about.[14] Topics were presented to respondents in random order, to avoid any question effects on respondents' selections. Subjects self-selected into three groups: those interested in receiving the stock market condition, those interested in the wages and income treatment, and those interested in unemployment.

The next step was to randomly assign these subjects to treatment and control conditions within their preference group. Fifty percent of subjects in each economic indicator condition were exposed to their preferred story, while the rest were exposed to a control condition which contained no economic information. In this way, study 5.2 allows us to examine the effects of learning about a preferred economic indicator, after accounting for the desire to select this information in the first place. In contrast to study 5.1, which assigned this information fully at random, we now have a more realistic experimental condition that engages the notion that different people willingly create differences in their economic information environment by seeking out different kinds of economic information.

Treatment conditions can be seen in table 5.3. The treatments once again expose respondents to information about a variety of economic topics. One marked difference between study 5.1 and study 5.2 is that the latter set of treatments is insensitive to the partisan congeniality of the content. In each case, both Republicans and Democrats were exposed to positive information, which is congenial to Democrats during the Obama administration, and disconfirming to Republicans.

The outcome of interest in the experiment is once again respondents' retrospective perceptions of the overall economy (the standard economic retrospection question examined in study 5.1 and elsewhere). In the results that follow, I examine the effects of the treatments on Republicans' and Democrats' beliefs that the economy had recently performed "better" or "the same" (1) relative to "worse" (0).

## Results: Study 5.2

Study 5.2's results provide support for the present hypotheses. First, I take up the question introduced by H4: When does partisan motivated reasoning drive respondents' interest in economic news topics? We expect partisans to choose topics in a biased fashion when their pre-existing knowledge of an indicator's recent performance is strong (a consequence of pretreatment exposure). When the indicator's performance is not well

Table 5.3. Experimental Treatment Conditions, Study 5.2

---

**Stock Market Treatment:**
NEW YORK—Stocks were up last week, lending further evidence that the markets are headed for even stronger gains. The Dow Jones rallied substantially in the past quarter, as investors displayed a growing appetite for risk and a striking lack of concern about any reversal of fortune. "Today's report continues to signal a solid investing environment that is likely to maintain its bullishness," said Omair Sharif, senior economist at RBS in Stamford, Connecticut.

**Wages and Income Treatment:**
NEW YORK—Wage growth strengthened last month, bolstering the view that American incomes will continue to gain steadily across a number of sectors. The median salary among workers in manufacturing increased 3 percent in the past quarter, and the rate was even higher among those working in service industries, the Labor Department said on Thursday. "Today's report continues to signal solid middle-class wage growth that is accompanied by remarkably low volatility," said Omair Sharif, senior economist at RBS in Stamford, Connecticut.

**Unemployment Treatment:**
NEW YORK—The number of Americans filing new claims for unemployment benefits fell more than expected last week, and the trend continued to support views that the labor market is strengthening. Initial claims for unemployment benefits fell 21,000 to a seasonally adjusted 311,000 for the past week, the Labor Department said on Thursday. "Today's report continues to signal a solid labor market that is experiencing a very low pace of layoffs," said Omair Sharif, senior economist at RBS in Stamford, Connecticut.

**Control:**
NEW YORK—Verizon once again has bragging rights in the wireless industry. The carrier took top honors in a new ranking of nationwide network performance by market research firm RootMetrics. Verizon ranked number one for reliability, speed, call and data performance, with AT&T a close second in all those categories. Those two firms held a significant advantage over third-ranked T-Mobile and fourth-ranked Sprint. RootMetrics conducted the study through the use of national surveys.

---

known, however, partisans will not possess the ability to select a topic based on its congeniality. Furthermore, we might also expect partisans to seek out information that they do not already know a great deal about, due to the inherent utility of learning as much as possible about economic conditions.

In January 2016, the stock market performed poorly, whereas unemployment improved, and wage growth remained flat. Based on these data, as well as the agenda-setting behavior of the press, we would expect the stock market to be a topic for which partisanship exerts a strong effect on respondents' choices. Republicans, aware of the stock market's recent troubles, should choose to learn about the topic more so than Democrats, who should seek to ignore the disconfirming nature of the stock market's recent slump. Next, unemployment is expected to be the second most partisan choice, followed by wage growth as the choice least influenced by partisan considerations due to its relatively rare inclusion in economic news reports. Figure 5.6 provides evidence that is largely consistent with this set of expectations.

Within the panels in figure 5.6, we see the effect of partisanship on willingness to choose news about stock market performance (leftmost panel), unemployment (center panel), and wage growth (rightmost panel). Whereas Republicans (23.9 percent) are more interested in the stock market than Democrats (15.3 percent) by a significant margin ($\delta$ = 8.59, p < 0.001), the partisan gap for unemployment news was still significant but much smaller ($\delta$ = 3.98, p < 0.01). We also see relatively more interest overall in unemployment, again supporting the notion that

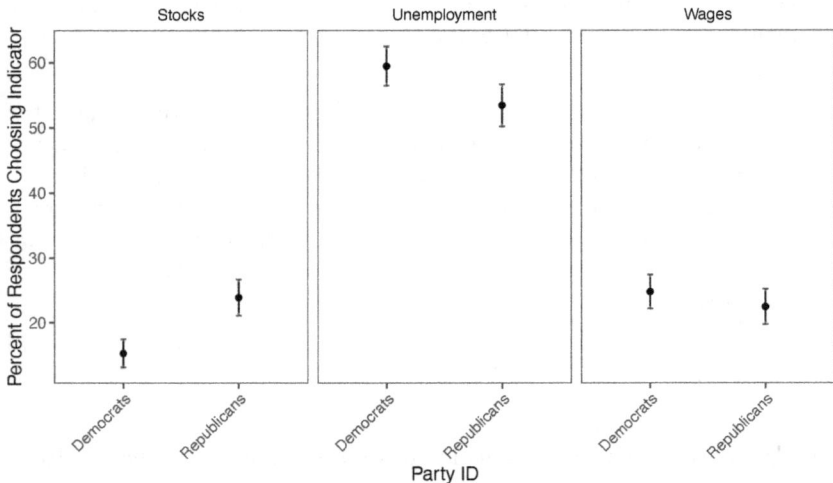

Figure 5.6. Percent of partisans choosing to read about three economic topics, study 5.2. *Source*: Author's own material.

respondents were pre-exposed to stock market information. Republicans and Democrats have likely been previously exposed to information about the stock market's recent performance, meaning that their willingness to learn new things about the indicator is shaped by partisan considerations.

In contrast to these two indicators, wage growth exhibited a non-significant difference between Democrats' and Republicans' rate of story selection ($\delta = 2.32$). It may be that because this indicator has *not* been the subject of pre-exposure, partisan respondents were unable to determine whether news about this topic would be congenial or not. And because the topic is so rarely covered in news, surprisingly few partisans on either side of the aisle were interested in learning about it—despite its pivotal importance for middle-class well-being.

Since pretreatment effects appear to influence partisans in a news choice environment, we should also expect experimental treatment effects in study 5.2 to follow a similar pattern as those seen in study 5.1. While the treatments in this case only expose Democrats to congenial information, the strongest evidence for treatment effects should still pertain to wage growth (a topic about which respondents knew little in advance), whereas stock market news should have a limited impact on partisans' beliefs about the economy. This pattern can be seen in figure 5.7.

The results presented in figure 5.7 once again show evidence that Republicans and Democrats were not strongly affected by the treatments they read about the stock market. In the left panel of the figure, we see that Republicans ($\delta = -0.14$) and Democrats ($\delta = 0.11$) adjusted their view of the economy only a small fraction of a point on a 1–5 scale. These effects are not statistically significant, reaffirming the view that pretreatment effects cause additional information about the stock market to have little impact on well-informed perceptions. We do see that partisans move in opposite directions on this scale, even though both Republicans and Democrats in the study learned something positive about stocks. The differences, however, are indistinguishable from random chance and should not be construed as a "backlash" effect among Republicans.

Under the unemployment and wage growth treatments, we see results that are more consistent with information updating. Exposure to a positive unemployment story increased the positivity of both Republicans' ($\delta = 0.19$) and Democrats' ($\delta = 0.16$) perceptions. These larger effects approach statistical significance among Democratic respondents ($p = 0.07$), consistent with the idea that congeniality helps to encourage a treatment effect. The relatively large number of respondents choosing

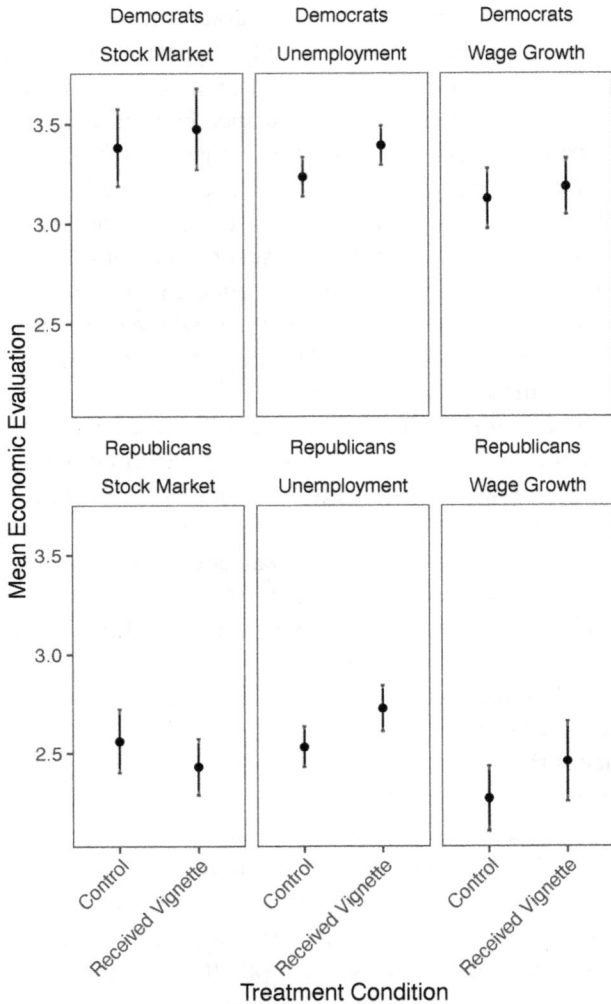

Figure 5.7. Effect of treatment conditions on partisans' economic perceptions, study 5.2. *Source*: Author's own material.

to learn about unemployment also helps increase the chances that we see a significant result for this group.

The results for wage growth, in contrast, are partially obscured by the fact that few participants chose to read about it. The results do, however, run in the expected direction and show large average effects. Republicans ($\delta = 0.19$, $p < 0.10$) increase their economic optimism in response to the story. Results for Democrats in this condition are closer to zero ($\delta = 0.06$), perhaps suggesting that for this small group of respondents, pre-treatment effects do exist due to greater interest in the subject. However, since the treatment and control conditions in these groups are so small, it is hard to draw strong conclusions about the specific point estimates. For unemployment, where we do observe an adequate sample size, the results are more consistent with our expectations.

## Conclusions

Together, the tests performed in chapters 2–4 have shown us that partisans' views of the economy are contingent upon several factors, including the information environment, incumbency, and the real economy. They show that partisan identities are powerful determinants of Americans' beliefs about the facts—until information saturation reins in partisans' ability to rationalize. None of these findings is particularly controversial given the findings in existing literature. But the discovery that different *types* of economic information are simultaneously more or less polarized in the minds of partisans reveals a variety of new directions for empirical research on motivated reasoning.

Based on these findings, we have more evidence in support of an agenda-setting explanation for polarized economic perceptions. The economic "information context," combined with the willingness or unwillingness of partisan elites to take up a specific indicator to suit a partisan narrative, are likely to combine to shape the contours of partisan motivated reasoning. The findings presented above may assuage readers concerned about the possibility that we are soon approaching the "end" of performance voting (Achen and Bartels 2017; Anderson 2007). Instead, it appears that ubiquitously mentioned economic indicators (principally the stock market) are invulnerable to framing efforts, even when accompanied by strong party elite cues.

But as Bisgaard (2015) helpfully reminds us, "bias will find a way." It remains to be seen how and whether entrepreneurial communicators in the post-2020 environment will expand the reach of their attempts at economic persuasion. As Donald Trump has recently taken on the stock market as a framing target, the rapidly shifting contours of elite communication mean that this topic will require ongoing empirical research in the near future.

The evidence contained in studies 5.1 and 5.2 highlight a second dimension of partisan motivated reasoning. When exposed to stories about two different economic indicators, Republicans and Democrats are willing to update their overall economic perceptions in light of what they have learned. But when constructing economic perceptions, partisans also construct different narratives that justify and support these associations. Stock prices and wage growth might both tell partisans something they like to hear. But the *meaning* of those movements for the lived experience of middle-class Americans is radically different. As partisanship infects Americans' "economic narratives," the meaning of economic perceptions changes. But so too has the economy itself experienced important changes over the past several decades, requiring us to think carefully about what economic perceptions mean for politics in an era of persistent inequality.

In this volume's concluding chapter, I take up the question of the stock market's broader political effects. In studies 5.1 and 5.2 we saw evidence that stock market perceptions predict respondents' *overall* economic evaluations, just as in study 4.3 we saw how the stock market matters more now than ever for Americans' judgments of political incumbents. Applying the lessons learned in this chapter and those before it sheds new light on the ways that Americans understand (and fail to understand) politics in an unequal American democracy.

# Conclusions

Perhaps the most distinctive feature of contemporary American politics is its intense partisan antipathy. Republican and Democratic Party identifiers have come to dislike each other more and more over recent decades, and there is little evidence to suggest that the trend will soon reverse (Mason 2018). Partisans find each other to be morally contemptible. They think their opponents are just about always wrong about how to make America better, perhaps because they possess the wrong values. Americans might not always find things to like about members of their own party, either. But even if partisans are vocally critical of their own party's elites, they almost always find even worse things to say about their opponents.

Despite increasing extremism among small factions of sophisticated, committed partisans, most Republicans and Democrats still have a great deal of common ground. Beyond ideological (dis)agreement, most Americans share basic material priorities. Partisans of all stripes often name the economy as the most important problem facing America today. They share the belief that economic growth is better than economic stagnation. They are concerned about the retrenchment of programs like social security.[1] They share a vision of the American dream that places prosperity for the middle class as the topmost priority. And while their beliefs about the past, present, and future performance of the economy can often conflict, Americans share a remarkably accurate and unbiased understanding of the roller-coaster fluctuations of US stock markets.

In this volume, we have seen what happens when antagonistic partisans, sharing in the pursuit of a more prosperous nation, wrestle with economic reality. Motivated reasoning causes partisans in similar economic circumstances to view the economy far differently. This is in part because the economy is more complex than most observers assume. As we have seen, the wide variety of economic data available to the public means that partisans can be picky about which facts to use in support of their beliefs. Often, economic topics can be framed in ways that make partisans feel good about themselves and their parties. Occasionally, however, economic information becomes difficult for partisans to rationalize away. The ubiquity of the stock market as a source of economic data, in particular, means that Republicans and Democrats often "follow the ticker" as a way to measure economic and political performance. When these citizens evaluate political incumbents, the movement of the stock market drives their enthusiasm—and their displeasure.

While we now know much more about the details of Americans' economic perceptions, the economy itself is currently evolving. Ongoing economic globalization means that domestic economic progress is becoming more strongly influenced by volatility and prosperity abroad. Along with exposure to the fluctuations of global markets, we are also witnessing the strengthening of capital as an influence on the domestic economy. In the ongoing COVID-19 pandemic, we are seeing the rapid acceleration of this long-term trend. While American industry has lagged in recent decades, finance has grown in its importance as a share of gross domestic product (GDP). In fact, the share of GDP jointly accounted for by finance, insurance, and real estate (FIRE) has more than doubled since 1947.[2]

In this concluding chapter, I comment upon the meaning of stock market perceptions for the future of American voting behavior. I assert that an increasingly financialized economy, paired with an increased focus on the stock market as a source of political evaluations, will bolster ongoing misperceptions about economic inequality. I further argue that the financialization of our economy may lead to newly "financialized citizens" who conceive of politics through a broader market-driven lens. Next, I discuss how the findings presented in this volume revise our understanding of partisan motivated reasoning, economic voting, and economic journalism.

Together, these observations make the case for continued research on stock market perceptions in a "two-speed" American economy. Rising inequality is a threat to Americans' ability to engage in meaningful performance voting, especially as motivated reasoning obfuscates the performance voting task. However, economic journalists can help Americans become more knowledgeable and accurate about the status of the middle-class economy, acting as pivotal agenda setters in a highly saturated media environment.

## Financialization and Political Accountability

As the American financial sector grows, the linkage between political decisions and economic outcomes is changing. Domestic and international financial markets are increasingly powerful vis-à-vis national governments, with major consequences for voting and accountability. Financial actors can reshape the sphere of policy making, putting constraints on governments' ability to steer the economy (Mosley 2003). These constraints can cause voters to discount incumbents' actions, as savvy citizens understand that incumbents lack the 'room to maneuver" around the needs of international investors (Hellwig and Samuels 2008). Increasingly, we see that global economies are constraining political decision makers.

Equity markets are particularly notable in their effects upon governments and the policy agendas of legislators. Mosley and Singer (2008) demonstrate that investors react to capital controls by divesting from nations' markets. These risks cause politicians to balance the priorities of investors and constituents when considering policy alternatives. As financial markets become important parts of domestic economies, they also put pressure on politicians to respond to their demands for a friendly investment climate.

Politicians also experience increased pressure from lobbyists associated with the financial sector, resulting in policies designed to protect and encourage particularly lucrative financial products (Witko 2016). The resulting economic deregulation drives inequality, counteracts efforts to secure higher wages for workers, and drowns out demands for protection against economic catastrophes. At each step in the democratic process, there is mounting evidence that financial interests are tipping the scales of policy making in their favor.

Before any policy making occurs, however, voters support or reject incumbents at the polls based on their performance in office. In this volume, we have seen that stock markets are often on the minds of ordinary Americans. While some middle-class Americans are becoming more active traders and investors, those who have little to no money invested are also exposed to a large volume of stock market news. As political elites seek "room to maneuver" around financial actors, the voters who provide them with the consent to govern are directly and indirectly influenced by the movement of stock market indicators.

Basic political accountability holds that voters reward and punish incumbents for their performance in office. As both voters and politicians turn their attention to the stock market, many observers have wondered whether the accountability linkage is affected by the movement of the stock market ticker. Notable among these voices is Piketty (2015), who provides a sweeping reinterpretation of the role of capital in driving neo-liberal politics and globalization. Lordon (2000) similarly observes that financialization has supplanted Fordism as the dominant mode of wealth accumulation in modern societies, as worker productivity and real wages diminish in importance relative to the value of investors' dividends (see also Lapavitsas 2013).

While these recent contributions suggest a role for stock markets in driving the politics of developed countries, the present study provides a more direct test of this premise. The present volume has shown that Americans' approval of incumbent presidents is increasingly aligned with the stock market. In keeping with studies of Americans' knowledge of inequality and middle-class economic performance, the results in this book show evidence that stock market news has a prevailing—and perhaps unwarranted—influence on Americans' political attitudes. Americans attend to economic information to help them make more informed political decisions. But despite the rise of social movements that point out the disconnect between the financial sector and the rest of the American economy, media agenda setting innocuously leads the stock market to occupy a "top-of-mind" position in the economic evaluations of many middle-class citizens.

## Financialized Citizens

To further examine the political consequences of financialization of the American economy, future research might consider how citizens trained to participate in a market environment come to view politics through a market-oriented lens. In his notable recent book, Porter (2020) asserts the rise of the "consumer citizen," a rational actor who makes political decisions based on the highly practiced behaviors native to the consumer context, rather than the political realm. The consequences of Americans' use of familiar consumer habits in political affairs are manifold and result in a variety of problems in the realms of public opinion, voting behavior, and participation in government-sponsored programs. Consumer citizens, having learned how to engage with public life through shopping experiences, appraise their government like a firm and are surprised and sometimes angered when government subverts their consumer expectations.

The central premise of Porter's (2020) volume—that citizens apply learned behaviors from an unrelated part of daily life to politics—resonates with the fact that many Americans are quickly becoming direct participants in the stock market. The rise of hands-on "retail investing" has been joined in recent times by widespread interest in cryptocurrency, nonfungible tokens (NFTs), and other unregulated, high-risk investment vehicles. Regardless of the type of investment, more so than ever, Americans are purchasing stocks, digital currencies, and financial assets themselves, rather than entrusting their savings to fund managers (to say nothing of the near nonexistence of contemporary pension funds). Presently, millions of Americans are rapidly gaining experience as do-it-yourself investors.

In addition to the consequences for political judgments that stem from unconscious *exposure* to stock market information, future researchers might also think about how conscious investor *experience* influences assumptions about the political world. For one thing, investing exposes participants to risk, which might spur an increased desire to maintain the status quo in the political realm (thus shielding investors from potential volatility). On the other hand, investing might teach participants to become more risk tolerant, leading Americans to seek out political causes that promise to "disrupt" the current political situation to their benefit. Further, investing might teach participants perverse lessons about short- and long-run gains, causing them to support candidates who propose immediate (but potentially ill-advised) solutions for complex, long-term political problems.

Whatever the specific outcome may be, it seems likely that future investment behavior will alter at least some individuals' ideological assumptions. For example, many cryptocurrency investors, spurred by a belief in the medium of exchange as an alternative to the monopoly on government control of currency, preach a libertarian, or even "anarcho-capitalist," view of politics (Bogost 2017). These political philosophies center the individual as the central nexus of politics, much in the same way that individual retail investing strips away the institutional support of fund managers and financial advisors. Retail trading premises a competition between the individual and rival market participants, with the goal of obtaining profit through savvy trading choices. We might theorize a wide variety of attitudinal and behavioral political consequences stemming from Americans' increased willingness to engage in this fundamentally atomistic form of economic interaction.

## Social Movements and Economic Attitudes

While individual investing is an atomizing experience, in recent years, cooperative social movements have also arisen in response to the perceived growth of finance's political influence. Occupy Wall Street is a global movement founded in 2011 that shuns hierarchical organization in favor of organic, consensus-based decision making. Its primary demands include the dismantling of corporate influence on the political process, a reduction of inequality within and across nations, debt relief, and the reform of the financial services sector (Calhoun 2013). As this movement has evolved, its purpose has clarified. Documents created by contributors to the movement have identified the capitalist underpinnings of modern liberal democracy as the source of widespread social ills. In France, for example, the "Nuit Debout" movement began in response to labor reforms supported by Emmanuel Macron, and shares elements of this sweeping critique of capital (Brustier 2016).

These anticapital and antiausterity demonstrations sought to raise awareness about the incompatibility of modern financial capitalism with egalitarian visions of democracy. Embedded in this critique is the simple lesson that "the stock market is not the economy." However, now more than ten years after the financial crisis of 2008, it is not clear that these lessons have been internalized by the majority of the American public. While candidates for office such as Bernie Sanders have incorporated the language of Occupy Wall Street in their communications, seeking to caution Americans that stock prices can be symptomatic of economic trends which do not portend prosperity for the middle class, the public opinion literature tells us that Americans have not become substantially more sympathetic to anti-inequality policy proposals over the past decade (K.-S. Trump 2018).

Nor, in fact, are Americans very good at understanding the contours of contemporary inequality in the first place. Gimpelson and Treisman (2018) examine data from the International Social Survey Project, which interviewed respondents across twenty-four countries about their incomes and the distribution of inequality in their countries. One particularly relevant item in the survey asked participants to think about five different shapes that describe income distributions. Some were thick at the bottom and narrow at the top, whereas others included an inverse triangle, a uniform distribution, a diamond, and an hourglass shape. Respondents were asked to report which of the shapes best reflected their society's wealth distribution. While some countries' respondents did well on the task, accurately identifying the shape that best corresponded to that nation's distribution of wealth as measured by the Gini coefficient, on average, Americans did only slightly better than guesswork. While partisan polarization might infect a wide variety of economic perceptions, Americans' misperceptions about inequality are also symptomatic of a widespread lack of knowledge about earnings and wealth.

Critiques of stock market-oriented politics have nevertheless begun to receive more mainstream attention on the left side of the American political spectrum. Critics like Raul Grijalva and Alexandria Ocasio-Cortez are leading a young crop of progressive Democrats in Congress, who are generally sympathetic to the goals of the Occupy movement. Consequently, we have seen increasing discussion on the floor of the House and Senate that the "stock market is not the economy." Critics such as Elizabeth Warren have laid out the case that the modern economy is treating middle- and lower-class Americans qualitatively and quantitatively differently than the wealthy. At the time of this writing, the Congressional Progressive Caucus includes ninety-eight members in the House and one member in the Senate. These incumbents agree upon a primary stated goal of "fighting for economic justice and security in the U.S. and global economies" (Congressional Progressive Caucus 2022). Economic perceptions, concerns about inequality, and critiques of the role of finance in the modern political system are becoming increasingly linked to partisan contestation.

## Stock Market Perceptions and the Depoliticization of Personal Experience

With this social and economic backstory in focus, we can better understand the consequences of Americans' preoccupation with the stock market as a source of economic information. While this indicator of economic progress has little to do with the day-to-day lived experience of members of the middle class, it stands out as a prime example of the "depoliticized" mediated information about the US economy that is so crucial to the process through which Americans construct their understanding of the economic past, present, and future (Mutz 1992). This learning process might paradoxically cause Americans to suffer from increasingly acute *mis*perceptions about economic inequality and the plight of working people.

In this volume, we have traced economic perceptions to their sources in national media and found that the agenda of economic news does not square well with the reality of the American economy. Most central to this critique is the notion that while economic news might tell us much about the performance of corporations and CEOs, on a day-to-day basis, it tells us very little about the economic conditions of wage earners. Consider a collection of hypothetical news stories. In one month, we might read that the Dow Jones experienced mixed performance, Jeff Bezos saw his wealth increase by billions, Amazon reported slower-than-expected earnings, and Amazon's warehouse employees were driven to the point of exhaustion after working in hazardous conditions. All these glimpses give us different impressions about the broader economy. But because of the psychological phenomena of priming and automaticity discussed in chapter 1, Americans will likely conjure the most *frequently* covered topic among these items when forming broader economic and political judgments.

Together, these four news items could help readers better understand the contours and contradictions of the contemporary economy. But when presented separately or incompletely, the lived economic experience of everyday Americans is more difficult to ascertain.

Concealed beneath the conventional economic statistics, the erosion of the quality of life of working-class Americans is best described by modern labor practices. The modern economy is rife with examples of cost-cutting innovations that have undermined the living conditions of traditional workers. The ride-sharing industry, including giants Uber and Lyft, has often been accused of having destroyed the livelihoods of cab drivers in major cities, often sparking protests and actions on the part of local policymakers (e.g., Malin and Chandler 2016). Major retailers' recent move towards hiring part-time workers has been adopted by many American universities, which have slowly replaced full-time faculty members with vulnerable adjuncts. The recent "Great Resignation," a post-COVID-19 trend in which workers are leaving their jobs *en masse* in search of higher pay and better working conditions, is a testament to this phenomenon.

These stories are not surprising to contemporary observers. After all, mistreatment of workers can make headlines if the specifics are sufficiently provocative. But along with the erosion of the power of contemporary unions, the dearth of political action on behalf of these workers can be explained at least in part by the way media represent the sociotropic US economy.

Trying to describe the 'two-speed" American economy is certainly an unenviable task. Economic journalists often do succeed in covering the plight of American workers in a sympathetic fashion. They also report core middle-class economic statistics like wage growth, whenever the data becomes available. But as we have seen, even subtle imbalances in the *persistent agenda* of economic news can powerfully reshape public opinion due to the psychology of information acquisition.

## New Directions in the Study of Motivated Reasoning

The implications of the present findings for political psychology are manifold. While motivated reasoning is currently receiving high levels of attention in political science, the most important contemporary question about the topic concerns its contours rather than its causes. In an era of "fake news," scholars need to know much more about how people process information that is patently untrue—and under what circumstances they will resist the development of misperceptions (Allcott and Gentzkow 2017).

The increasingly tense relationship between new and traditional media organizations and recent presidential administrations has showcased the difficulty of reporting the facts in an era of intense framing efforts. Social media companies like Facebook and Twitter have been forced to think carefully about the implications of textual and audiovisual communications on their platforms, given the risk of the spread of political disinformation. Public debate about factual inaccuracies is widespread, as many Americans are concerned about the effects of mis- and disinformation for the health of democracy. Consequently, many Americans are becoming less trusting of traditional media, paradoxically hampering their ability to accurately identify misinformation (e.g., Van Duyn and Collier 2019). "Polarizing cues" from ideological media sources are also playing a greater role in driving bias in factual perceptions (Nicholson 2011).

While these insights deserve continued attention in the literature, we must also take a more encompassing view of media agenda setting to better understand when and where bias is most and least prevalent. The present findings show that persistent, long-term media agenda setting is an important determinant of bias in economic perceptions. Journalists' repeated, long-term agenda practices matter for the factual accuracy of citizens' beliefs, perhaps even more than efforts to disinform in the realm of the economy. However, agenda setting itself is currently in a state of flux. As new technologies challenge the ways in which traditional media sources attract and retain audiences, the agenda-setting and framing behavior of mainstream journalists is also evolving. Are these online communication strategies more likely to foster accurate economic perceptions? While this volume has advanced our understanding of the contingent nature of motivated reasoning, there are many additional dimensions of the information environment that deserve exploration in the future.

Attempts to use new media to combat misperceptions have been widespread in recent years. Some organizations have launched efforts to create platforms where information can be verified and then propagated. Verrit, for example, was a now-defunct website created by former Hillary Clinton campaign staffers which purported to verify information using authentication codes (Stein 2017). Snopes.com is a website with more currency in the fact-checking business, featuring an easy-to-use interface that allows users to quickly identify falsehoods and half-truths. Despite a contemporary Internet experience that is inundated with competing political claims, many interested parties have taken an interest in bias-free browsing.

But as we have seen, persistent agenda-setting constitutes a subtler, but more powerful, form of influence than the use of partisan frames or the repetition of misinformation. Do journalistic norms have an impact on growing platforms for online news and conversation? Aggregators such as Reddit and Twitter, for example, have exploded in popularity. Such websites feature agenda-setting mechanisms that deviate strongly from the practices of contemporary journalists.

Instead, on many online platforms the agenda is set by a combination of user interest and algorithm-driven personalization. In part, popularity drives the visibility of a given piece of content (be it a news story, a meme, a video, a link to an opinion article, or simply a text-based post). This "front page" content eventually sinks back into digital oblivion, as new content rises in user popularity to replace it. News about the American economy, in this context, should reflect the things that the average user finds to be most provocative, interesting, exciting, or alarming—in short, anything worthy of an upvote, a favorite, or a retweet.

Accessing information through peer-to-peer platforms like this should ideally dampen motivated reasoning, as the popularity-based agenda will expose users to various, potentially disconfirming, sources of economic data. However, we still know little about the effects of platform design on the maintenance of economic attitudes and misperceptions. Repetitive presentation of factual information seems to play an important role in minimizing partisan disagreement. However, as many traditional and social media platforms are designed specifically *not* to present their users with repetitive content, innovations in this realm may work against the goal of partisan agreement rather than towards it. And with the rise of stock market–focused subredits and user groups like the "wallstreetbets" community, stock market news is breaking into the mainstream on social media platforms anyway. Thanks to the priorities of vocal retail investors, the economic agenda on social media may become even less balanced than the agenda of traditional news sources.

Nevertheless, online aggregators are still highly reliant upon the news agendas of traditional sources (Choi and Kim 2017; Vonbun, Königslöw, and Schoenbach 2016). Without economic news stories provided by journalists at reputable news sources, there would be little new content for users to post. Combined with the self-policing nature of moderated online platforms, these playing fields might also tilt towards giving journalists continued agenda-setting power.

Despite the plausibility of these assertions, we currently lack empirical evidence to support them. Future research is poised to better understand how online aggregators and other modern newsfeeds influence citizens' economic perceptions. Many scholars are currently measuring media exposure more directly than ever before, using evidence collected from passive listening devices and other technologies. Armed with these and other methods, the future of research on the moderators of motivated reasoning is bright.

## Economic Journalism and Persistent Agenda Setting

The preceding discussion has returned our attention to the central role of economic journalists in shaping economic perceptions. Given this important role, one pressing question is how journalists might revise their practices in the future. What recommendations for economic journalism can we draw from the present findings?

As described in chapter 1, journalists' agenda-setting behavior is shaped by the daily availability of new economic data. Many economic "indicator stories" report on daily aggregated economic data (such as commodity prices and the stock market) because they are continuously available. It is much more difficult to write consistently about economic data that are aggregated on monthly or quarterly bases. After all, journalists are focused on reporting *new* developments, and a jobs report from three weeks ago would certainly not fit many reporters' definition of "newsworthiness."

Given these incentives, it is unlikely that the public's unbalanced diet of "indicator stories" will change anytime soon. Instead of a call to reshape journalists' fundamental approach to story selection, I suggest that journalists continue to rethink the way they *compose* "indicator stories." In chapter 1, I provided a series of examples of this common format for reporting economic news. Indicator stories often focus on a specific trend or development in economic data, providing a few snippets of context and interpretation along the way to help readers understand the broader implications of a given data release.

These indicator stories often contain brief mentions of other sources of economic data at their conclusions. These bullet-point style reports are usually presented without interpretation, instead leaving the reader to decipher the arcane and technical data contained within. Interested readers might read an indicator story about rising home prices and then scroll to the bottom to find brief mentions of RV sales, beef futures, and the cost of airfare. For some readers, the meaning of these less-vital economic statistics will be highly evident. For others, the content can be safely skipped over.

I recommend that in keeping with this style, economic journalists consider including a snapshot of the "middle-class economy" at the conclusion of daily reports. This snapshot may not change each day, as it will likely rely upon monthly and quarterly economic reports. For example, a story about rising gas prices might be accompanied by the most recent wage-growth data and the most recent unemployment data. These reflexive mentions of important data sources might cause the tail ends of economy stories to be repetitive from day to day. After all, if the next month's wage-growth estimates have not been released, these numbers might not have changed for up to thirty days.

Nevertheless, making repetitive mentions of core "middle-class" indicators is no less reflexive than economic journalists' penchant for "doing the numbers;" that is, reporting stock market conditions on a daily basis. By pointing to core middle-class economic indicators each day, however briefly, we might help Americans gain a more rounded understanding of the economic conditions facing average Americans. Mentions of wage-growth data, in particular, might help counteract politicians' efforts to frame this critical indicator (as seen in chapter 3).

## Conclusion: Economic Voting and Accountability

Ultimately, partisans' beliefs about the economy are important because they are useful criteria for judging incumbents' performance in office. In modern democracy, it should come as no surprise that more complex forms of political accountability are relatively rare (Lewis-Beck et al. 2008). Only the most sophisticated citizens can link the policy priorities of incumbents to the outcomes experienced by everyday Americans (Gomez and Wilson 2001). Few Americans understand how ideologies and values fit together into coherent political logics; instead, an inattentive and dis-affected public often falls back on basic cues to make political judgments (Nicholson 2011). One such cue is party attachment. Another is the state of the American economy.

Among "unsophisticated" citizens, partisanship and economic per-formance are not always opposing influences on voting behavior. Often, partisanship easily prevails over the influence of simple accountability cues as the lens of motivated reasoning reshapes citizens' understanding of objective economic reality. In short, partisans find ways to justify the belief the economy is better under co-partisan presidents than under out-partisan presidents. But sometimes, incumbent performance is seen for what it is. Occasionally, Americans eschew their partisan lenses to accurately appraise incumbent performance.

Nevertheless, the present volume has shown that these accura-cy-driven judgments might not always be true to the complexities of economic reality. They might obscure the plight of low-income Americans by focusing unduly upon stock market fluctuations that mean little for the economy in the long run. But if partisans punish their own party's incumbents, or reward members of the out-party on this basis, the result is nevertheless an example of democratic accountability in action.

While this vision of democracy might be a far cry from the standard proposed by older, more optimistic theories, it reflects the contemporary landscape of public opinion research. Some scholars posit that widespread democratic accountability is possible; that even a myopic, ill-informed public can behave rationally due to the simplicity of performance cues.[3] Others argue that accountability is impossible for such an ill-equipped electorate and that elections in modern times are more or less random coin-flips between Republican and Democratic candidates (Achen and Bartels 2017).[4] While one school sees a silver lining for democracy hidden within the cloudy discoveries of the rational ignorance approach, the other suggests that this lining is brittle and ephemeral.

I stake out a position in between these competing democratic visions. As we have seen, digging beneath the surface of economic perceptions reveals that the public can extract relatively accurate, unbiased signals about American economic performance. However, these signals are weak indicators of middle-class economic performance. Economic accountability is a highly imperfect, but functioning, mechanism for judging incumbent politicians. While the stock market is surely not the economy, and our economic perceptions are surely imperfect reflections of real-world economic performance, we may still be able to reward and punish incumbents on the margin despite our abiding national impulse to "follow the ticker" at the expense of other relevant forms of economic news.

# Appendices

## Appendices for Chapter 2

In chapter 2, I explore two datasets. The first is a large-scale repository of *New York Times* articles about the economy, aggregated on a daily basis, from 1980 through 2020. The second is a database consisting of news stories from a variety of sources collected from 2015 through 2020. Below, I provide details about each dataset, including the data collection effort, filtering, processing, and a presentation of descriptive statistics.

STUDY 2.1

In study 2.1, I searched LexisNexis Academic for *New York Times* articles across quarters, from January 1980 to July 2020 which satisfied the following criteria:

> TERMS (ECONOMY & ECONOMIC INDICATORS) OR
> TERMS (ECONOMIC NEWS) OR TERMS (ECONOMIC
> CONDITIONS) OR TERMS (ECONOMIC INDICATORS)
> OR TERMS (ECONOMY)

The search yielded 50,071 total economy-focused articles across the period in question. Below, figure A.1 shows the over-time distribution of these articles. In some cases, the total number of articles selected for a given time period was smaller than the total number of articles written across a quarter.

Figure A.1 shows that while there are in many cases ceiling effects on the data collection process stemming from the method of scraping

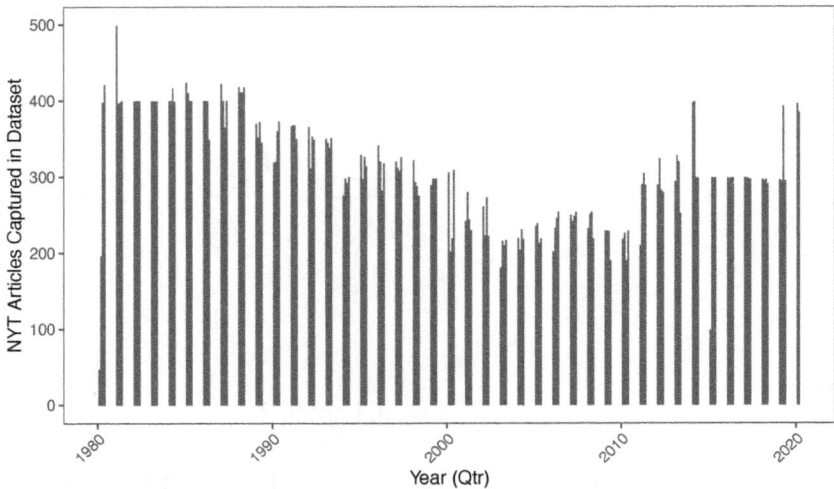

Figure A.1. *New York Times* economy articles per quarter, 1980–2020. *Source*: Author's own material.

LexisNexis employed in the study, there is good coverage across the period. There is at least some evidence that economic news in total fluctuates across the period, as, for example, the ceiling is not reached in the mid-2000s, when the economy was performing well. These imbalances in the counts of economic news stories are natural, however, and better reflect the economic agenda across the period. In quarters when data collection was limited by ceiling effects, we have no reason to suspect that articles left out of the collection would be significantly different in terms of economic topic.

Batch text files were broken into individual articles using regular expression algorithms. Each article was stored in a separate folder, with its year and quarter reflected in the file name. The articles were individually stripped of stopwords, made lowercase, were stripped of punctuation and were cleared of excess white space. While the resulting plain text was not always completely free of certain defects (including, for instance, metadata related to the article's publication date and other details), these additions were not necessary to remove due to the simple nature of the dictionary-based approach used in the study. The resulting texts were then individually evaluated by searching the (nonstemmed) terms contained in the text for key words and N-grams contained in a dictionary.

ECONOMIC LEXICON

The economic lexicon used in studies 2.1, 2.2 and in chapters 3 and 4 was constructed and validated in several steps. First a subset of the articles gathered for study 2.1 were randomly selected in order to make up a training set for the purposes of dictionary assembly. This training set included 250 randomly selected articles.

Coders were next enlisted to perform a number of tasks. First, the coders were asked to read each article in the training set and to identify the topic of the article from a list of possibilities including the stock market, unemployment, wages, prices, sales, goods, and manufacturing, trade, consumer sentiment, economic growth, credit, and debt. If an article did not have a clearly identifiable economic focus, but was still focused on the subject of the economy and its performance, the article was coded as "general economy." If the article had no discernible economic focus and was therefore apparently mislabeled by LexisNexis, the article was coded as "noneconomic."

Next, coders went in order through the list of random articles with the intention of finding N-grams that described any of the economic topics mentioned in the paragraph above. Coders included the first instance of each N-grams identified in the list of articles and did not repeat them. For example, the word "Dow" to represent the Dow Jones Industrial Average would be coded under "markets," and would not be included again in this category even if "Dow" was present in the next article read by the coder. This process was adopted in order to save time and to alleviate the tedious nature of the task for the coders.

Once the lexicon was assembled, it was tested in a variety of ways. First, intercoder reliability was assessed using basic tools. The first was to assess whether the coders had identified the same terms. This was accomplished by including all coders' lexicons together in a bag-of-words text corpus and treating each coder's lexicon as a separate text. Then, the proportion of terms that featured positive identification across all coders was taken. Because one coder identified almost all the terms identified by other coders, measures like Cronbach's alpha are inappropriate. Instead, the common code proportion was reported as 75.1 percent. These common codes were retained, while others, which did not feature cross-coder agreement, were removed.

This first stage resulted in a set of 289 remaining N-grams. As a reminder, these N-grams were not stemmed because the sense of each N-gram could change according to the specifics of the word's usage (for example, "inflate" and "inflation" may have very different senses, the former often being noneconomic in nature, and the latter being frequently economic in nature).

To that end, coders also assessed the *context* of terms that had been included in the first stage of the lexicon's development. This step was performed by searching a second set of two hundred randomly selected news articles for all the words in the initial lexicon. For each term, all sentences containing that term were stored in a comma-separated file. Next, coders went back through these sentences and manually identified whether the term in question was used to refer to an economic indicator or if the term was used in a different sense. For example, the term "stock" could have appeared in a sentence like this one: "One stock to watch this week is Kronos Worldwide (NYSE: KRO), a titanium dioxide firm which has witnessed explosive growth over the last quarter."

In this case, the term "stock" is being used in the correct sense, to refer to a public stock offering by a company. However, we can also consider a second sentence: "After taking stock of the damage, Governor Hogan has chosen to declare a state of emergency in historic Ellicott City."

In the second sentence, the term "stock" is used in a different, noneconomic sense. The ultimate question being answered by this training-set validation exercise is which terms in the lexicon have inappropriately low rates of "correct" economic usage and which do not possess frequently used alternative senses which detract from those terms' overall utility. It should come as no surprise that the word "stock" was dropped from the set, whereas N-grams like "stock market" were retained due to their inherently lower likelihood of being used in reference to other concepts. While no clear benchmark exists for these purposes, any term which was identified as having a noneconomic sense more than 10 percent of the time across the validation set were excluded from the final lexicon.

The resulting lexicon contained 241 N-grams, with a training-set accuracy rate of 97 percent. N-grams that were included in the final set were used in the validation set for economic purposes 97 percent of the time, while 3 percent of the time, these terms referred to noneconomic topics. Each topic did not contain the same number of terms—in fact, the largest lexical diversity of references to indicators occurred in the topic of market indicators, while the lowest number of terms in a category belonged to mentions of consumer behavior. While some may see this as an indication that the dictionary is biased in favor of the former economic topic, this imbalance reflects the ways in which journalists described the economy in our training set.

There are simply far more ways in which journalists discuss topics like the stock market, given their complexity (and the massive quantity of data which can describe their performance) than other indicators. This assertion is in line with the theory advanced in chapter 1. Table A.1 on pages 204–207 shows the complete lexicon.

TIME SERIES ANALYSIS: STUDY 2.1

To verify that the appropriate parameters were used for the ARIMA models introduced in study 2.1, I used several time series diagnostics. First, the results of KPSS tests indicated that the stock market time series required differencing to achieve stationarity (KPSS Level = 0.73, p = 0.01). The unemployment time series also required differencing due to a similar rejection of the null hypothesis of stationarity (KPSS Level = 1.65, p < 0.01).

As a result, the series were differenced and F-tests for autoregressive order were performed using the *auto.arima* library in R. The results of these tests for stock market and unemployment data were ARIMA(0,1,2) and ARIMA(0,1,1), respectively.

Next, I checked to verify that the residuals of the resultant models did not show additional autocorrelation or any other model violations. Using the *checkresiduals* command in the *forecast* library in R, I produce evidence below that for both models 2.2 and 2.3, specifications exist that fail to reject the null hypothesis that the AR errors resemble white noise. In model 2.3, diagnostic tests prefer an ARIMA(0,1,2) model, though this test rejects the Ljung-Box test for white noise (p < 0.02). An alternative model specification, ARIMA(2,0,3) passes the test ($Q^* = 5.7$, p = 0.12). This latter specification provides results that are robust to the model presented in the text. Results are robust to the model presented in-text based on an alternate specification for model 2.2 using ARIMA(2,0,3).

STUDY 2.2

In study 2.2, I searched the LexisNexis Academic database for news articles that satisfied the following criteria:

- TERMS(ECONOMY & ECONOMIC INDICATORS) OR TERMS(ECONOMIC NEWS) OR TERMS(ECONOMIC CONDITIONS) OR TERMS(ECONOMIC INDICATORS) OR TERMS(ECONOMY)

- Article must be full-text (no abstract-only files)

Table A.1. Composition of Economic Term Lexicon

| Employment | Prices | Mfg. and Sales | Wages | Growth | Credit | Markets | Consumers | Trade |
|---|---|---|---|---|---|---|---|---|
| manufacturing jobs | oil revenue | manufacture | salaries | economic output | housing | stock market | consumer confidence | imports |
| job placement | oil price | retail | wages | recession | home price | wall street | consumer spending | trade |
| unemployment rate | benchmark crude | service sector | household income | growth rate | student debt | investors | leadership certainty | foreign exchange rates |
| jobless rate | brent crude | consumer habits | income growth | annual growth | loan defaults | investor | consumers | free trade |
| full employment | crude oil | domestic consumption | wage gap | productivity growth | credit card debt | financial markets | consumer sentiment | trading practices |
| work force | inflation rate | factory activity | income gap | productivity | new homes | dow jones | | foreign firms |
| workforce | price hikes | manufacturing sector | hourly wage growth | gross domestic product | creditors | nasdaq | | exports |
| hiring | pricing | manufacturing | cost of living | economic growth | lenders | global market | | global economy |
| rate unemployment | college costs | new orders | income inequality | rate of expansion | debt rating | global markets | | chinas economy |
| part time | cost of college | oil production | gratuities | gdp growth | mortgage rates | portfolio | | chinese economy |
| salary worker | afford college | barrels per day | low income | gdp | home loan | portfolios | | mexico economy |

| salary workers | inflation | start ups | middle income | global growth | home buyers | bond investors | mexican | economy |
|---|---|---|---|---|---|---|---|---|
| job growth | gas prices | startup | affluent | economic output | total homebuyers | stock indexes | | india economy |
| labor market | commodity prices | start up | wage inflation | economic gains | mortgages | market crash | | eu economy |
| job creation | borrowing costs | goods and services | wages adjusted for inflation | economic losses | mortgage | traders | | european economy |
| jobless claim | interest rates eurozone | heavy industry | real wages | business activity index | | cost of construction | | bank stocks |
| jobless claims | gasoline prices | consumer electronics | weekly earnings | leading economic index | residential housing market | financial sector | | german economy |
| unemployment benefits | medical costs | car industry | upper income | | real estate | government bonds | | protectionism |
| reducing staff | cpi | auto industry | labor costs | | personal debt | treasury notes | | globalization |
| staff reductions | natural gas | automobile industry | living standards | | bond financing | long term yields | trade barriers | |
| staff reduction | energy prices | industry | median household income | | apr | portfolios | | tariffs |
| nonfarm payroll | price energy | auto sales | paychecks | | auto loan market | dividend yield | | barriers trade |
| full-time work | interest rate | car sales | full time | | property values | currency | | regional trade |

*continued on next page*

Table A.1. Continued.

| Employment | Prices | Mfg. and Sales | Wages | Growth | Credit | Markets | Consumers | Trade |
|---|---|---|---|---|---|---|---|---|
| employees | rate hike | retailers | incomes | | property value | currencies | | world trade |
| employee | north slope crude | consumer demand | income | | housing costs | share prices | | capital outflow |
| supply labor | shale oil | | | | cost housing | share price | | capital inflow |
| factory worker | fed rate | | | | credit card | market confidence | | trade imbalance |
| jobs data | federal funds rate | | | | credit cards | tech stocks | | |
| job data | consumer price index | | | | residential property | tech stock | | |
| jobless aid | | | | | student loan debt | fortune 500 | | |
| job cuts | | | | | student loans | private equity | | |
| layoffs | | | | | real estate trust | sell off | | |
| jobs | | | | | home sales | stocks traded | | |
| | | | | | car loan | stock funds | | |
| | | | | | car loans | municipal bonds | | |
| | | | | | payday loan | treasury bonds | | |
| | | | | | payday loans | pace of investment | | |

banking sector

stock exchange

stock exchanges

currency
market

stocks

markets

These news articles were drawn from all daily newspapers in the dataset with full-text coverage spanning January 3, 2015 to July 1, 2020. These newspapers were as follows:

- *Atlanta Journal-Constitution*
- *Christian Science Monitor*
- *NY Daily News*
- *Daily Oklahoman*
- *New York Post*
- *The New York Times*
- *Philadelphia Inquirer*
- *Pittsburgh Post-Gazette*
- *St. Louis Post-Dispatch*
- *Minneapolis Star-Tribune*
- *Tampa Bay Times*
- *USA Today*
- *The Washington Post*

In addition, I drew cable news transcripts from the following sources:

- MSNBC
- FOX News Channel

Altogether, the dataset comprised 4,196 articles and cable TV transcripts and yielded 22,654 mentions of economic topics on cable TV and 119,345 mentions of economic topics in daily newspapers. To perform analyses on the articles, an identical process to the one described for study 2.1 was applied: articles were made lowercase, stripped of unnecessary punctuation and whitespace, but were not stemmed.

In figure A.2, we see that the economic terms search yielded a very large number of transcripts in the spring of 2020, during the COVID-19 pandemic. However, this increased density of economy stories is in keeping with the real economic coverage patterns of journalists in response to economic reality.

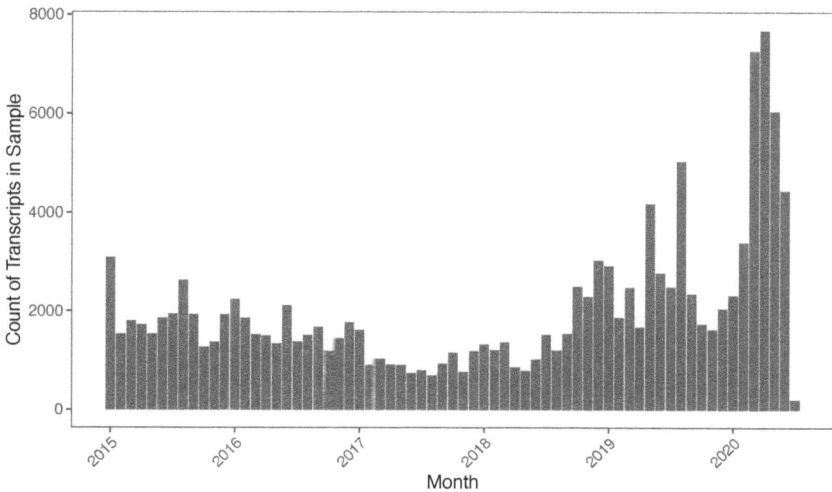

Figure A.2. Count of economic news mentions, study 2.2 sample. *Source*: Author's own material.

# Appendices for Chapter 3

Study 3.1 also relied upon the economic lexicon created from newspaper articles described above. However, in this analysis, the lexicon was applied to a large corpus of tweets from senators and representatives from 2015 through 2020. These tweets were gathered using the *twitteR* software library for the R environment and altogether included roughly 445,000 individual records of senators' tweets, as well as roughly 849,000 tweets from the House of Representatives. The *twitteR* library contains code which allows users to access the timelines of specific accounts. Using a comprehensive list of all official twitter accounts of sitting and former senators, I captured as many tweets as possible from each timeline. Then I excluded tweets from all MCs which had been written before January 1, 2015.

Next, to ensure that tweets from before or after an MC's term in office were not accidentally included, I matched the date range of tweets to the date range of terms in office for all MCs in the dataset. The same strategy was deployed in 2017 and in 2020, meaning that I was able to gather a longer timeframe of tweets than other studies which are limited by Twitter's caps on timeline scraping (as of this writing, 3,200 tweets).

Next, the tweets were preprocessed, including removing punctuation and making all text lowercase. The same N-gram search algorithm described for chapter 2 above was next applied to the tweets. If a tweet contained no economic N-grams, it was excluded from the analysis. If it did include an economic mention, it was retained in the dataset.

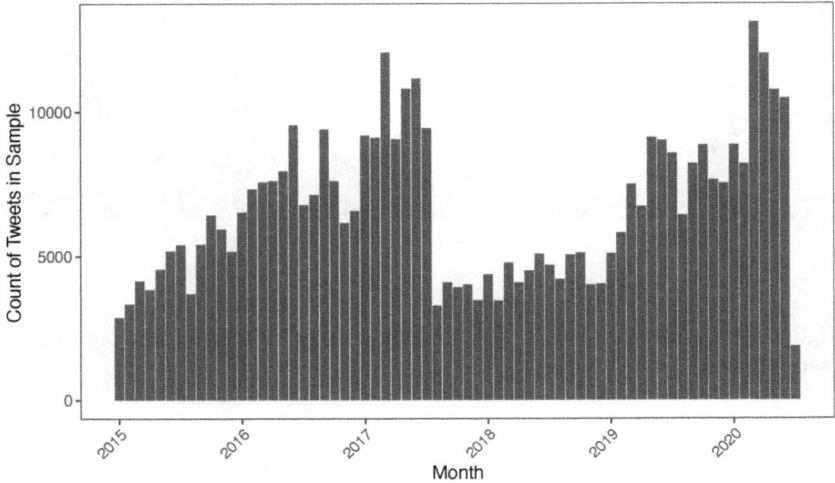

Figure A.3. Histogram, tweets by month, Senate tweets dataset. *Source*: Author's own material.

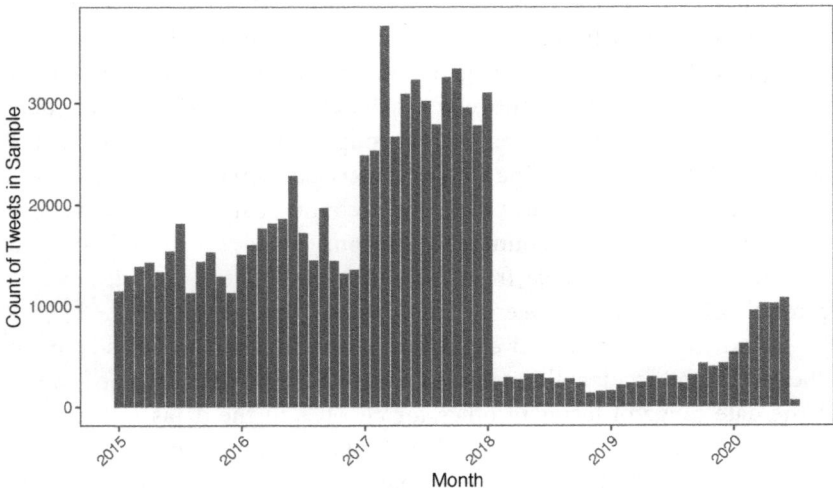

Figure A.4. Histogram, tweets by month, House tweets dataset. *Source*: Author's own material.

## Appendices for Chapter 4

Chapter 4 relied on data collected from dozens of public opinion surveys, which included economic perceptions and partisanship data. Below, I include table A.2, which describes the details of these surveys, including their sources, the number of observations, question wording, and dates of distribution.

## Appendices for Chapter 5

The experimental data for study 5.1 was gathered in July of 2018. At that time, 1,560 people responded to an invitation to participate in a survey on Amazon MTurk. Respondents were offered one dollar to complete a roughly six-minute survey. Respondents were first asked to complete a demographic question battery, which included partisanship alongside standard questions like age, sex, race, formal education, and household income. Next, a short task was implemented that was designed to clear the respondents' working memories.

Afterwards, respondents were randomly exposed to one of the experimental treatments described in chapter 5. Finally, a variety of outcome questions, including overall economic perceptions and stock market perceptions, were presented to all respondents. The wording of the treatment variable is included in table A.3.

MTurk surveys are notably unrepresentative of the broader US population. However, the demographics of the partisan groups in the study were not particularly out of step with our expectations about the modern Republican and Democratic parties. While the demographics of the overall sample show that the sample trends younger, more liberal, less racially diverse, and more male than the national population, Republicans were older, more conservative, less racially diverse, and more male than the Democrats in the sample on average.

TABULAR RESULTS FOR STUDY 5.1

Below we see a description of the study 5.1 sample, contained in table A.4. The table shows us that while not representative, the sample has good coverage on variables such as ideology, education, and news exposure, among other demographics.

Table A.2. List of Survey Items Used in Economic Indicator Dataset

| Source | Date | Indicator | Perspective | N | Method |
|---|---|---|---|---|---|
| ANES | 11/1/1980 | Economy | Retrospective | 1614 | Face-to-Face |
| NBC/WSJ | 10/18/1982 | Unemployment | Prospective | 1595 | Landline |
| NBC/WSJ | 10/18/1982 | Economy | Prospective | 1595 | Landline |
| NBC/WSJ | 10/18/1982 | Inflation | Prospective | 1595 | Landline |
| ANES | 11/1/1982 | Economy | Retrospective | 1418 | Face-to-Face |
| ANES | 11/1/1984 | Economy | Retrospective | 2257 | Face-to-Face |
| ANES | 11/1/1986 | Economy | Retrospective | 2176 | Face-to-Face |
| ANES | 11/1/1986 | Unemployment | Retrospective | 2176 | Face-to-Face |
| ANES | 11/1/1986 | Inflation | Retrospective | 2176 | Face-to-Face |
| ANES | 11/1/1988 | Economy | Retrospective | 2040 | Face-to-Face |
| ANES | 11/1/1988 | Unemployment | Retrospective | 2040 | Face-to-Face |
| ANES | 11/1/1988 | Inflation | Retrospective | 2040 | Face-to-Face |
| ANES | 12/1/1988 | Unemployment | Retrospective | 2040 | Face-to-Face |
| ANES | 12/1/1988 | Inflation | Retrospective | 2040 | Face-to-Face |
| ANES | 11/1/1990 | Economy | Retrospective | 1980 | Face-to-Face/Landline |
| ANES | 11/1/1992 | Economy | Retrospective | 2485 | Face-to-Face/Landline |
| ANES | 11/1/1992 | Unemployment | Retrospective | 2485 | Face-to-Face/Landline |
| ANES | 11/1/1992 | Inflation | Retrospective | 2485 | Face-to-Face/Landline |
| ANES | 11/1/1994 | Economy | Retrospective | 1795 | Face-to-Face/Landline |
| ANES | 11/1/1996 | Economy | Retrospective | 1714 | Face-to-Face/Landline |
| Gallup | 11/6/1997 | Economy | Current | 1003 | Landline |
| Gallup | 11/6/1997 | Stock Market | Current | 1003 | Landline |
| CBS | 5/19/1998 | Economy | Current | 1080 | Landline |

| | | | | | |
|---|---|---|---|---|---|
| CBS | 5/19/1998 | Stock Market | Current | 1080 | Landline |
| CBS/NYT | 9/19/1998 | Economy | Current | 944 | Landline |
| CBS/NYT | 9/19/1998 | Stock Market | Current | 944 | Landline |
| ANES | 11/1/1998 | Economy | Retrospective | 1281 | Face-to-Face/Landline |
| CBS | 9/28/1999 | Stock Market | Current | 1652 | Landline |
| CBS | 9/28/1999 | Economy | Current | 1652 | Landline |
| CBS | 4/15/2000 | Stock Market | Prospective | 1150 | Landline |
| CBS/NYT | 5/10/2000 | Economy | Current | 947 | Landline |
| CBS/NYT | 5/10/2000 | Stock Market | Current | 947 | Landline |
| ANES | 11/1/2000 | Economy | Retrospective | 1807 | Face-to-Face/Landline |
| CBS | 3/8/2001 | Economy | Current | 1105 | Landline |
| CBS | 3/8/2001 | Stock Market | Current | 1105 | Landline |
| CBS | 3/8/2001 | Stock Market | Current | 1086 | Landline |
| CBS | 3/8/2001 | Economy | Current | 1086 | Landline |
| CBS | 4/23/2001 | Economy | Current | 921 | Landline |
| CBS | 4/23/2001 | Stock Market | Current | 921 | Landline |
| CBS/NYT | 8/28/2001 | Economy | Current | 850 | Landline |
| CBS/NYT | 8/28/2001 | Stock Market | Current | 850 | Landline |
| CBS | 1/15/2002 | Economy | Current | 1030 | Landline |
| CBS | 1/15/2002 | Stock Market | Current | 1030 | Landline |
| NBC/WSJ | 7/19/2002 | Economy | Current | 1014 | Landline |
| NBC/WSJ | 7/19/2002 | Stock Market | Current | 1014 | Landline |
| LA Times | 8/22/2002 | Stock Market | Prospective | 1372 | Landline |
| LA Times | 8/22/2002 | Economy | Current | 1372 | Landline |
| NBC/WSJ | 9/3/2002 | Economy | Current | 1011 | Landline |

continued on next page

Table A.2. Continued.

| Source | Date | Indicator | Perspective | N | Method |
|---|---|---|---|---|---|
| ANES | 11/1/2002 | Economy | Retrospective | 1511 | Landline |
| NBC/*WSJ* | 1/19/2003 | Economy | Prospective | 1025 | Landline |
| CBS | 4/26/2003 | Economy | Current | 925 | Landline |
| CBS | 4/26/2003 | Stock Market | Current | 925 | Landline |
| CBS | 8/11/2003 | Economy | Current | 798 | Landline |
| CBS | 8/11/2003 | Stock Market | Current | 798 | Landline |
| NBC/*WSJ* | 11/8/2003 | Economy | Current | 1003 | Landline |
| NBC/*WSJ* | 11/8/2003 | Stock Market | Current | 1003 | Landline |
| Gallup | 8/1/2004 | Stock Market | Prospective | 804 | Landline |
| Gallup | 8/1/2004 | Economy | Prospective | 804 | Landline |
| Gallup | 8/1/2004 | Unemployment | Prospective | 804 | Landline |
| Gallup | 8/1/2004 | Inflation | Prospective | 804 | Landline |
| ANES | 11/1/2004 | Economy | Retrospective | 1212 | Landline |
| ANES | 11/1/2004 | Unemployment | Retrospective | 1212 | Face-to-Face/Landline |
| ANES | 11/1/2004 | Inflation | Retrospective | 1212 | Face-to-Face/Landline |
| Pew | 5/11/2005 | Economy | Current | 1502 | Landline |
| Pew | 5/11/2005 | Stock Market | Current | 1502 | Landline |
| Pew | 5/11/2005 | Unemployment | Current | 1502 | Landline |
| Pew | 5/11/2005 | Inflation | Current | 1502 | Landline |
| Pew | 5/11/2005 | Gas Prices | Current | 1502 | Landline |
| AP/IPSOS | 8/1/2005 | Stock Market | Prospective | 1000 | Landline |
| AP/IPSOS | 8/1/2005 | Housing Prices | Prospective | 1000 | Landline |
| Pew | 1/4/2006 | Economy | Current | 1503 | Landline |

| | | | | | |
|---|---|---|---|---|---|
| Pew | 1/4/2006 | Unemployment | Current | 1503 | Landline |
| Pew | 1/4/2006 | Inflation | Current | 1503 | Landline |
| Pew | 1/4/2006 | Housing Prices | Current | 1503 | Landline |
| Pew | 1/4/2006 | Gas Prices | Current | 1503 | Landline |
| Pew | 1/4/2006 | Stock Market | Current | 1503 | Landline |
| LA Times | 2/25/2006 | Stock Market | Prospective | 2563 | Landline |
| LA Times | 2/25/2006 | Economy | Retrospective | 2563 | Landline |
| LA Times | 2/25/2006 | Housing Prices | Prospective | 2563 | Landline |
| CCES | 10/7/2006 | Economy | Retrospective | 36421 | Online |
| CBS/NYT | 12/1/2006 | Economy | Current | 922 | Landline |
| CBS/NYT | 12/1/2006 | Stock Market | Current | 922 | Landline |
| CBS/NYT | 12/1/2006 | Housing Prices | Prospective | 922 | Landline |
| NBC/WSJ | 3/2/2007 | Stock Market | Prospective | 1007 | Landline |
| AP/IPSOS | 4/2/2007 | Stock Market | Prospective | 1000 | Landline |
| AP/IPSOS | 4/2/2007 | Housing Prices | Prospective | 1000 | Landline |
| AP/IPSOS | 5/7/2007 | Stock Market | Prospective | 1000 | Landline |
| AP/IPSOS | 5/7/2007 | Housing Prices | Prospective | 1000 | Landline |
| AP/IPSOS | 6/4/2007 | Stock Market | Prospective | 1000 | Landline |
| AP/IPSOS | 6/4/2007 | Stock Market | Prospective | 1000 | Landline |
| AP/IPSOS | 6/4/2007 | Housing Prices | Prospective | 1000 | Landline |
| Pew | 9/12/2007 | Economy | Current | 1501 | Landline |
| Pew | 9/12/2007 | Stock Market | Current | 1501 | Landline |
| AP/IPSOS | 10/1/2007 | Stock Market | Prospective | 1005 | Landline |
| AP/IPSOS | 10/1/2007 | Housing Prices | Prospective | 1005 | Landline |
| CCES | 11/9/2007 | Economy | Retrospective | 9999 | Online |

continued on next page

Table A.2. Continued.

| Source | Date | Indicator | Perspective | N | Method |
|---|---|---|---|---|---|
| Pew | 1/30/2008 | Economy | Retrospective | 1502 | Landline |
| Pew | 1/30/2008 | Inflation | Retrospective | 1502 | Landline |
| Pew | 1/30/2008 | Stock Market | Retrospective | 1502 | Landline |
| AP/IPSOS | 4/7/2008 | Stock Market | Prospective | 1005 | Landline |
| AP/IPSOS | 4/7/2008 | Housing Prices | Prospective | 1005 | Landline |
| AP/IPSOS | 7/31/2008 | Stock Market | Prospective | 1002 | Landline |
| AP/IPSOS | 7/31/2008 | Housing Prices | Prospective | 1002 | Landline |
| NBC/WSJ | 9/19/2008 | Stock Market | Retrospective | 1157 | Landline/Cell |
| CCES | 10/8/2008 | Economy | Retrospective | 32800 | Online |
| ANES | 11/1/2008 | Economy | Retrospective | 2322 | Face-to-Face/Online |
| ANES | 11/1/2008 | Unemployment | Retrospective | 2322 | Face-to-Face/Online |
| ANES | 11/1/2008 | Inflation | Retrospective | 2322 | Face-to-Face/Online |
| CBS | 12/4/2008 | Economy | Current | 1390 | Landline/Cell |
| CBS | 12/4/2008 | Stock Market | Current | 1390 | Landline/Cell |
| Pew | 3/9/2009 | Economy | Current | 1308 | Landline/Cell |
| Pew | 3/9/2009 | Stock Market | Current | 1308 | Landline/Cell |
| Pew | 3/9/2009 | Housing Prices | Current | 1308 | Landline/Cell |
| Gallup | 5/29/2009 | Stock Market | Prospective | 1015 | Landline/Cell |
| Gallup | 5/29/2009 | Inflation | Prospective | 1015 | Landline/Cell |
| Gallup | 5/29/2009 | Economy | Prospective | 1015 | Landline/Cell |
| Gallup | 5/29/2009 | Unemployment | Prospective | 1015 | Landline/Cell |
| CNN/ORC | 9/11/2009 | Stock Market | Prospective | 1012 | Landline/Cell |

| | | | | | |
|---|---|---|---|---|---|
| CCES | 11/5/2009 | Economy | Retrospective | 13800 | Online |
| Gallup | 12/11/2009 | Stock Market | Prospective | 1025 | Landline/Cell |
| CCES | 10/1/2010 | Economy | Retrospective | 55400 | Online |
| CBS/60 Minutes/ Vanity Fair | 11/1/2010 | Economy | Current | 1137 | Landline/Cell |
| CCES | 11/9/2011 | Economy | Retrospective | 20150 | Online |
| Pew | 2/8/2012 | Unemployment | Current | 1501 | Landline/Cell |
| Pew | 2/8/2012 | Economy | Current | 1501 | Landline/Cell |
| CBS | 7/26/2012 | Unemployment | Prospective | 1027 | Landline/Cell |
| CBS | 7/26/2012 | Economy | Prospective | 1027 | Landline/Cell |
| CCES | 10/1/2012 | Economy | Retrospective | 54535 | Online |
| ANES | 11/1/2012 | Economy | Retrospective | 5914 | Face-to-Face/Online |
| CBS | 3/1/2013 | Economy | Current | 1181 | Landline/Cell |
| CBS | 3/1/2013 | Stock Market | Current | 1181 | Landline/Cell |
| Pew | 6/6/2013 | Economy | Current | 1004 | Landline/Cell |
| Pew | 6/6/2013 | Stock Market | Current | 1004 | Landline/Cell |
| Pew | 6/6/2013 | Unemployment | Current | 1004 | Landline/Cell |
| Pew | 6/6/2013 | Gas Prices | Current | 1004 | Landline/Cell |
| Pew | 6/6/2013 | Housing Prices | Current | 1004 | Landline/Cell |
| CBS | 7/1/2013 | Economy | Current | 1036 | Landline/Cell |
| CBS | 7/1/2013 | Stock Market | Current | 1036 | Landline/Cell |
| CBS | 7/1/2013 | Unemployment | Current | 1036 | Landline/Cell |
| CCES | 11/6/2013 | Economy | Retrospective | 16400 | Online |
| Gallup | 1/5/2014 | Stock Market | Prospective | 1018 | Landline/Cell |

continued on next page

Table A.2. Continued.

| Source | Date | Indicator | Perspective | N | Method |
|--------|------|-----------|-------------|---|--------|
| CBS | 1/17/2014 | Economy | Retrospective | 1018 | Landline/Cell |
| CBS | 1/17/2014 | Stock Market | Current | 1018 | Landline/Cell |
| CBS | 1/17/2014 | Housing Prices | Current | 1018 | Landline/Cell |
| CBS | 1/17/2014 | Unemployment | Current | 1018 | Landline/Cell |
| Pew | 2/6/2014 | Economy | Current | 1004 | Landline/Cell |
| Pew | 2/6/2014 | Stock Market | Current | 1004 | Landline/Cell |
| Pew | 2/6/2014 | Housing Prices | Current | 1004 | Landline/Cell |
| Pew | 2/6/2014 | Inflation | Current | 1004 | Landline/Cell |
| Pew | 2/6/2014 | Unemployment | Current | 1004 | Landline/Cell |
| Pew | 2/6/2014 | Gas Prices | Current | 1004 | Landline/Cell |
| CBS | 5/1/2014 | Economy | Current | 1009 | Landline/Cell |
| Pew | 7/31/2014 | Economy | Current | 1002 | Landline/Cell |
| Pew | 7/31/2014 | Stock Market | Current | 1002 | Landline/Cell |
| Pew | 7/31/2014 | Housing Prices | Current | 1002 | Landline/Cell |
| Pew | 7/31/2014 | Inflation | Current | 1002 | Landline/Cell |
| Pew | 7/31/2014 | Unemployment | Current | 1002 | Landline/Cell |
| Pew | 7/31/2014 | Gas Prices | Current | 1002 | Landline/Cell |
| CCES | 10/1/2014 | Economy | Retrospective | 56200 | Online |
| Pew | 2/5/2015 | Stock Market | Current | 1003 | Landline/Cell |
| Pew | 2/5/2015 | Housing Prices | Current | 1003 | Landline/Cell |
| Pew | 2/5/2015 | Inflation | Current | 1003 | Landline/Cell |
| Pew | 2/5/2015 | Unemployment | Current | 1003 | Landline/Cell |
| Pew | 2/5/2015 | Gas Prices | Current | 1003 | Landline/Cell |

| Pollster | Date | Topic | Orientation | Sample | Mode |
|---|---|---|---|---|---|
| CBS | 2/13/2015 | Economy | Retrospective | 1006 | Landline/Cell |
| CBS | 2/13/2015 | Stock Market | Retrospective | 1006 | Landline/Cell |
| CBS | 2/13/2015 | Housing Prices | Retrospective | 1006 | Landline/Cell |
| CBS | 2/13/2015 | Gas Prices | Retrospective | 1006 | Landline/Cell |
| Pew | 2/18/2015 | Economy | Current | 1504 | Landline/Cell |
| Pew | 2/18/2015 | Housing Prices | Retrospective | 1504 | Landline/Cell |
| Pew | 2/18/2015 | Stock Market | Retrospective | 1504 | Landline/Cell |
| Pew | 2/18/2015 | Unemployment | Retrospective | 1504 | Landline/Cell |
| Pew | 2/18/2015 | Income | Retrospective | 1504 | Landline/Cell |
| CCES | 11/6/2015 | Economy | Retrospective | 14250 | Online |
| Work Trends Poll | 8/3/2016 | Economy | Retrospective | 822 | Online |
| Work Trends Poll | 8/3/2016 | Unemployment | Current | 822 | Online |
| CNN/ORC | 9/1/2016 | Economy | Retrospective | 1001 | Landline/Cell |
| CCES | 9/28/2016 | Economy | Retrospective | 64600 | Online |
| Kaiser Family Foundation | 10/12/2016 | Unemployment | Retrospective | 1205 | Landline/Cell |
| Kaiser Family Foundation | 10/12/2016 | Inflation | Retrospective | 1205 | Landline/Cell |
| Kaiser Family Foundation | 10/12/2016 | Gas Prices | Retrospective | 1205 | Landline/Cell |
| ANES | 11/1/2016 | Economy | Retrospective | 4270 | Face-to-Face/Online |
| CNN/ORC | 11/17/2016 | Economy | Retrospective | 1001 | Landline/Cell |
| CNN/ORC | 1/12/2017 | Economy | Retrospective | 1000 | Landline/Cell |
| CCES | 11/8/2017 | Economy | Retrospective | 18200 | Online |
| CCES | 9/27/2018 | Economy | Retrospective | 60000 | Online |
| Fox News | 3/21/2020 | Stock Market | Current | 1011 | Online |
| AP/NORC | 1/16/2019 | Stock Market | Current | 1062 | Telephone/Online |

Table A.3. Full Experimental Question Wording, Study 5.1

**Treatment 1 (Republicans):**
NEW YORK. Stocks were up last week, lending further evidence that the markets are headed for even stronger gains. The Dow Jones rallied substantially in the past quarter as investors displayed a growing appetite for risk and a disregard for worries about any potential downturns. "Today's report continues to signal a solid investing environment," said Bruce Sittenfeld, senior economist at RBS in Stamford, Connecticut.

**Treatment 1 (Democrats):**
NEW YORK—Stocks dipped sharply last week, adding to growing concerns that the markets are headed for even bigger losses in the near future. The Dow Jones has experienced worrying volatility in the past quarter, as investors displayed a growing aversion to risk and a striking amount of concern towards potential reversals of fortune. "Today's report continues to signal an unsteady investing environment," said Bruce Sittenfeld, senior economist at RBS in Stamford, Connecticut.

**Treatment 2 (Republicans):**
NEW YORK—Last week's income report showed strengthening wage growth, lending mounting evidence to the view that American incomes will continue to gain steadily across a number of sectors this year. The median salary among nonfarm employees increased 3 percent in the past quarter, and the rate was even higher among those working in service industries, the Labor Department said on Thursday. "Today's report continues to signal solid middle-class wage growth," said Bruce Sittenfeld, senior economist at RBS in Stamford, Connecticut.

**Treatment 2 (Democrats):**
NEW YORK—Last week's income report showed weakening wage growth, lending mounting evidence to the view that American incomes will continue to fall across a number of sectors this year. The median salary among non-farm workers decreased 3 percent in the past quarter, and the rate was even higher among those working in service industries, the Labor Department said on Thursday. "Today's report continues to signal faltering middle-class wage growth," said Bruce Sittenfeld, senior economist at RBS in Stamford, Connecticut.

**Treatment 3 (Republicans):**
WASHINGTON—Congressional Republicans are enthusiastic about the stock market. "Stocks were up last week, lending further evidence that the markets are headed for even stronger gains," Speaker of the House Paul Ryan said in a prepared statement. "The Dow Jones rallied substantially in the past quarter, as investors displayed a growing appetite for risk and a disregard for worries about any potential downturns. Today's report continues to signal a solid investing environment."

**Treatment 3 (Democrats):**
WASHINGTON—Congressional Democrats are worried about the stock market. "Stocks dipped sharply last week, adding to growing concerns that the markets are headed for even bigger losses in the near future," House minority leader Nancy Pelosi said in a prepared statement. "The Dow Jones has experienced worrying volatility in the past quarter, as investors displayed a growing aversion to risk and a striking amount of concern towards potential reversals of fortune. Today's report continues to signal an unsteady investing environment."

**Treatment 4 (Republicans):**
WASHINGTON—Congressional Republicans are enthusiastic about wages. "Last week's income report showed strengthening wage growth, lending mounting evidence to the view that American incomes will continue to gain steadily across a number of sectors this year," Speaker of the House Paul Ryan said in a prepared statement. "The median salary among nonfarm employees increased 3% in the past quarter, and the rate was even higher among those working in service industries. Today's report continues to signal solid middle-class wage growth."

**Treatment 4 (Democrats):**
WASHINGTON—Congressional Democrats are worried about wages. "Last week's income report showed weakening wage growth, lending mounting evidence to the view that American incomes will continue to fall across a number of sectors this year," House minority leader Nancy Pelosi said in a prepared statement. "The median salary among non-farm workers decreased 3% in the past quarter, and the rate was even higher among those working in service industries. Today's report continues to signal faltering middle-class wage growth."

Table A.4. Descriptive Statistics, Study 5.1

| Statistic | N | Mean | SD | Min | 25% | 75% | Max |
|---|---|---|---|---|---|---|---|
| Republican | 1,560 | 0.276 | 0.447 | 0 | 0 | 1 | 1 |
| Democrat | 1,560 | 0.406 | 0.491 | 0 | 0 | 1 | 1 |
| Income | 1,560 | 5.938 | 2.957 | 1 | 4 | 8 | 12 |
| Age | 1,560 | 18.979 | 11.626 | 1 | 11 | 24 | 63 |
| Male | 1,560 | 1.451 | 0.498 | 1 | 1 | 2 | 2 |
| Education | 1,560 | 5.422 | 1.421 | 1 | 4 | 6 | 8 |
| Ideology | 1,558 | 3.539 | 1.728 | 1.000 | 2.000 | 5.000 | 7.000 |
| News Exposure | 1,560 | 6.019 | 2.130 | 1 | 4 | 8 | 8 |

Next, table A.5 shows the results of the experiment conducted in study 5.1 for Democrats only, while table A.6 shows the results for Republicans only. We see in this table that overall economic perceptions are moved in congenial directions by the treatments, with positive coefficients indicating more positive evaluations, and negative coefficients indicating more negative evaluations.

Table A.7 shows the effects of the treatments on the stock market perceptions of Democrats. In this case we see that treatment 3 has a strong and significant positive effect on the outcome (a difference of roughly 0.27 points; $p < 0.001$).

Next, in table A.8, we see tabular results for the effects of the treatments on stock market perceptions among Republicans. The results show in this case that while treatments 1 and 2 have the strongest negative effect on perceptions, the effect is close to statistically significant but does not exceed the $p < 0.05$ level.

TABULAR RESULTS FOR STUDY 5.2

In table A.9, we see a summary of descriptive statistics for the nationally representative TESS sample used for study 5.2.

Table A.5. Treatment Effects, Study 5.1: Democrats

|  | Democratic Respondents: Overall Economy |
|---|---|
| Treatment 1 | −0.063 |
|  | (0.100) |
| Treatment 2 | 0.094 |
|  | (0.099) |
| Treatment 3 | 0.006 |
|  | (0.100) |
| Treatment 4 | 0.140 |
|  | (0.098) |
| Constant | 3.000*** |
|  | (0.070) |
| N | 825 |
| R-squared | 0.006 |
| Adj. R-squared | 0.002 |
| Residual Std. Error | 0.901 (df = 820) |
| F Statistic | 1.338 (df = 4; 820) |

Note: ***$p < 0.001$.

Table A.6. Treatment Effects, Study 5.1: Republicans

|  | Republican Respondents: Overall Economy |
|---|---|
| Treatment 1 | −0.029 |
|  | (0.098) |
| Treatment 2 | −0.066 |
|  | (0.099) |
| Treatment 3 | −0.059 |
|  | (0.100) |
| Treatment 4 | −0.053 |
|  | (0.104) |
| Constant | 2.189*** |
|  | (0.069) |
| N | 559 |
| R-squared | 0.001 |
| Adj. R-squared | −0.006 |
| Residual Std. Error | 0.760 (df = 554) |
| F Statistic | 0.147 (df = 4; 554) |

*Note:* ***$p < 0.001$.

Table A.7. Treatment Effects on Stock Market Perceptions of
Democrats, Study 5.1

|  | Democratic Respondents: Stock Market Perceptions |
|---|---|
| Treatment 1 | 0.160 |
|  | (0.103) |
| Treatment 2 | 0.134 |
|  | (0.101) |
| Treatment 3 | 0.274*** |
|  | (0.103) |
| Treatment 4 | 0.053 |
|  | (0.101) |
| Constant | 2.695*** |
|  | (0.072) |
| N | 825 |
| R-squared | 0.010 |
| Adj. R-squared | 0.005 |
| Residual Std. Error | 0.926 (df = 820) |
| F Statistic | 2.102* (df = 4; 820) |

*Note:* ***$p < .01$; **$p < .05$; *$p < 0.1$.

Table A.8. Treatment Effects on Stock Market Perceptions of Republicans, Study 5.1

|  | Republican Respondents: Stock Market Perceptions |
|---|---|
| Treatment 1 | −0.103 |
|  | (0.103) |
| Treatment 2 | −0.104 |
|  | (0.104) |
| Treatment 3 | −0.077 |
|  | (0.105) |
| Treatment 4 | −0.085 |
|  | (0.109) |
| Constant | 2.262*** |
|  | (0.072) |
| N | 559 |
| R-squared | 0.003 |
| Adj. R-squared | −0.005 |
| Residual Std. Error | 0.796 (df = 554) |
| F Statistic | 0.348 (df = 4; 554) |

Note: ***p < .01; **p < .05; *p < 0.1.

Table A.9. Descriptive Statistics, Study 5.2

| Statistic | N | Mean | St. Dev. | Min | Pctl. (25) | Pctl. (75) | Max |
|---|---|---|---|---|---|---|---|
| Republican | 1,946 | 0.462 | 0.499 | 0.000 | 0.000 | 1.000 | 1.000 |
| Democrat | 1,946 | 0.538 | 0.499 | 0.000 | 0.000 | 1.000 | 1.000 |
| Income | 2,033 | 12.094 | 4.565 | 1 | 9 | 16 | 19 |
| Age | 2,033 | 4.093 | 1.741 | 1 | 3 | 5 | 7 |
| Female | 2,033 | 0.511 | 0.500 | 0 | 0 | 1 | 1 |
| Nonwhite | 2,033 | 0.253 | 0.435 | 0 | 0 | 1 | 1 |
| Education | 2,033 | 2.848 | 0.965 | 1 | 2 | 4 | 4 |
| Ideology | 2,022 | 4.181 | 1.521 | 1.000 | 3.000 | 5.000 | 7.000 |
| Married | 2,033 | 0.553 | 0.497 | 0 | 0 | 1 | 1 |
| Homeowner | 2,033 | 0.716 | 0.451 | 0 | 0 | 1 | 1 |
| Employed | 2,033 | 0.565 | 0.496 | 0 | 0 | 1 | 1 |
| Retirement Accts. | 1,425 | 1.512 | 1.482 | 0.000 | 0.000 | 3.000 | 5.000 |
| Active Stock Market Investor | 1,481 | 0.258 | 0.438 | 0.000 | 0.000 | 1.000 | 1.000 |
| Savings Level | 1,212 | 6.012 | 3.243 | 1.000 | 3.000 | 9.000 | 11.000 |

Finally, table A.10 provides tabular estimates of the various treatment effects in study 5.2. This interactive model shows the baseline results of treatments 1, 2, and 3 on economic perceptions for Republicans. The intercept shows the baseline difference in this outcome for Republicans, and the interactive terms shows the difference between Democratic (baseline) and Republican treatment effect estimates for each treatment. In addition, the model compensates for story selection by including coefficients for whether a respondent intentionally sought out the specific economic information they received.

Table A.10. Effects of Treatment Effects and Preferences on Economic Perceptions, Republicans and Democrats, Study 5.2

| | Dependent variable: |
| --- | --- |
| | Retrospective Economic Eval. |
| Democrat | 0.928*** |
| | (0.099) |
| Sought Treatment 1 | 0.133* |
| | (0.072) |
| Sought Treatment 2 | −0.133 |
| | (0.086) |
| Sought Treatment 3 | 0.115** |
| | (0.058) |
| Received Preferred Treatment | −0.247** |
| | (0.106) |
| Democrat x Treatment 1 | −0.141 |
| | (0.123) |
| Democrat x Treatment 2 | 0.009 |
| | (0.080) |
| Democrat x Treatment 3 | 2.438*** |
| | (0.066) |
| Observations | 1,936 |
| $R^2$ | 0.170 |
| Adjusted $R^2$ | 0.167 |
| Residual Std. Error | 0.873 (df = 1928) |
| F Statistic | 56.235*** (df = 7; 1928) |

Note: *$p < 0.05$; **$p < 0.01$; ***$p < 0.01$.

# Notes

## Introduction

1. @realDonaldTrump, April 8, 2020 and April 10, 2020.

2. Scholars of economic voting have produced a vast amount of work on the subject. See Anderson (2007) for a partial review.

3. In the highly technical literature on the subject, this point is known as the "Kramer problem" (Kramer 1983; Lewis-Beck and Stegmaier 2013).

4. A short is "an investing or trading strategy that speculates on the decline in a stock or other security's price" (Hayes 2021). When hedge funds shorted GameStop's stock, retail investors attempted to create a "short squeeze," in which short-selling firms would be obligated to buy additional shares to cover their shorts (hence driving up the price of the stock, to the benefit of those who had previously purchased shares).

5. Valence issues are often defined in political science literature as those issues upon which Americans can generally agree. For example, it is assumed that Americans unanimously prefer low unemployment to high unemployment (Stokes 1963).

6. A great deal of political science research has attempted to measure whether presidents can manipulate the business cycle. Results are mixed, and many scholars remain skeptical that administrations can have a major influence on the pace and timing of economic downturns or upswings (e.g., Nordhaus 1975).

7. For a partial introduction to this literature, see Boydstun (2013) and McCombs (2018).

## Chapter 1

1. Fact checking is one other way in which journalists might fulfill their "social responsibility." Attempts to correct misperceptions have been especially

salient in recent years, as public discussion has centered on "fake news" and its potential role in tipping the scales in favor of Donald Trump in the 2016 presidential election (Allcott and Gentzkow 2017; Fridkin, Kenney, and Wintersieck 2015; Nyhan and Reifler 2010, Nyhan and Reifler 2015). Social scientists and commentators alike have wondered whether it is possible to "inoculate" or otherwise prevent people from believing information stemming from groups who are intent upon misleading the American public for a variety of political purposes. The answer appears to be relatively unclear at this stage, with some studies showing a good deal of success in correcting misperceptions through fact-checking, and others showing more doubtful results.

2. While journalists might describe news values as "gut feelings" that help them engage in story selection, scholars have described them as "highly regulated procedures" that drive the news agenda forward through habits and pragmatic routines (Harcup and O'Neill 2017).

3. See Chong and Druckman (2007), Borah (2011), and Nelson (2019) for partial reviews of this voluminous literature.

4. Valence issues are those issues on which most Americans can agree about what constitutes "positive" and "negative" performance (Stokes 1963). The canonical literature on this subject has identified economic progress and military casualties as central examples.

5. Another example of misinformation that has been scrutinized by scholars is the (non)existence of weapons of mass destruction (WMDs) in Iraq prior to Operation Iraqi Freedom in 2003 (Gaines et al. 2007; Kull, Ramsay, and Lewis 2003).

6. Some readers may wonder whether Republicans were sincere in their beliefs about the size of the crowd at Trump's inauguration ceremony. This idea, of "expressive responding" or insincere "cheerleading," has recently occupied the attention of several researchers (e.g., Prior, Sood, and Khanna 2015). While some studies have been able to successfully limit the amount of directional bias in survey respondents' beliefs about facts using specialized interventions, others suggest that the existence of widespread "cheerleading" in the electorate is unlikely.

7. See, for relevant examples spanning the recent history of public opinion research, Converse (1964), Green, Palmquist, and Schickler (2004), and Mason (2018).

8. Of course, partisans often have unbalanced news diets that allow them to consume party-congenial information more often than disconfirming information. This pattern of selective exposure, beyond the confines of the present thought experiment, that explains how motivated reasoning is perpetuated in the realm of factual perceptions. I return to the topic of selective exposure later in the chapter.

9. This observation has raised important questions in recent years about the sincerity of biased economic beliefs. See Bullock and Lenz (2019) for a review.

10. Related studies which similarly examine the information context include those of Erisen, Redlawsk, and Erisen (2018), Jerit and Barabas (2012), Braman and Nelson (2007), and Parker-Stephen (2013).

11. While the nature and extent of mass polarization is the subject of much ongoing debate in political science, elite polarization is often assumed (Hetherington 2001).

## Chapter 2

1. I do not intend to say that journalists necessarily have a choice when it comes to this agenda-setting behavior. Because many core economic indicators are aggregated on a monthly or quarterly basis, journalists seeking to inform audiences of the day's economic events turn to daily-aggregated indicators on most days as a matter of course.

2. This means that wire services might play an outsized role in determining which economic indicators are talked about even by the largest and most prominent news outlets.

3. One of the most noteworthy recent examples of this trend concerns the Sinclair Broadcast Group, which has sought to inject right-leaning coverage into Americans' news diets at the local, rather than national, level. They have accomplished this goal in many media markets through aggressive acquisitions of existing media enterprises in local marketplaces (Merced and Fandos 2017).

4. We know this in part thanks to the inventive study of Gentzkow and Shapiro (2010), who show that demand for ideological coverage tends to drive newspaper ideology, and not vice versa.

5. Rather than machine learning methods which discover new language features indicating the presence of topics in text, these methods rely on the assumption that a dictionary of known terms is sufficient to identify topics. This kind of assumption makes more sense when trying to determine mentions of economic indicators compared to other research questions. For example, a dictionary-based method might struggle to place the left-right ideology of party manifestos, which would benefit from algorithms accounting for language features in an unsupervised or semi-unsupervised fashion, or from human coding (e.g., Hjorth et al. 2015; Mikhaylov, Laver, and Benoit 2012.)

6. These categories are as follows: "employment," "prices," "sales, goods, and manufacturing," "wages," "growth," "credit and household debt," "stock markets," "consumers," and "trade."

7. As Lewis-Beck, Martini, and Kiewiet (2013) show, there is some evidence that uncorrected versions of these indicators, that is, statistics as they were reported at the time, yield stronger relationships with media coverage than corrected figures. Many economic indicators are updated years after they are first

reported to the public, which means that people at the time did not receive the same information that is contained in currently available economic data tables. It is very difficult to assemble fully uncorrected reports in this analysis, as the data series cover economic data since 1980.

8. All series were coded so that increases in the indicator's value signaled positive developments. For example, unemployment, which usually signals bad news upon increasing, was reverse-coded.

9. Modeling was performed using the LPM package in R.

10. Data were collected from Nexis Uni. The newspaper data include the following sources: *Daily News* (NY), the *Los Angeles Times*, the *Pittsburgh Post-Gazette*, the *St. Louis Post-Dispatch*, the *Minneapolis Star Tribune*, the *Tampa Bay Times*, the *Atlanta Journal-Constitution*, the *Christian Science Monitor*, the *Daily Oklahoman*, the *New York Post*, the *Philadelphia Inquirer*, the *Washington Post*, and *USA Today*. The cable news transcripts were drawn from Fox News Network and MSNBC.

11. As the American economy continues to shift from one driven primarily by manufacturing and natural resources to one in which banks and financial organizations are incredibly important, perhaps it is only logical that our news reflects this shift in terms of its agenda.

## Chapter 3

1. Because Twitter limited scraping to user profiles' most recent thirty-two hundred tweets when this analysis was performed, the 2018 data collection contained too few tweets from the 111th Congress for reliable analysis.

2. In this chapter, I deal specifically with legislators' discussion of developments in news, which can be distinguished from broader arguments about position taking (e.g., Mayhew 1974).

3. Other work has also contended with symbolic speeches made by legislators on the floor of the House and Senate. Hill and Hurley (2002), for example, show how the "home style" of legislators, among other predictable patterns of behavior, are visible in the amount, timing, and topics of floor speeches (Fenno 1978). See also Grimmer (2013) for similar evidence of home style in the case of press releases. Proksch and Slapin (2012) examine floor debate in parliaments, showing that in this context, multiple strategic considerations emerge from the rules of a given legislature, the rank of a given MC, and the ideological distance between members and their party leadership.

4. For an introduction to the discussion of the inability of incumbents to manipulate the political business cycle, see Chappell and Keech (1985) for a partial discussion.

5. The actions of the Federal Reserve Board represent an increasingly important subject in political science research. See, for example, Jacobs and King (2018), who introduce a recent symposium on the topic.

6. I used the R programming environment and associated libraries. Data collection was performed using the *twitteR* library, the *tidytext* library, and the tidyverse approach to text mining (Wickham and Grolemund 2016).

7. Official twitter accounts were identified by the language present in the account's descriptive bio. It is possible that this timeline search missed a significant number of tweets, especially if MCs deleted tweets after posting them. The Twitter API currently prevents other forms of large-scale scraping. Retweets were included, given that these mentions also form part of MCs' twitter agendas.

8. Each tweet was made lowercase, was cleaned of common stopwords, and was stripped of excess whitespace, punctuation, and unreadable symbols.

9. Independent legislators were excluded from the analysis.

10. See the appendix for a discussion of false positives and false negatives in the tweet dataset.

11. It is unclear why the Twitter data do not reflect a stronger increase in unemployment-related tweets among members of Congress in early 2020. For the subset of tweets after the COVID-19 unemployment rate hit 14.8 percent in April of 2020, up to the end of the time series in July of 2020 (around 66,000 tweets total), unemployment is mentioned roughly 4 percent of the time, which is higher than average, but not an immense shift in the agenda. It may be that MCs chose to frame the situation not by mentioning the unemployment rate itself, but by discussing the stimulus bills. We also see a substantial uptick in the overall volume of tweets, meaning that unemployment's salience may be balanced by an increasing willingness to tweet about other issues relevant to COVID-19. Regardless, we do see many tweets in the data related to the effects of COVID-19 on jobs, such as Representative Peter DeFazio's assertion on April 2, 2020, that "Any future economic stimulus bill must include ways to create JOBS."

12. @RepJimRenacci, August 27, 2018.

13. Negative binomial models are preferred to standard Poisson regression models for these count data, based on tests for overdispersion (Cameron and Trivedi 1990).

14. Independent variables in this model include MC partisanship, Trump tweet volume, and MC tweet volume. Because the series only analyzes the Trump administration, the model excludes presidential incumbency.

15. This data collection was performed in July of 2020, before Donald Trump was banned from Twitter and before his historical tweets were removed from the platform.

## Chapter 4

1. See Matthews and Pickup (2018) for an important exception from the literature on Canadian politics.

2. See Bisgaard and Slothuus (2018) for another study that examines a sudden shift in the economic perceptions of partisans after a specific exogenous shock; in this case, a prominent Danish party's policy reversal.

3. See also Weatherford (1983) and Wlezien, Franklin, and Twiggs (1997) for additional resources on the contextual limits of partisan biases.

4. By cognitive resources, I refer to the scarce mental capacity of humans to self-regulate—a capacity that can be depleted when we engage in effortful cognitive tasks like self-reflection and decision making (Muraven, Tice, and Baumeister 1998).

5. I compute these predictions using R's ggpredict library and visualize them using ggplot.

6. For ease of interpretation, I divide these raw quarterly counts by one hundred, meaning that the coefficients presented below measure the effects of every one hundred additional tweets on economic evaluations.

7. Results are robust to the use of ordered logistic regression, which is a more appropriate modeling strategy for the trichotomous dependent variable, but one that is far more difficult to interpret.

## Chapter 5

1. In some recent studies experimental conditions have included more realistic features, relying on methods like field experiments (e.g., Gerber, Huber, and Washington 2010).

2. The act reformed the U.S. tax code, and strongly impacted economic conditions and budgetary considerations (Mertens 2018).

3. @realDonaldTrump, January 4, 2018.

4. By acceptance and rejection, I refer to the R-A-S model pioneered by Zaller (1992).

5. Some readers may anticipate that exposure to disconfirming information will cause a "backlash" effect among partisans, in which the disconfirming information causes motivated reasoners to move further away from the valence of the news story (and towards the congenial position). However, consistent with work by Wood and Porter (2019) and others, backlash effects appear to be virtually nonexistent in the prior studies on the topic.

6. See Chong and Druckman (2010). Pretreatment exposure could upwardly or downwardly bias the experimental treatment effects we are trying to estimate in our studies.

7. Barabas and Jerit (2010), for example, show that contemporaneous survey and natural experiments can reveal substantially different treatment effects.

8. Despite these low costs, it is important to treat MTurk workers ethically. Marinova (2016) provides a useful overview of the ethics of online surveys, arguing that livable wage equivalents should be used to inform MTurk workers' compensation for survey completion.

9. For full question wording please see the appendix.

10. For ease of interpretation, in some subsequent analyses I dichotomize these scales into "same/better" vs. "worse" classifications.

11. Respondents' working memory was cleared before treatment exposure by asking them to complete a simple memory-based task.

12. Because the overall economy was performing quite well during the implementation of the survey, the Republican group is at risk of "ceiling effects," in which the control group's responses are already so positive that a treatment contrast in this direction is necessarily limited in magnitude.

13. This experiment was fielded thanks to the generosity of the Time Sharing Experiments in the Social Sciences (TESS) program (www.tessexperiments.org).

14. "In a moment, we'd like you to read a short news article. Please indicate which of the following you would be interested in reading about. You may not receive your preferred topic."

## Conclusion

1. Kinder and Kalmoe (2017) shows that many Americans can be considered "operationally liberal," though many of these same Americans report conservative ideological identifications.

2. In 1947 FIRE accounted for around 10% of GDP, a figure which had increased to over 20 percent by 2005 (Witko 2016).

3. This literature can trace its roots to the work of Erikson, MacKuen, and Stimson (2002) and Page and Shapiro (2010), among others.

4. See, for example, the work of Kuklinski et al. (2000) and Caplan (2011), which informs perhaps the most impactful recent examples in this vein. But see Fowler and Hall (2018) for a recent counterargument.

# Works Cited

Abramowitz, Alan I. 2018. *The Great Alignment: Race, Party Transformation, and the Rise of Donald Trump*. Yale University Press.

Achen, Christopher H., and Larry M. Bartels. 2017. *Democracy for Realists: Why Elections Do Not Produce Responsive Government*. Princeton University Press.

Allcott, Hunt, and Matthew Gentzkow. 2017. "Social Media and Fake News in the 2016 Election." *Journal of Economic Perspectives* 31 (2): 211–36.

Alt, James E. 1979. *The Politics of Economic Decline: Economic Management and Political Behaviour in Britain Since 1964*. Cambridge University Press.

Alt, James E., John Marshall, and David D. Lassen. 2016. "Credible Sources and Sophisticated Voters: When Does New Information Induce Economic Voting?" *The Journal of Politics* 78 (2): 327–42.

Amsalem, E., and A. Zoizner. 2022. "Real, But Limited: A Meta-Analytic Assessment of Framing Effects in the Political Domain." *British Journal of Political Science* 52 (1): 221–37.

Anderson, Cameron. 2020. "(Re) Considering the Sources of Economic Perceptions." *Social Science Quarterly* 101 (4): 1314–25.

Anderson, Christopher J. 2000. "Economic Voting and Political Context: A Comparative Perspective." *Electoral Studies* 19 (2): 151–70.

Anderson, Christopher J. 2007. "The End of Economic Voting? Contingency Dilemmas and the Limits of Democratic Accountability." *Annual Review of Political Science* 10: 271–96.

Ansolabehere, Stephen, Marc Meredith, and Erik Snowberg. 2014. "Mecro-Economic Voting: Local Information and Micro-Perceptions of the Macro-Economy." *Economics & Politics* 26 (3): 380–410.

Anson, Ian G. 2016. "Just the Facts? Partisan Media and the Political Conditioning of Economic Perceptions." *Political Research Quarterly* 69 (3): 444–56.

Anson, Ian G. 2017. "'That's Not How It Works': Economic Indicators and the Construction of Partisan Economic Narratives." *Journal of Elections, Public Opinion and Parties* 27 (2): 213–34.

Anson, Ian G. 2018. "Taking the Time? Explaining Effortful Participation among Low-Cost Online Survey Participants." *Research & Politics* 5 (3). https://doi.org/10.1177%2F2053168018785483.

Arceneaux, Kevin, and Martin Johnson. 2013. *Changing Minds or Changing Channels?: Partisan News in an Age of Choice*. University of Chicago Press.

Arceneaux, Kevin, and Ryan J. Vander Wielen. 2017. *Taming Intuition: How Reflection Minimizes Partisan Reasoning and Promotes Democratic Accountability*. Cambridge University Press.

Associated Press. 2018. "About Us." The Associated Press. Last modified April 27, 2022. http://www.ap.org/about.

Baker, C. Edwin. 2006. *Media Concentration and Democracy: Why Ownership Matters*. Cambridge University Press.

Barabas, Jason, and Jennifer Jerit. 2010. "Are Survey Experiments Externally Valid?" *American Political Science Review* 104 (2): 226–42.

Barberá, Pablo, John T. Jost, Jonathan Nagler, Joshua A. Tucker, and Richard Bonneau. 2015. "Tweeting from Left to Right: Is Online Political Communication More Than an Echo Chamber?" *Psychological Science* 26 (10): 1531–42.

Bargh, John A., and Melissa J. Ferguson. 2000. "Beyond Behaviorism: On the Automaticity of Higher Mental Processes. *Psychological Bulletin* 126 (6): 925.

Bartels, Larry M. 2002. "Beyond the Running Tally: Partisan Bias in Political Perceptions." *Political Behavior* 24 (2): 117–50.

Bartels, Larry M. 2009. *Unequal Democracy: The Political Economy of the New Gilded Age*. Princeton University Press.

Bartels, Larry, and Nancy Bermeo. 2013. *Mass Politics in Tough Times: Opinions, Votes and Protest in the Great Recession*. Oxford University Press.

Baum, Matthew A., and Tim Groeling. 2009. "Shot by the Messenger: Partisan Cues and Public Opinion Regarding National Security and War." *Political Behavior* 31 (2): 157–86.

Baumohl, Bernard. 2012. *The Secrets of Economic Indicators: Hidden Clues to Future Economic Trends and Investment Opportunities*. FT Press.

Berinsky, Adam J. 2018. "Telling the Truth about Believing the Lies? Evidence for the Limited Prevalence of Expressive Survey Responding." *The Journal of Politics* 80 (1): 211–24.

Bisgaard, Martin. 2015. "Bias Will Find a Way: Economic Perceptions, Attributions of Blame, and Partisan-Motivated Reasoning During Crisis." *The Journal of Politics* 77 (3): 849–60.

Bisgaard, Martin. 2019. "How Getting the Facts Right Can Fuel Partisan-Motivated Reasoning." *American Journal of Political Science* 63 (4): 824–39.

Bisgaard, Martin, and Rune Slothuus. 2018. "Partisan Elites as Culprits? How Party Cues Shape Partisan Perceptual Gaps." *American Journal of Political Science* 62 (2): 456–69.

Bisgaard, Martin, Kim M. Sønderskov, and Peter T. Dinesen. 2016. "Reconsidering the Neighborhood Effect: Does Exposure to Residential Unemployment

Influence Voters' Perceptions of the National Economy?" *The Journal of Politics* 78 (3): 719–32.

Blount, Simon. 2002. "Unemployment and Economic Voting." *Electoral Studies* 21 (1): 91–100.

Bogost, Ian. 2017. "Cryptocurrency Might Be a Path to Authoritarianism." *The Atlantic,* May 30. https://www.theatlantic.com/technology/archive/2017/05/blockchain-of-command/528543/.

Bolsen, Toby, James N. Druckman, and Fay Lomax Cook. 2014. "The Influence of Partisan Motivated Reasoning on Public Opinion." *Political Behavior* 36 (2): 235–62.

Borah, Porismita. 2011. "Conceptual Issues in Framing Theory: A Systematic Examination of a Decade's Literature." *Journal of Communication* 61 (2): 246–63.

Boskin, Michael J. 2018. "Why the Economy's Strength Won't Help Republicans in November." *Marketwatch,* August 21, https://www.marketwatch.com/story/why-the-economys-strength-wont-help-republicans-in-november-2018-08-21.

Boydstun, Amber E. 2013. *Making the News: Politics, the Media, and Agenda Setting.* University of Chicago Press.

Boyle, Thomas P. 2001. "Intermedia Agenda Setting in the 1996 Presidential Election." *Journalism & Mass Communication Quarterly* 78 (1): 26–44.

Brady, David W., John A. Ferejohn, and Brett Parker. 2022. "Cognitive Political Economy: A Growing Partisan Divide in Economic Perceptions." *American Politics Research* 50 (1): 3–16.

Braman, Eileen, and Thomas E. Nelson. 2007. "Mechanism of Motivated Reasoning? Analogical Perception in Discrimination Disputes." *American Journal of Political Science* 51 (4): 940–56.

Brown, Adam R. 2010. "Are Governors Responsible for the State Economy? Partisanship, Blame, and Divided Federalism." *The Journal of Politics* 72 (3): 605–15.

Brustier, Gaël. 2016. # *Nuit Debout: Que Penser?* Editions du Cerf.

Bucy, Erik P., Walter Gantz, and Zheng Wang. 2007. "Media Technology and the 24-hour News Cycle." In *Communication Technology and Social Change: Theory and Implications,* edited by Carolyn A. Lin and David J. Atkin. Taylor & Francis. 143–63.

Bullock, John G. 2011. "Elite Influence on Public Opinion in an Informed Electorate." *American Political Science Review* 105 (03): 496–515.

Bullock, John G., and Gabriel Lenz. 2019. "Partisan Bias in Surveys." *Annual Review of Political Science* 22: 325–42.

Bureau of Economic Analysis. 2022. "GDP by Industry," https://www.bea.gov/data/gdp/gdp-industry.

Bureau of Labor Statistics. 2018. "Table A-15. Alternative Measures of Labor Underutilization," https://www.bls.gov/news.release/empsit.t15.htm.

Bureau of Labor Statistics. 2018a. "Consumer Price Index," https://www.bls.gov/cpi/home.htm.

Bureau of Labor Statistics. 2018b. "Labor Force Statistics from the Current Population Survey," https://www.bls.gov/cps.

Cacioppo, John T., and Richard E. Petty. 1982. "The Need for Cognition." *Journal of Personality and Social Psychology* 42 (1): 116–32.

Calhoun, Craig. 2013. "Occupy Wall Street in Perspective." *British Journal of Sociology* 64 (1): 26–38.

Cameron, A. Colin, and Pravin K. Trivedi. 1990. "Regression-Based Tests for Overdispersion in the Negative Binomial Model." *Journal of Econometrics* 46 (3): 347–64.

Campbell, Angus, Philip E. Converse, Warren E. Miller, and Donald E. Stokes. 1960. *The American Voter*. New York: John Wiley.

Campbell, David E., Geoffrey C. Layman, John C. Green, and Nathanael G. Sumaktoyo. 2018. "Putting Politics First: The Impact of Politics on American Religious and Secular Orientations." *American Journal of Political Science* 62 (3): 551–65.

Caner, Asena, and Edward N. Wolff. 2004. *Asset Poverty in the United States: Its Persistence in an Expansionary Economy*. Public Policy Brief #76, Jerome Levy Economics Institute of Bard College.

Caplan, Bryan. 2011. *The Myth of the Rational Voter: Why Democracies Choose Bad Policies* (2nd Ed.). Princeton University Press.

Chappell, Henry W., and William R. Keech. 1985. "A New View of Political Accountability for Economic Performance." *American Political Science Review* 79 (1): 10–27.

Chen, Emily, Herbert Chang, Ashwin Rao, Kristina Lerman, Geoffrey Cowan, and Emilio Ferrara. 2021. "COVID-19 Misinformation and the 2020 U.S. Presidential Election." *The Harvard Kennedy School Misinformation Review* 1 (7): https://doi.org/10.37016/mr-2020-57.

Choi, Sujin, and Jeongseob Kim. 2017. "Online News Flow: Temporal/Spatial Exploitation and Credibility." *Journalism* 18 (9): 1184–1205.

Chong, Dennis, and James N. Druckman. 2010. "Dynamic Public Opinion: Communication Effects over Time." *American Political Science Review* 104 (4): 663–80.

Chzhen, Kat, Geoffrey Evans, and Mark Pickup. 2014. "When Do Economic Perceptions Matter for Party Approval?" *Political Behavior* 36 (2): 291–313.

Clark, Nicholas, and Todd Makse. 2019. "Local Media Tone, Economic Conditions, and the Evaluation of Us Governors." *Journal of Elections, Public Opinion and Parties* 29 (1): 82–101.

Clarke, Harold D., and Marianne C. Stewart. 1994. "Prospections, Retrospections, and Rationality: The 'Bankers' Model of Presidential Approval Reconsidered." *American Journal of Political Science* 38 (4): 1104–23.

Clifford, Scott, Ryan M. Jewell, and Philip D. Waggoner. 2015. "Are Samples Drawn from Mechanical Turk Valid for Research on Political Ideology?" *Research & Politics* 2 (4): 2053168015622072.

Congressional Progressive Caucus. 2022. "A Fair Economy," https://progressives. house.gov/a-fair-economy

Conover, Pamela J. 1984. "The Influence of Group Identifications on Political Perception and Evaluation." *The Journal of Politics* 46 (3): 760–785.

Converse, Philip E. 1964. "The Nature of Belief Systems in Mass Publics." In *Ideology and Discontent*, edited by David Apter. New York: Free Press of Glencoe.

Conway, Bethany Anne, Kate Kenski, and Di Wang. 2013. "Twitter Use by Presidential Primary Candidates during the 2012 Campaign." *American Behavioral Scientist* 57 (11): 1596–1610.

Dahl, Robert A. 2008. *On Democracy*. Yale University Press.

Damstra, Alyt, and Mark Boukes. 2021. "The Economy, the News, and the Public: A Longitudinal Study of the Impact of Economic News on Economic Evaluations and Expectations." *Communication Research* 48 (1): 26–50.

Dassonneville, Ruth, and Charles Tien. 2021. "Introduction to Forecasting the 2020 US Elections." *PS: Political Science & Politics* 54 (1): 47–51.

Davidson, Paul. 2009. "On the Road Again: RV Sales See an Upswing." *USA Today*, September, Page 1B.

De Vries, Catherine E, Sara B Hobolt, and James Tilley. 2018. "Facing up to the Facts: What Causes Economic Perceptions?" *Electoral Studies* 51: 115–122.

Delli Carpini, Michael X., and Scott Keeter. 1997. *What Americans Know about Politics and Why It Matters*. Yale University Press.

Dickerson, Bradley. 2016. "Economic Perceptions, Presidential Approval, and Causality: The Moderating Role of the Economic Context." *American Politics Research* 44 (6): 1037–65.

Dickerson, Bradley T., and Heather L. Ondercin. 2017. "Conditional Motivated Reasoning: How the Local Economy Moderates Partisan Motivations in Economic Perceptions." *Political Research Quarterly* 70 (1): 194–208.

Ditto, Peter H., and David F. Lopez. 1992. "Motivated Skepticism: Use of Differential Decision Criteria for Preferred and Nonpreferred Conclusions." *Journal of Personality and Social Psychology* 63 (4): 568.

Donovan, Kathleen, Paul M. Kellstedt, Ellen M, Key, and Matthew J. Lebo. 2020. "Motivated Reasoning, Public Opinion, and Presidential Approval." *Political Behavior* 42: 1201–20.

Druckman, James N. 2001. "On the Limits of Framing Effects: Who Can Frame?" *Journal of Politics* 63 (4): 1041–66.

Druckman, James N., Erik Peterson, and Rune Slothuus. 2013. "How Elite Partisan Polarization Affects Public Opinion Formation." *American Political Science Review* 107 (1): 57–79.

Druckman, James N., and Kjersten R. Nelson. 2003. "Framing and Deliberation: How Citizens' Conversations Limit Elite Influence." *American Journal of Political Science* 47 (4): 729–45.

Druckman, James N., and Michael Parkin. 2005. "The Impact of Media Bias: How Editorial Slant Affects Voters." *The Journal of Politics* 67 (4): 1030–49.

Druckman, James N., and Thomas J. Leeper. 2012. "Learning More from Political Communication Experiments: Pretreatment and Its Effects." *American Journal of Political Science* 56 (4): 875–96.

Egan, Matt. 2016. "Wild January Stock Market Ends on a High Note." *CNN Business,* January 31, https://money.cnn.com/2016/01/29/investing/doEw-january-2016-worst-month/.

Entman, Robert M. 1993. "Framing: Toward Clarification of a Fractured Paradigm." *Journal of Communication* 43 (4): 51–58.

Erikson, Robert S., and Rocío Titiunik. 2015. "Using Regression Discontinuity to Uncover the Personal Incumbency Advantage." *Quarterly Journal of Political Science* 10 (1): 101–119.

Erikson, Robert S., Michael B. MacKuen, and James A. Stimson. 2002. *The Macro Polity*. Cambridge University Press.

Erisen, Cengiz, David P. Redlawsk, and Elif Erisen. 2018. "Complex Thinking as a Result of Incongruent Information Exposure." *American Politics Research* 46 (2): 217–45.

Evans, Geoffrey, and Mark Pickup. 2010. "Reversing the Causal Arrow: The Political Conditioning of Economic Perceptions in the 2000–2004 U.S. Presidential Election Cycle." *The Journal of Politics* 72 (4): 1236–51.

Evans, Geoffrey, and Robert Andersen. 2006. "The Political Conditioning of Economic Perceptions." *Journal of Politics* 68 (1): 194–207.

Evans, Heather K., Kayla J. Brown, and Tiffany Wimberly. 2018. " 'Delete Your Account:' The 2016 Presidential Race on Twitter." *Social Science Computer Review* 36 (4): 500–508.

Ezrow, Lawrence, and Timothy Hellwig. 2014. "Responding to Voters or Responding to Markets? Political Parties and Public Opinion in an Era of Globalization." *International Studies Quarterly* 58 (4): 816–27.

Fallows, James M. 1996. *Breaking the News: How the Media Undermine American Democracy*. Vintage.

Feldman, Stanley, Leonie Huddy, and George E. Marcus. 2012. "Limits of Elite Influence on Public Opinion." *Critical Review* 24 (4): 489–503.

Fenno, Richard F. 1978. Home *Style: Representatives in Their Districts*. Boston: Little, Brown.

Ferre, Ines. 2021. "GameStop Saga Is about 'Working Class v. Hedge Funds': Reddit WSB User." *Yahoo!Finance,* January 27, https://finance.yahoo.com/news/game-stop-phenomena-is-about-the-poor-vs-rich-reddit-wsb-user-204822769.html.

Fiorina, Morris P. 1981. *Retrospective Voting in American National Elections*. Yale University Press.

Fitzgerald, Maggie. 2021. "GameStop Shares Soar More Than 100% Amid Executive Shuffle." *CNBC.com.* February 24, https://www.cnbc.com/2021/02/24/gamestop-shares-soar-more-than-80percent-in-late-afternoon-trading.html.

Flynn, D. J., Brendan Nyhan, and Jason Reifler. 2017. "The Nature and Origins of Misperceptions: Understanding False and Unsupported Beliefs about Politics." *Political Psychology* 38 (S1): 127–50.

Fogarty, Brian J. 2005. "Determining Economic News Coverage." *International Journal of Public Opinion Research* 17 (2): 149–72.

Fowler, Anthony, and Andrew B. Hall. 2018. "Do Shark Attacks Influence Presidential Elections? Reassessing a Prominent Finding on Voter Competence." *The Journal of Politics* 80 (4): 1423–37.

Fowler, Anthony, and B. Pablo Montagnes. 2015. "College Football, Elections, and False-Positive Results in Observational Research." *Proceedings of the National Academy of Sciences* 112 (45): 13800–13804.

Fowler, Erika Franklin, Laura M. Baum, Colleen L. Barry, Jeff Niederdeppe, and Sarah E. Gollust. 2017. "Media Messages and Perceptions of the Affordable Care Act during the Early Phase of Implementation." *Journal of Health Politics, Policy and Law* 42 (1): 167–95.

Fridkin, Kim, Patrick J. Kenney, and Amanda Wintersieck. 2015. "Liar, Liar, Pants on Fire: How Fact-Checking Influences Citizens' Reactions to Negative Advertising." *Political Communication* 32 (1): 127–51.

Gaines, Brian J., James H. Kuklinski, Paul J. Quirk, Buddy Peyton, and Jay Verkuilen. 2007. "Same Facts, Different Interpretations: Partisan Motivation and Opinion on Iraq." *The Journal of Politics* 69 (4): 957–74.

Gamson, William A., and Micah L. Sifry. 2013. "The Occupy Movement: An Introduction." *The Sociological Quarterly* 54 (2): 159–63.

Gans, Herbert J. 1979. *Deciding What's News: A Study of CBS Evening News, NBC Nightly News, Newsweek, and Time.* Pantheon Books.

Geithner, Timothy F. 2014. *Stress Test: Reflections on Financial Crises.* Broadway Books.

Gelman, Andrew, and Jennifer Hill. 2006. *Data Analysis Using Regression and Multilevel/Hierarchical Models.* Cambridge University Press.

Gentzkow, Matthew, and Jesse M. Shapiro. 2006. "Media Bias and Reputation." *Journal of Political Economy* 114 (2): 280–316.

Gentzkow, Matthew, and Jesse M. Shapiro. 2010. "What Drives Media Slant? Evidence from US Daily Newspapers." *Econometrica* 78 (1): 35–71.

Gerber, Alan S., and Donald Green. 1999. "Misperceptions about Perceptual Bias." *Annual Review of Political Science* 2 (1): 189–210.

Gerber, Alan S., and Gregory A. Huber. 2010. "Partisanship, Political Control, and Economic Assessments." *American Journal of Political Science* 54 (1): 153–73.

Gerber, Alan S., Gregory A. Huber, and Ebonya Washington. 2010. "Party Affil-iation, Partisanship, and Political Beliefs: A Field Experiment." *American Political Science Review* 104 (4): 720–44.

Gil de Zúñiga, H., B. Weeks, and A. Ardèvol-Abreu. 2017. "Effects of the News-Finds-Me Perception in Communication: Social Media Use Implications for News Seeking and Learning about Politics." *Journal of Computer-Mediated Communication* 22 (3): 105–123.

Gimpelson, Vladimir, and Daniel Treisman. 2018. "Misperceiving Inequality." *Economics & Politics* 30 (1): 27–54.

Glazier, Rebecca A., and Amber E. Boydstun. 2012. "The President, the Press, and the War: A Tale of Two Framing Agendas." *Political Communication* 29 (4): 428–46.

Godbout, Jean-François, and Éric Bélanger. 2006. "Cognitive Heterogeneity and Economic Voting: A Comparative Analysis of Four Democratic Electorates." *American Journal of Political Science* 50 (1): 127–45.

Godbout, Jean-François, and Éric Bélanger. 2007. "Economic Voting and Political Sophistication in the United States: A Reassessment." *Political Research Quarterly* 60 (3): 541–54.

Goidel, Kirby, Stephen Procopio, Dek Terrell, and H. Denis Wu. 2010. "Sources of Economic News and Economic Expectations." *American Politics Research* 38 (4): 759–77.

Goidel, Robert K., and Ronald E. Langley. 1995. "Media Coverage of the Economy and Aggregate Economic Evaluations: Uncovering Evidence of Indirect Media Effects." *Political Research Quarterly* 48 (2): 313–28.

Golan, Guy. 2006. "Inter-Media Agenda Setting and Global News Coverage: Assessing the Influence of the New York Times on Three Network Television Evening News Programs." *Journalism Studies* 7 (2): 323–33.

Gomes, Carlos F. A., Charles J. Brainerd, and Lilian M. Stein. 2013. "Effects of Emotional Valence and Arousal on Recollective and Nonrecollective Recall." *Journal of Experimental Psychology: Learning, Memory, and Cognition* 39 (3): 663.

Gomez, Brad T., and J. Matthew Wilson. 2001. "Political Sophistication and Economic Voting in the American Electorate: A Theory of Heterogeneous Attribution." *American Journal of Political Science* 45 (4), 899–914.

Green, Donald P., Bradley Palmquist, and Eric Schickler. 2004. *Partisan Hearts and Minds: Political Parties and the Social Identities of Voters.* Yale University Press.

Grieco, Elizabeth, Nami Sumida, and Sophia Fedeli. 2018. "About a Third of Large U.S. Newspapers Have Suffered Layoffs Since 2017." *Pew Research Center*, July 23, http://www.pewresearch.org/fact-tank/2018/07/23/about-a-third-of-large-u-s-newspapers-have-suffered-layoffs-since-2017/.

Grimmer, Justin. 2013. "Appropriators, Not Position Takers: The Distorting Effects of Electoral Incentives on Congressional Representation." *American Journal of Political Science* 57 (3): 624–42.

Grimmer, Justin, Sean J. Westwood, and Solomon Messing. 2014. *The Impression of Influence: Legislator Communication, Representation, and Democratic Accountability*. Princeton University Press.

Groenendyk, Eric. 2013. *Competing Motives in the Partisan Mind: How Loyalty and Responsiveness Shape Party Identification and Democracy*. Oxford University Press.

Gross, Justin H., and Kaylee T. Johnson. 2016. "Twitter Taunts and Tirades: Negative Campaigning in the Age of Trump." *PS: Political Science & Politics* 49 (4): 748–54.

Guay, Brian, and Christopher D Johnston. 2022. "Ideological Asymmetries and the Determinants of Politically Motivated Reasoning." *American Journal of Political Science* 66 (2): 267–534.

Guess, Andrew M. 2015. "Measure for Measure: An Experimental Test of Online Political Media Exposure." *Political Analysis* 23 (1): 59–75.

Hacker, Jacob S., and Paul Pierson. 2010. "Winner-Take-All Politics: Public Policy, Political Organization, and the Precipitous Rise of Top Incomes in the United States." *Politics & Society* 38 (2): 152–204.

Hamilton, James. 2004. *All the News That's Fit to Sell: How the Market Transforms Information into News*. Princeton University Press.

Hansford, Thomas G., and Brad T. Gomez. 2015. "Reevaluating the Sociotropic Economic Voting Hypothesis." *Electoral Studies* 39: 15–25.

Harcup, Tony, and Deirdre O'Neill. 2017. "What Is News? News Values Revisited (Again)." *Journalism Studies* 18 (12): 1470–88.

Harsgor, Liran. 2018. "The Partisan Gender Gap in the United States: A Generational Replacement?" *Public Opinion Quarterly* 82 (2): 231–51.

Hart, P. Sol. 2013. "The Role of Numeracy in Moderating the Influence of Statistics in Climate Change Messages." *Public Understanding of Science* 22 (7): 785–98.

Hayes, Adam. 2021. "Short Selling." *Investopedia*, March 13, https://www.investopedia.com/terms/s/shortselling.asp.

Hayes, Danny, and Jennifer L. Lawless. 2015. "As Local News Goes, so Goes Citizen Engagement: Media, Knowledge, and Participation in U.S. House Elections." *The Journal of Politics* 77 (2): 447–62.

Hayes, K. 2014. *Business Journalism: How to Report on Business and Economics*. Apress.

Healy, Andrew, and Neil Malhotra. 2013. "Retrospective Voting Reconsidered." *Annual Review of Political Science* 16: 285–306.

Healy, Andrew J., Neil Malhotra, and Cecilia Hyunjung Mo. 2010. "Irrelevant Events Affect Voters' Evaluations of Government Performance." *Proceedings of the National Academy of Sciences* 107 (29): 12804–09.

Hellwig, Timothy T. 2001. "Interdependence, Government Constraints, and Economic Voting." *The Journal of Politics* 63 (4): 1141–62.

Hellwig, Timothy. 2014. *Globalization and Mass Politics: Retaining the Room to Maneuver*. New York: Cambridge University Press.

Hellwig, Timothy, and David Samuels. 2008. "Electoral Accountability and the Variety of Democratic Regimes." *British Journal of Political Science* 38 (1): 65–90.

Herrnson, Paul S. 2015. *Congressional Elections: Campaigning at Home and in Washington*. CQ Press.

Hester, Joe B., and Rhonda Gibson. 2003. "The Economy and Second-Level Agenda Setting: A Time-Series Analysis of Economic News and Public Opinion about the Economy." *Journalism & Mass Communication Quarterly* 80 (1): 73–90.

Hetherington, Marc J. 2001. "Resurgent Mass Partisanship: The Role of Elite Polarization." *American Political Science Review* 95 (3): 619–31.

Hill, Kim Quaile, and Patricia A. Hurley. 2002. "Symbolic Speeches in the Us Senate and Their Representational Implications." *The Journal of Politics* 64 (1): 219–31.

Hjorth, Frederik, Robert Klemmensen, Sara Hobolt, Martin Ejnar Hansen, and Peter Kurrild-Klitgaard. 2015. "Computers, Coders, and Voters: Comparing Automated Methods for Estimating Party Positions." *Research & Politics* 2 (2): 2053168015580476.

Hobolt, Sara B., and James Tilley. 2014. "Who's in Charge? How Voters Attribute Responsibility in the European Union." *Comparative Political Studies* 47 (6): 795–819.

Hopkins, Daniel J. 2018. *The Increasingly United States: How and Why American Political Behavior Nationalized*. University of Chicago Press.

Huddy, Leonie. 2001. "From Social to Political Identity: A Critical Examination of Social Identity Theory." *Political Psychology* 22 (1): 127–56.

Huff, Connor, and Dustin Tingley. 2015. "'Who Are These People?' Evaluating the Demographic Characteristics and Political Preferences of MTurk Survey Respondents." *Research & Politics* 2 (3): 2053168015604648.

Iyengar, Shanto. 1990. "Framing Responsibility for Political Issues: The Case of Poverty." *Political Behavior* 12 (1): 19–40.

Jacobs, Lawrence R., and Desmond King. 2018. "The Fed's Political Economy." *PS: Political Science & Politics* 51 (4): 727–31.

Jacobson, Gary C. 2017. "The Triumph of Polarized Partisanship in 2016: Donald Trump's Improbable Victory." *Political Science Quarterly* 132 (1): 9–41.

Jerit, Jennifer. 2008. "Issue Framing and Engagement: Rhetorical Strategy in Public Policy Debates." *Political Behavior* 30 (1): 1–24.

Jerit, Jennifer, and Jason Barabas. 2012. "Partisan Perceptual Bias and the Information Environment." *The Journal of Politics* 74 (3): 672–84.

Jungherr, Andreas. 2016. "Twitter Use in Election Campaigns: A Systematic Literature Review." *Journal of Information Technology & Politics* 13 (1): 72–91.

Kahan, Dan M. 2015. "The Politically Motivated Reasoning Paradigm, Part 1: What Politically Motivated Reasoning Is and How to Measure It." *Emerging Trends in the Social and Behavioral Sciences: An Interdisciplinary, Searchable, and Linkable Resource*. 1–16.

Kam, Cindy D. 2005. "Who Toes the Party Line? Cues, Values, and Individual Differences." *Political Behavior* 27 (2): 163–82.

Kang, Taewoo, Erika Franklin Fowler, Michael M Franz, and Travis N. Ridout. 2018. "Issue Consistency? Comparing Television Advertising, Tweets, and E-Mail in the 2014 Senate Campaigns." *Political Communication* 35 (1): 32–49.

Kinder, Donald R., and D. Roderick Kiewiet. 1981. "Sociotropic Politics: The American Case." *British Journal of Political Science* 11 (2): 129–61.

Kinder, Donald R., and Nathan P. Kalmoe. 2017. *Neither Liberal nor Conservative: Ideological Innocence in the American Public*. University of Chicago Press.

Knight, Brian. 2006. "Are Policy Platforms Capitalized into Equity Prices? Evidence from the Bush/Gore 2000 Presidential Election." *Journal of Public Economics* 90 (4–5): 751–73.

Knobloch-Westerwick, Silvia, Mothes, Cornelia, and Nick Polavin. 2020. "Confirmation Bias, Ingroup Bias, and Negativity Bias in Selective Exposure to Political Information." *Communication Research* 47 (1): 104–24.

Kramer, Gerald H. 1983. "The Ecological Fallacy Revisited: Aggregate-Versus Individual-Level Findings on Economics and Elections, and Sociotropic Voting." *American Political Science Review* 77 (1): 92–111.

Krosnick, Jon A. 1991. "Response Strategies for Coping with the Cognitive Demands of Attitude Measures in Surveys." *Applied Cognitive Psychology* 5 (3): 213–36.

Krugman, Paul. 2020. "Crashing Economy, Rising Stocks: What's Going On?" *The New York Times*, April 30, https://www.nytimes.com/2020/04/30/opinion/economy-stock-market-coronavirus.html.

Krupnikov, Yanna, and Adam Seth Levine. 2014. "Cross-Sample Comparisons and External Validity." *Journal of Experimental Political Science* 1 (1): 59–80.

Kuklinski, James H., Paul J. Quirk, Jennifer Jerit, David Schwieder, and Robert F. Rich. 2000. "Misinformation and the Currency of Democratic Citizenship." *The Journal of Politics* 62 (3): 790–816.

Kull, Steven, Clay Ramsay, and Evan Lewis. 2003. "Misperceptions, the Media, and the Iraq War." *Political Science Quarterly* 118 (4): 569–98.

Kunda, Ziva. 1990. "The Case for Motivated Reasoning." *Psychological Bulletin* 108 (3): 480–98.

Lapavitsas, Costas. 2013. "The Financialization of Capitalism: 'Profiting without Producing.'" *City* 17 (6): 792–805.

Larcinese, Valentino, Riccardo Puglisi, and James M. Snyder Jr. 2011. "Partisan Bias in Economic News: Evidence on the Agenda-Setting Behavior of U.S. Newspapers." *Journal of Public Economics* 95 (9–10): 1178–89.

Lau, Richard R., and David P. Redlawsk. 2001. "Advantages and Disadvantages of Cognitive Heuristics in Political Decision Making." *American Journal of Political Science* 45 (4): 951–71.

Lavine, Howard G., Christopher D. Johnston, and Marco R. Steenbergen. 2012. *The Ambivalent Partisan: How Critical Loyalty Promotes Democracy*. Oxford University Press.

Lawrence, Eric D., and John Sides. 2014. The Consequences of Political Innumeracy. *Research & Politics* 1 (2): 2053168014545414.

Layman, Geoffrey C., Thomas M. Carsey, and Juliana M. Horowitz. 2006. "Party Polarization in American Politics: Characteristics, Causes, and Consequences." *Annual Review of Political Science* 9: 83–110.

Lecheler, Sophie, and Claes H. De Vreese. 2012. "News Framing and Public Opinion: A Mediation Analysis of Framing Effects on Political Attitudes." *Journalism & Mass Communication Quarterly* 89 (2): 185–204.

Lecheler, Sophie, and Claes H. De Vreese. 2019. *News Framing Effects*. Routledge.

Leeper, Thomas J, and Rune Slothuus. 2014. "Political Parties, Motivated Reasoning, and Public Opinion Formation." *Political Psychology* 35 (S1): 129–56.

Leonhardt, David. 2012."Obamanomics: A Counterhistory." *The New York Times,* September 30.

Lerer, Lisa, and Astead W. Herndon. 2021. "When Ted Cruz and AOC Agree: Yes, the Politics of GameStop are Confusing." *The New York Times,* January 31, https://www.nytimes.com/2021/01/31/us/politics/gamestop-robinhood-democrats-republicans.html.

Levendusky, Matthew. 2009. *The Partisan Sort: How Liberals Became Democrats and Conservatives Became Republicans.* University of Chicago Press.

Levendusky, Matthew S. 2018. "Americans, Not Partisans: Can Priming American National Identity Reduce Affective Polarization?" *The Journal of Politics* 80 (1): 59–70.

Lewis-Beck, Michael S., and Mary Stegmaier. 2013. "The VP-Function Revisited: A Survey of the Literature on Vote and Popularity Functions After over 40 Years." *Public Choice* 157 (3–4): 367–85.

Lewis-Beck, Michael S., and Tom W. Rice. 1982. "Presidential Popularity and Presidential Vote." *Public Opinion Quarterly* 46 (4): 534–37.

Lewis-Beck, Michael S., Helmut Norpoth, William G. Jacoby, and Herbert F. Weisberg. 2008. *The American Voter Revisited.* University of Michigan Press.

Lewis-Beck, Michael S., Nicholas F. Martini, and D. Roderick Kiewiet. 2013. "The Nature of Economic Perceptions in Mass Publics." *Electoral Studies* 32 (3): 524–28.

Linos, Katerina, and Kimberly Twist. 2018. "Diverse Pre-Treatment Effects in Survey Experiments." *Journal of Experimental Political Science* 5 (2): 148–58.

Lordon, Frédéric. 2000. *Fonds de Pension, Piège à Cons: Mirage de la Démocratie Actionnariale.* Raisons d'Agir.

Lowrey, Annie. 2018. "Left Economy, Right Economy." *The Atlantic,* June 4, https://www.theatlantic.com/politics/archive/2018/06/two–economies/561929/.

MacKuen, Michael B., Robert S. Erikson, and James A. Stimson. 1992. "Peasants or Bankers? The American Electorate and the U.S. Economy." *American Political Science Review* 86 (3): 597–611.

Malin, Brenton J., and Curry Chandler. 2016. "Free to Work Anxiously: Splintering Precarity among Drivers for Uber and Lyft." *Communication, Culture & Critique* 10 (2): 382–400.

Margolis, Michele F. 2018. "How Politics Affects Religion: Partisanship, Socialization, and Religiosity in America." *The Journal of Politics* 80 (1): 30–43.

Marinova, Dani M. 2016. "On the Use of Crowdsourcing Labor Markets in Research." *Perspectives on Politics* 14 (2): 422–31.

Martin, Paul S. 2008. "The Mass Media as Sentinel: Why Bad News about Issues Is Good News for Participation." *Political Communication* 25 (2): 180–93.

Mason, Lilliana. 2016. "A Cross-Cutting Calm: How Social Sorting Drives Affective Polarization." *Public Opinion Quarterly* 80 (S1): 351–77.

Mason, Lilliana. 2018. *Uncivil Agreement: How Politics Became Our Identity.* University of Chicago Press.

Matsa, Katerina Eva. 2017. "Buying Spree Brings More Local TV Stations to Fewer Big Companies." *Pew Research Center*, May 11, http://www.pewresearch. org/fact-tank/2017/05/11/buying-spree-brings-more-local-tv-stations-to-fewer-big-companies/.

Matthews, J. Scott, and Mark Pickup. 2018. "Rational Learners or Impervious Partisans? Economic News and Partisan Bias in Economic Perceptions." *Canadian Journal of Political Science* 52 (2): 1–19.

Mayhew, David R. 1974. *Congress: The Electoral Connection.* Yale University Press.

McCarty, Nolan, Keith T. Poole, and Howard Rosenthal. 2016. *Polarized America: The Dance of Ideology and Unequal Riches.* MIT Press.

McCombs, Maxwell. 2018. *Setting the Agenda: Mass Media and Public Opinion.* John Wiley & Sons.

McCombs, Maxwell E., Donald L. Shaw, and David H. Weaver. 2013. *Communication and Democracy: Exploring the Intellectual Frontiers in Agenda-Setting Theory.* Routledge.

McDevitt, Michael. 2003. "In Defense of Autonomy: A Critique of the Public Journalism Critique." *Journal of Communication* 53 (1): 155–64.

Meraz, Sharon. 2009. "Is There an Elite Hold? Traditional Media to Social Media Agenda Setting Influence in Blog Networks." *Journal of Computer-Mediated Communication* 14 (3): 682–707.

Merced, Michael J., and Nicholas Fandos. 2017. "Fox's Unfamiliar but Powerful Television Rival: Sinclair." *The New York Times*, May 3, https://www. nytimes.com/2017/05/03/business/dealbook/sinclair-media-expansion-fox-conservative-media.html

Merkley, Eric. 2019. "Partisan Bias in Economic News Content: New Evidence." *American Politics Research* 47 (6): 1303–23.

Mertens, Karel. 2018. "The Near Term Growth Impact of the Tax Cuts and Jobs Act." *Federal Reserve Bank of Dallas Working Paper*, no. 1803.

Messing, Solomon, and Sean J. Westwood. 2014. "Selective Exposure in the Age of Social Media: Endorsements Trump Partisan Source Affiliation When Selecting News Online." *Communication Research* 41 (8): 1042–63.

Mikhaylov, Slava, Michael Laver, and Kenneth R. Benoit. 2012. "Coder Reliability and Misclassification in the Human Coding of Party Manifestos." *Political Analysis* 20 (1): 78–91.

Morrissey, Monique. 2016. "The State of American Retirement: How 401(k)s Have Failed Most American Workers." *Economic Policy Institute*, March 1, https://www.epi.org/publication/retirement-in-america/#charts.

Mosley, Layna. 2003. *Global Capital and National Governments.* Cambridge University Press.

Mosley, Layna, and David Andrew Singer. 2008. "Taking Stock Seriously: Equity-Market Performance, Government Policy, and Financial Globalization." *International Studies Quarterly* 52 (2): 405–25.

Mullinix, Kevin J. 2016. "Partisanship and Preference Formation: Competing Motivations, Elite Polarization, and Issue Importance." *Political Behavior* 38 (2): 383–411.

Muraven, Mark, Dianne M. Tice, and Roy F. Baumeister. 1998. "Self-Control as a Limited Resource: Regulatory Depletion Patterns." *Journal of Personality and Social Psychology* 74 (3): 774.

Mutz, D. C. 1998. *Impersonal Influence: How Perceptions of Mass Collectives Affect Political Attitudes.* Cambridge University Press.

Mutz, Diana C. 1992. "Mass Media and the Depoliticization of Personal Experience." *American Journal of Political Science* 36 (2): 483–508.

Nadeau, Richard, Andre Blais, Neil Nevitte, and Elisabeth Gidengil. 2000. "It's Unemployment, Stupid! Why Perceptions about the Job Situation Hurt the Liberals in the 1997 Election." *Canadian Public Policy/Analyse de politiques* 26 (1): 77–93.

Nadeau, Richard, Richard G. Niemi, David P. Fan, and Timothy Amato. 1999. "Elite Economic Forecasts, Economic News, Mass Economic Judgments, and Presidential Approval." *The Journal of Politics* 61 (1): 109–35.

Nelson, Thomas E. 2019. "Emphasis Framing and Political Decision Making." In *Oxford Research Encyclopedia of Politics*, edited by William Thompson. Oxford University Press, https://doi.org/10.1093/acrefore/9780190228637.013.965.

Nicholson, Stephen P. 2011. "Dominating Cues and the Limits of Elite Influence." *The Journal of Politics* 73 (04): 1165–77.

Noam, Eli M. 2016. *Who Owns the World's Media?: Media Concentration and Ownership around the World.* Oxford University Press.

Nordhaus, William D. 1975. "The Political Business Cycle." *The Review of Economic Studies* 42 (2): 169–90.

Nyhan, B., and J. Reifler. 2015. "Does Correcting Myths about the Flu Vaccine Work? An Experimental Evaluation of the Effects of Corrective Information." *Vaccine* 33 (3): 459–64.

Nyhan, Brendan, and Jason Reifler. 2010. "When Corrections Fail: The Persistence of Political Misperceptions." *Political Behavior* 32 (2): 303–30.

Okun, Arthur M. 1970. *The Political Economy of Prosperity*. Washington, DC: Brookings Institute Press.

Ostini, Jennifer, and Anthony Y. H. Ostini. 2002. "Beyond the Four Theories of the Press: A New Model of National Media Systems." *Mass Communication and Society* 5 (1): 41–56.

Page, Benjamin I., and Robert Y Shapiro. 1984. "Presidents as Opinion Leaders: Some New Evidence." *Policy Studies Journal* 12 (4): 649–61.

Page, Benjamin I., and Robert Y. Shapiro. 2010. *The Rational Public: Fifty Years of Trends in Americans' Policy Preferences*. University of Chicago Press.

Pardos-Prado, Sergi, and Iñaki Sagarzazu. 2016. "The Political Conditioning of Subjective Economic Evaluations: The Role of Party Discourse." *British Journal of Political Science* 46 (4): 799–823.

Park, Chang Sup, and Barbara K. Kaye. 2020. "What's This? Incidental Exposure to News on Social Media. News-Finds-Me Perception, News Efficacy, and News Consumption." *Mass Communication and Society* 23 (2): 157–180.

Parker, Kim and Richard Fry. 2020. "More than half of U.S. Households Have Some Investment in the Stock Market." *Pew Research Center*, https://www.pewresearch.org/fact-tank/2020/03/25/more-than-half-of-u-s-households-have-some-investment-in-the-stock-market/.

Parker-Stephen, Evan. 2013. "Tides of Disagreement: How Reality Facilitates (and Inhibits) Partisan Public Opinion." *The Journal of Politics* 75 (4): 1077–88.

Pennycook, Gordon, and David G. Rand. 2019. "Lazy, Not Biased: Susceptibility to Partisan Fake News Is Better Explained by Lack of Reasoning Than by Motivated Reasoning." *Cognition* 188: 39–50.

Petrocik, John R. 1996. "Issue Ownership in Presidential Elections, with a 1980 Case Study." *American Journal of Political Science* 40 (3): 825–50.

Piketty, Thomas. 2015. "Putting Distribution Back at the Center of Economics: Reflections on Capital in the Twenty-First Century." *Journal of Economic Perspectives* 29 (1): 67–88.

Piketty, Thomas, and Emmanuel Saez. 2006. "The Evolution of Top Incomes: A Historical and International Perspective." *American Economic Review* 96 (2): 200–205.

Piketty, Thomas, and Emmanuel Saez. 2014. "Inequality in the Long Run." *Science* 344 (6186): 838–43.

Porter, Ethan. 2020. *The Consumer Citizen*. Oxford University Press.

Poterba, James M. 2000. "Stock Market Wealth and Consumption." *Journal of Economic Perspectives* 14 (2): 99–118.

Poterba, James, Steven Venti, and David A. Wise. 2007. "The Changing Landscape of Pensions in the United States." *National Bureau of Economic Research Working Paper No. 13381*, https://doi.org/10.3386/w13381.

Powell Jr, G. Bingham, and Guy D. Whitten. 1993. "A Cross-National Analysis of Economic Voting: Taking Account of the Political Context." *American Journal of Political Science* 37 (2): 391–414.

Price, Vincent, and Edward J. Czilli. 1996. "Modeling Patterns of News Recognition and Recall." *Journal of Communication* 46 (2): 55–78.

Prior, Markus. 2007. *Post-Broadcast Democracy: How Media Choice Increases Inequality in Political Involvement and Polarizes Elections.* Cambridge University Press.

Prior, Markus, Gaurav Sood, and Kabir Khanna. 2015. "You Cannot Be Serious: The Impact of Accuracy Incentives on Partisan Bias in Reports of Economic Perceptions." *Quarterly Journal of Political Science* 10 (4): 489–518.

Proksch, Sven-Oliver, and Jonathan B. Slapin. 2012. "Institutional Foundations of Legislative Speech." *American Journal of Political Science* 56 (3): 520–37.

Redlawsk, David P., Andrew J. W. Civettini, and Karen M. Emmerson. 2010. "The Affective Tipping Point: Do Motivated Reasoners Ever 'Get It'?" *Political Psychology* 31 (4): 563–93.

Rudolph, Thomas J. 2003. "Who's Responsible for the Economy? The Formation and Consequences of Responsibility Attributions." *American Journal of Political Science* 47 (4): 698–713.

Rudolph, Thomas J. 2016. "The Meaning and Measurement of Responsibility Attributions." *American Politics Research* 44 (1): 106–30.

Ryssdal, Kai. 2018. "The Market Is Not the Economy . . ." *NPR Marketplace*, February 2, https://www.marketplace.org/2018/02/02/economy/weekly-wrap/market-not-economy.

Sabato, Larry. 1991. *Feeding Frenzy: How Attack Journalism Has Transformed American Politics.* Free Press.

Sances, Michael W. 2021. "Presidential Approval and the Inherited Economy." *American Journal of Political Science* 65 (4): 938–53.

Sanders, David. 2000. "The Real Economy and the Perceived Economy in Popularity Functions: How Much Do Voters Need to Know?: A Study of British Data, 1974–97." *Electoral Studies* 19 (2–3): 275–94.

Sanders, David, and Neil Gavin. 2004. "Television News, Economic Perceptions and Political Preferences in Britain, 1997–2001." *The Journal of Politics* 66 (4): 1245–66.

Schaffner, Brian F., and Samantha Luks. 2018. "Misinformation or Expressive Responding? What an Inauguration Crowd Can Tell Us about the Source of Political Misinformation in Surveys." *Public Opinion Quarterly* 82 (1): 135–47.

Scheufele, Dietram A. 1999. "Framing as a Theory of Media Effects." *Journal of Communication* 49 (1): 103–22.

Scheufele, Dietram A., and David Tewksbury. 2006. "Framing, Agenda Setting, and Priming: The Evolution of Three Media Effects Models." *Journal of Communication* 57 (1): 9–20.

Schickler, Eric. 2013. "New Deal Liberalism and Racial Liberalism in the Mass Public, 1937–1968." *Perspectives on Politics* 11 (1): 75–98.

Shaw, Ibrahim S. 2015. *Business Journalism: A Critical Political Economy Approach.* Routledge.

Shell, Adam. 2017. "Stock Markets Start January with a Bang; For First Time Since '13, S&P 500 Posts Gains on First Trading Day." *USA Today*, January 4, Money, p. 1B.

Simonovits, Gabor. 2015. "An Experimental Approach to Economic Voting." *Political Behavior* 37 (4): 977–94.

Singer, Jane B. 2018. "Transmission Creep: Media Effects Theories and Journalism Studies in a Digital Era." *Journalism Studies* 19 (2): 209–26.

Slothuus, Rune. 2016. "Assessing the Influence of Political Parties on Public Opinion: The Challenge from Pretreatment Effects." *Political Communication* 33 (2): 302–27.

Slothuus, Rune, and Claes H. De Vreese. 2010. "Political Parties, Motivated Reasoning, and Issue Framing Effects." *The Journal of Politics* 72 (3): 630–45.

Slothuus, Rune, Thomas J. Leeper, and James N. Druckman. 2018. "Motivated Responses to Political Communications: Framing, Party Cues, and Science Information." In *The Feeling, Thinking Citizen: Essays in Honor of Milton Lodge*, edited by Howard Lavine and Charles S. Taber, 125–50. Routledge.

Snowberg, Erik, Justin Wolfers, and Eric Zitzewitz. 2007. "Partisan Impacts on the Economy: Evidence from Prediction Markets and Close Elections." *The Quarterly Journal of Economics* 122 (2): 807–29.

Sorkin, Andrew R., Jason Karaian, Michael J. de la Merced, Lauren Hersch, and Ephrat Livni. 2021. "Something Very Wrong Happened Here: A High-Profile Hearing Criticized Robinhood's Business Model." *The New York Times*, February 19, https://www.nytimes.com/2021/02/19/business/dealbook/robinhood-hearing-congress.html.

Soroka, Stuart, and Stephen McAdams. 2015. "News, Politics, and Negativity." *Political Communication* 32 (1): 1–22.

Soroka, Stuart, Mark Daku, Dan Hiaeshutter-Rice, Lauren Guggenheim, and Josh Pasek. 2018. "Negativity and Positivity Biases in Economic News Coverage: Traditional Versus Social Media." *Communication Research* 45 (7): 1078–98.

Soroka, Stuart N. 2006. "Good News and Bad News: Asymmetric Responses to Economic Information." *Journal of Politics* 68 (2): 372–85.

Soroka, Stuart N., Dominik A. Stecula, and Christopher Wlezien. 2015. "It's (Change in) the (Future) Economy, Stupid: Economic Indicators, the Media, and Public Opinion." *American Journal of Political Science* 59 (2): 457–74.

Southwell, Brian G., Emily A. Thorson, and Laura Sheble. 2018. *Misinformation and Mass Audiences.* University of Texas Press.

Stanig, Piero. 2013. "Political Polarization in Retrospective Economic Evaluations during Recessions and Recoveries." *Electoral Studies* 32 (4): 729–45.

Stein, Jeff. 2017. "Verrit, the New Website for Hillary Clinton Superfans, Explained." *Vox,* September 8, https://www.vox.com/policy-and-politics/2017/9/8/16257502/verrit-peter-daou-aweseomeStein, Robert M. 1990. "Economic Voting for Governor and US Senator: The Electoral Consequences of Federalism." *The Journal of Politics* 52 (1): 29–53.

Stewart, Emily. 2020. "You Can't Turn the Economy Back on Like a Light Switch." *Vox,* May 21, https://www.vox.com/2020/5/21/21263934/economy-reopening-stock-market-v-shape-recovery-jerome-powell.

Stokes, Donald E. 1963. "Spatial Models of Party Competition." *American Political Science Review* 57 (2): 368–77.

Storm, Servaas. 2017. "The New Normal: Demand, Secular Stagnation, and the Vanishing Middle Class." *International Journal of Political Economy* 46 (4): 169–210.

Stroud, Natalie Jomini. 2008. "Media Use and Political Predispositions: Revisiting the Concept of Selective Exposure." *Political Behavior* 30 (3): 341–66.

Stroud, Natalie Jomini. 2010. "Polarization and Partisan Selective Exposure." *Journal of Communication* 60 (3): 556–76.

Taber, Charles S., and Milton Lodge. 2006. "Motivated Skepticism in the Evaluation of Political Beliefs." *American Journal of Political Science* 50 (3): 755–69.

Tavits, Margit. 2007. "Clarity of Responsibility and Corruption." *American Journal of Political Science* 51 (1): 218–29.

Thorson, Emily. 2016. "Belief Echoes: The Persistent Effects of Corrected Misinformation." *Political Communication* 33 (3): 460–80.

Tilley, James, and Sara B Hobolt. 2011. "Is the Government to Blame? An Experimental Test of How Partisanship Shapes Perceptions of Performance and Responsibility." *The Journal of Politics* 73 (2): 316–30.

Trump, Kris-Stella. 2018. "Income Inequality Influences Perceptions of Legitimate Income Differences." *British Journal of Political Science* 48 (4): 929–52.

Udland, Myles. 2019. "The Stock Market Is Not the Economy. The Labor Market Is." *Yahoo Finance,* January 4, https://finance.yahoo.com/news/stock-market-not-economy-labor-184609482.html.

Van Duyn, Emily, and Jessica Collier. 2019. "Priming and Fake News: The Effects of Elite Discourse on Evaluations of News Media." *Mass Communication and Society* 22 (1): 29–48.

Vasileiadou, Eleftheria, and Rens Vliegenthart. 2014. "Studying Dynamic Social Processes with ARIMA Modeling." *International Journal of Social Research Methodology* 17 (6): 693–708.

Vliegenthart, Rens, Alyt Damstra, Mark Boukes, and Jeroen Jenkman. 2021. *Economic News: Antecedents and Effects.* Cambridge University Press.

Vonbun, Ramona, Katharina Kleinen-von Königslöw, and Klaus Schoenbach. 2016. "Intermedia Agenda-Setting in a Multimedia News Environment." *Journalism* 17 (8): 1054–73.

Wagner, Michael W. 2007. "The Utility of Staying on Message: Competing Partisan Frames and Public Awareness of Elite Differences on Political Issues." *The Forum* 5 (3), doi.org/10.2202/1540-8884.1197.

Weatherford, M. Stephen. 1983. "Economic Voting and the 'Symbolic Politics' Argument: A Reinterpretation and Synthesis." *American Political Science Review* 77 (1): 158–74.

Whitford, Andrew B., and Jeff Yates. 2009. *Presidential Rhetoric and the Public Agenda: Constructing the War on Drugs.* Johns Hopkins University Press.

Wickham, Hadley, and Garrett Grolemund. 2016. *R for Data Science: Import, Tidy, Transform, Visualize, and Model Data.* O'Reilly.

Wilcox, Nathaniel, and Christopher Wlezien. 1993. "The Contamination of Responses to Survey Items: Economic Perceptions and Political Judgments." *Political Analysis* 5: 181–213.

Witko, Christopher. 2016. "The Politics of Financialization in the United States, 1949–2005." *British Journal of Political Science* 46 (2): 349–70.

Wlezien, Christopher, Mark Franklin, and Daniel Twiggs. 1997. "Economic Perceptions and Vote Choice: Disentangling the Endogeneity." *Political Behavior* 19 (1): 7–17.

Wolff, Edward. N. 2017. "Household Wealth Trends in the United States, 1962 to 2016: Has Middle Class Wealth Recovered?" *National Bureau of Economic Research Working Paper No. 24085.*

Wood, Thomas, and Ethan Porter. 2019. "The Elusive Backfire Effect: Mass Attitudes' Steadfast Factual Adherence." *Political Behavior* 41 (1): 135–63.

Wooley, John, and Gerhard Peters. 2018. "The American Presidency Project," http://www.presidency.ucsb.edu/data/popularity.php.

Xu, Qian. 2013. "Social Recommendation, Source Credibility, and Recency: Effects of News Cues in a Social Bookmarking Website." *Journalism & Mass Communication Quarterly* 90 (4): 757–75.

Yakabuski, Conrad, and Kevin Carmichael. 2012. "Jobs Report Gives Obama a Lift." *The Globe and Mail (Canada)*, October 5, https://www.theglobeandmail.com/news/world/us-jobs-report-gives-obama-a-lift/article4593576/.

Zaller, John R. 1992. *The Nature and Origins of Mass Opinion.* Cambridge University Press.

Zukin, Cliff, and Robin Snyder. 1984. "Passive Learning: When the Media Environment Is the Message." *Public Opinion Quarterly* 48 (3): 629–38.

# Index

www.ingramcontent.com/pod-product-compliance
Lightning Source LLC
Chambersburg PA
CBHW020341270326
41926CB00007B/274